# DRUMMERS CALL

# DRUMMERS CALL

An Anthology of Writings
While
Following the Drum

Lieutenant General NS Brar, PVSM, AVSM, VSM
Indian Army (Retired)

www.drummerscall.com

THE BROWSER
www.thebrowser.org
Publishers and Booksellers

End page: Types of the Indian Army by AC Lovett 1888 : Bengal Army

Rear (Left to Right):
Daffadar 13 Duke of Connaught's Bengal Lancers (6 Lancers Pak Army), Sowar 19(Fane's Horse) Bengal Lancers (19 Lancers Pak Army), Native Officer 55 Coke's Rifles [7 (Coke's) FF Regiment Pak Army], Gunner 4 (Hazara) Mountain Battery (56 Field Regiment)

Front (Left to Right):
Native Officer Queen's Own Corps of Guides (Infantry) (2 FF Regiment Pak Army), Sepoy 4 Gurkha Rifles (4 Gurkha Rifles), Native Officer Queen's Own Corps of Guides (Cavalry) [Guides Cavalry (FF) Pak Army], Sepoy 45 Rrattray's Sikh (3 Sikh), Sowar 3 Bengal Cavalry (Skinners Horse), Sowar 1 Punjab Cavalry [11 Cavalry (FF) Pak Army], Piper 1 Sikh Infantry (3 FF Regiment Pak Army), Sowar Viceroy's Body Guard (President's Body Guard), Native Officer 18 Bengal Infantry (Disbanded), Sowar 15 (Multani) Cavalry (20 Lancers), Sowar 1 Bengal Cavalry (Skinners Horse)

First Published in India by **The Browser** 2019
(An imprint of J.G.S. Enterprises Pvt. Ltd.)
SCO 14-15, Sector 8-C, Chandigarh 160 009
Email: service@thebrowser.org



ISBN 978-93-88150-00-2

Printed in India by Replika Press Pvt. Ltd.



THE BROWSER
www.thebrowser.org

TO THE INDIAN ARMY
And
Its men I had the honour to serve with

*I have eaten your bread and salt.*
*I have drunk your water and wine.*
*The deaths ye died I have watched beside,*
*And the lives ye led were mine.*

*Was there aught that I did not share*
*In vigil or toil or ease .....*

—Rudyard Kipling, *Departmental Ditties*

# CONTENTS

# DRUMMERS CALL

Of all musical instruments associated with martial music, the drum is unique. Through the ages, it has found such usage in all societies. 'War Drums' are thus universal and most inspiring. Being intimately linked with soldiering, they have lent themselves to coinage of such military terms as 'Drumhead Court Martial' – quick and summary military justice, 'Drum Fire' – massed artillery fire with a rolling sound, 'Drum Major' – leader of a military band and 'Following The Drum' – military service. Army wives have an adage, 'If you marry the drum you got to follow it'.

Drums are integral to military ceremonials. The drum major, in his elaborate uniform and holding a silver-mounted staff, is 'the prince of pomp and circumstance' on such occasions. They find an honourable place during colour presentation parades when drums are 'piled' and the colours laid on them and consecrated before being presented. Besides the colours, a unit's battle honours are also inscribed on the drums. Captured enemy drums are prized war trophies. When a soldier departs for 'Valhalla', the drums are 'muffled' with black cloth at the funeral.

*The muffled drum's sad roll has beat the soldier's last tattoo;*
*No more on Life's parade shall meet the brave and fallen few.*
—Theodore O'Hara, *The Bivouac of the Dead*

The foundation of formal and standardised British military drumming was drawn up in an 1810 publication titled *The Art of Beating the Drum.* Drums regulated the soldier's day by beating calls from 'Reveille' to 'Retreat' or 'Lights Out' and all parades and activities in between. In camp, the drums would sound 'Camp Taps' before reveille from one end to the other and back again and in battle sound commands for 'Advance', 'Retreat', 'Commence Firing', 'Cease Firing' and so on. It was 'Drummed' into the troops to respond explicitly to orders conveyed through drum beats. They also set the step and pace while marching. The shrill sound of the bugle being easier to be heard above the din of battle, it gradually replaced the drum for conveying orders.

Drummers were usually the youngest in a military unit, often teenage boys and sons of serving soldiers of the unit, or of those killed in battle, referred to as 'born in the regiment'. They were also trained as buglers and later graduated to the band.

The Drummer Boys were also the company commander's aides; runners to carry messages and other errands, sounding his orders on the drums and informing him of orders relayed by other drums. As close attendants, they managed his horse on manoeuvres or in action and often provided him protection.

Flogging, when ordered, was administered by the drummers. A maximum of 1000 lashes could be administered for an offence and by the time of its abolition, it was restricted to 50. The drum major carried the whip – 'cat-o-nine-tails' – in a bag, thus when 'the cat was out of the bag' it meant trouble. It was quite common in the British Army where it was abolished in 1868 and rare in the Indian Army until it was abolished in 1835. If flogged, a man was invariably dismissed from service in the Indian Army. The culmination of a court-martial saw what was called 'John Drum's Entertainment'. The man dismissed by a court-martial was 'drummed out' at a promulgation parade where the drummer if required, executed the flogging called 'going to the triangle'. After the man was stripped of his uniform he was led out of the unit by the junior most drummer while the band played *The Rogue's March*:

*Twenty I got for selling my coat*
*Twenty for selling my blanket*
*If ever I 'list for a soldier again*
*The devil shall be my sergeant*

The ancient convention of suspending fighting and returning to camp at sunset now finds expression in the military ceremonial of 'Beating the Retreat' by military bands. The grand finale and most stirring part of this ceremony, before the buglers sound retreat and flags are lowered, is played out when the drummers come forward to weave patterns to their beat and having formed up in a hollow square lead through their delightful repertoire – *The Drummers Call*!

I was born what is today called an 'Army Brat' and what a pre-Independence British Indian Army Tommy would call a 'Barrack Chokra' or 'Line Boy'. While my father 'followed the drum', I grew up hearing tales of the Frontier and Burma, seeing remote areas, travelling in Army convoys, and living in thatched *bashas,* tents, converted temporary barracks and huge colonial bungalows. The sound of a bugler, drummer or band practising, rifle fire on the range (*chandmari)* or the shouts on the regimental training grounds or playfields was never far away. The Army had its unique charm and flavour which could not but rub off on me. I too 'followed the drum'.

Much like the myriad beats and rolls of the drums, this anthology is a result of varied writings over the years while following the drum.

# THE OLD SOLDIER

He stood at my office door one morning in July 1994, seeking permission to enter. A ramrod-straight figure with silvery-white beard and moustache and dressed in spotlessly clean clothes. He saluted smartly and introduced himself, 'Saab, I am Jemadar Kirpal Singh, retired from the Sikh Regiment. You would call me a Naib Subedar today.' I offered him a chair and a cup of tea, for he was an old soldier. He had come to collect his entitlement of liquor from the canteen and intended to look up my predecessor, who had joined his battalion as a subaltern when he was about to hang his uniform. Well, his *Saab Bahadur* too had retired after nearly 30 years of service. As he prepared to depart, I insisted that he sit down and tell me something about himself – his countenance and simplicity struck me.

'I am a much contended retired soldier and by the grace of God have no worries or troubles', he said. 'I was a good soldier in a good paltan and have been amply rewarded for my endeavours. My means are adequate and more than meet my ends. What extra I have, I give to my daughter, my only surviving child of my six children. I came home on a pension of fifty-nine rupees per month, today I get fifteen-hundred'. 'Whereabout is your village?', I asked. 'It's an hour by the Roadways bus and twelve rupees fare away.' After a while he begged to take leave, not wanting to take up more of my time. When I urged that he come again, he promised to do so the following month. His visits became a monthly feature thereafter, and unwittingly, he recounted a piece of history every time we met.

He could recall dates with uncanny ability. 'On 01 October 1946,

I along with two others from my village came to Ferozepur to seek enrolment into the police', he told me on his next visit. 'Seeing some soldiers on training in Ferozepur we decided that the Army would be better. As recruitment was then done only at Jallandhar, we caught the first train next morning to Jallandhar. Having paid the tonga driver two annas each we reached the recruiting office temporarily set up at the King George's School, the present day location of Headquarters 11 Corps. I was enrolled the same day and put on the night mail train to Naushera, the then Sikh Regimental Centre', he recounted. 'The train took us through Amritsar, Lahore and Sialkot and the next day we arrived at Naushera.' He had entered the brotherhood of arms.

By the time he finished his recruits training, talk of independence, the creation of Pakistan and rumours of communal tension were rife. He went on to recount, 'In July 1947, as part of a draft for the 2nd Battalion of the Sikh Regiment, I was placed under a JCO with orders to proceed to Bombay where my unit was located. Fear and panic prevailed all around, and by then, movement of refugees had already begun. Our train only moved in fits and starts, so after four days we reached Bombay. My unit was at Colaba, and I was seeing the sea for the first time. Then in October 1947, we were sent to Junagadh to amalgamate it into the Indian Union, but were back in Bombay by the year-end. We immediately got down to practising ceremonial drill as we had been nominated to present a guard of honour to a departing British battalion. And a few days later we did form part of a grand guard of honour presented near the Gateway of India'.

Without realizing it, Jemadar Kirpal Singh witnessed the end of the military saga in India of one of the greatest empires the world had seen – a significant event of removing the 'Jewel in the Crown.' The last British unit to leave India was the 1st Battalion The Somerset Light Infantry. It was ceremonially seen off at the Gateway of India and presented a guard of honour on 28 Feb 1948 commanded by Lieutenant Colonel Prithipal Singh of the Sikh Regiment and made up of detachments drawn from 2 Sikh, 1 Maratha Light Infantry, 3/5 Gurkha Rifles (Frontier Force), 3 Grenadiers, The Bombay Sappers and the Indian Navy. The bands played *God Save the King* and *Vande Matram.* Marching down through the Gateway of India to the strains of *Auld Lang Syne* the departing troops had been ferried by boats to the waiting troopship *Empress of Australia* and sailed out towards the Suez. For the British, the East began and ended at Port Said. On crossing the Suez at Port Said, the battalion drew up on the deck of the troopship, and at a given signal, tossed their *Sola Topees* (pith hats) into the sea. The British Army's association of nearly two hundred years with the 'Heat and Dust' of the sub-continent was finally over. On parting, the last British battalion had been presented a silver replica of the Gateway of India, inscribed 1757-1947. He was witness to Rudyard Kipling's *Troopin'* being enacted one last time:

*We're goin' 'ome, we're goin' 'ome,*
*Our ship is at the shore,*
*An' you must pack your 'aversack,*
*For we won't come back no more.*

*They'll turn us out at Portsmouth wharf in cold an' wet an' rain,*
*All wearin' Injian cotton kit, but we will not complain;*
*They'll kill us of pneumonia—for that's their little way—*
*But damn the chills and fever, men, we're goin' 'ome today!*

The next two years saw Kirpal Singh restoring law and order in 'Aid to Civil Authority' in Junagadh, followed by the Hyderabad Police Action in September 1948 as part of 1 Armoured Division. In 1949, he was in Jutogh in the Simla Hills. Travelling back and forth from the hills while on training or on leave, he saw the proposed layout of Chandigarh marked with flags and stone pillars. 'I understand it's a big modern city today though I have had no occasion to go there', he remarked.

'In 1956, we moved to the Naga Hills, where we lost about 30 men. On 22 October 1961, I with my battalion set sail from Bombay for Gaza to form part of the United Nations Emergency Force, Gaza. General Harbaksh Singh, the Colonel of our Regiment, bid farewell to the battalion. We disembarked on 08 November 1961, but when the Chinese attacked India in October 1962, orders came to sail back home. By the time we hit the shores at Bombay, the ceasefire came about'. He then showed me his Omega Seamaster wristwatch, which each man of his unit had been allowed to purchase in Gaza, still in perfect working condition.

On his subsequent visit, he came carrying a bag, one that was full of memories. Pulling out a framed photograph which showed him receiving a prize, he explained, 'I was the Divisional 400-meter champion in 1950 and had the honour of being presented this prize by the Maharaja of Patiala, the Honorary Colonel of our Regiment'. The next photograph showed him in battle dress firing a sten-gun. He then pulled out a beautiful silver medal and proudly narrated how he'd won the medal competing with international contingents in the UN Emergency Force Gaza Sten Firing Competition in 1961. The reverse carried the inscription UNEF GAZA FIRING – 1961 WINNER SGT KIRPAL SINGH.

We could not meet when he came next as I was away on a training exercise. 'Away on make-believe war', he asked me with a twinkle in his eyes when we caught up, and added, 'the make-believe is sometimes more taxing than the actual one'. He narrated his experience of actual combat. 'On 30 August 1965, we were moved to Poonch. The Pak piquets of Raja and Chand Tekri had been attacked twice without success. Lieutenant Colonel NN Khanna, our Commanding Officer, had undertaken to capture Raja Piquet. The attack got underway on night 5/6 September 1965 but stalled short of the objective due to very heavy enemy fire. The CO then moved amongst us, rallying all the men and exhorting them forward by reminding them of the Battalion's glorious past and saying that the future generations would not forgive us if we failed. He raised his white-and-green mountaineering pullover above his head, waving it to urge the men forward. The Battalion surged forward with the CO leading. He was cut down by a Medium Machine Gun burst and lay dying. As he was being evacuated, his only query was if the objective had been captured. As his life ebbed away, he was told that victory was ours. He died soon after, saying "Give my *Shabash* and *Fateh* to the boys". We suffered very heavy casualties, forty killed and over a hundred wounded, but the CO carried the day'.

Hajipir Pass had been captured by the Indian Army on 28 August 1965. Capture of these piquets opened the way for linking up with our troops from Uri on 10 September 1965. The entire Hajipir Bulge was in Indian hands, an outstanding achievement of the 1965 War.

Kirpal Singh also manned the defences at Nathu La in Sikkim soon after the clash with the Chinese in 1967. The next year he bid farewell to arms. To my inevitable question about what was different in the Army of his days, he summed it up succinctly by saying, 'Discipline in those days was more taut, while the sense of propriety is more ambivalent today'.

Over a couple of months, he had narrated his experiences of life with the colours. He would proudly carry these memories, till one day, he would fade away as the good old soldier that he was.

Ten years later, having been posted again to Ferozepur as the General Officer Commanding of the Division, I sent word to the canteen to send the Old Soldier to me whenever he came to collect his monthly entitlement of liquor. Within days, he was at my office door, straight as ever and beaming with pleasure at meeting me again. Thankfully, he hadn't faded away just yet.

# FRONTIER CENTURY

## Indian Army and the North-West Frontier 1838-1947

> Terrible country, harsh, fierce, and jagged; rocky peak, serrated ridge, dry icy upland, stony breathless valley that pent up the heat; a marksman behind every rock; a war of sniping and ambush and long marches at night, occasionally the rush of yelling fanatics sworn to die for the faith of Mohammad... the extraordinary part about these wars is the spirit in which they are fought; death is real enough, exhaustion, hunger, thirst and above all courage, but across this harsh and bitter landscape will flash suddenly a jagged lightning-streak of humour. It is a game – a contest with rules in which men kill without compunction and die in order to win, in which kinship and friendship count less than winning – but without malice when the whistle blows and the game is over.
>
> —Philip Mason

There were two 'Frontiers' of undivided India, the North-West – full of romance and danger and deeds of derring-do, and the North-East – virtually ignored and largely unexplored till the Second World War. The North-West Frontier is one of the most legendary places on Earth, and the Khyber one of very few places that have seen such a constant succession of marching troops and horsemen pass through. No area of comparable size has witnessed so much action, bloodshed, intrigue, gallantry, suffering or sacrifice.

On 27 December 1979, in one of the biggest airlifts since the Berlin Blockade, the Russians landed at Kabul, enacting yet another scene in what Kipling called the 'Great Game', and what the Russians called 'A Tournament of Shadows'. Afghanistan, by virtue of its location between Safavid Persia and Moghul India, and later between Czarist Russia and Imperialist British-India, became the arena of their conflicting interests. With its rugged, savagely independent and desperately unpredictable warriors and wily amirs, living constantly on the brink of eternity, with a proud heritage of not having been subjugated by any foreign power in recorded history, it was not a country that would easily accommodate and accept outside influence and tutelage. A Pathan saying goes: 'The invader may have the watches but we have the time'. All these made for a turbulent and active arena of military activity. The Americans were to learn this following their entry in 2001. To quote Alexander the Great: 'May God keep you away from the venom of a cobra, the teeth of a tiger and the revenge of an Afghan'.

> *This is the land of the Afghans and the sons of this soil cannot be deceived,*
> *Therefore withhold your hand, as your agents cannot succeed.*
> *Listen, oh child of imperialism, to my views and thoughts:*
> *Don't play with fire, and sit quietly,*
> *For I am the Afghan who made the British flee.*
> —An Afghan Song

Afghans saw the Oxus in the North and the Indus in the East as the traditional extent of their country. On 14 January 1761, Ahmed Shah Abdali defeated the Maratha Confederacy at Panipat extending the Durrani Afghan Empire to Delhi. After nearly four decades of anarchy in North India, Ranjit Singh took over Lahore on 07 July 1799, and by 1819, he had pushed the Pathans beyond the Khyber and captured Kashmir. This was to remain the frontier till the arrival of the British and for the successor state of Pakistan after Independence. Only three things were exchanged between the Sikhs and the Pathans – the knife, rope or bullet.

The Indian Army's century of involvement in the North-West Frontier began in 1838. The Amir of Afghanistan, Dost Mohammad's request for British help to recover Peshawar, captured by the Sikhs in 1834, having been turned down, he sought a Russo-Persian alliance which entailed their presence in Herat. In December 1838, Lord Auckland, the Governor-General of India, perceiving Russian ingress into Herat as threatening British interests, decided to intervene militarily with the intention of installing the pro-British Shah Shuja in place of Dost Mohammad on the throne of Kabul.

Shah Shuja had been in exile in Ludhiana for thirty years. Ranjit Singh had extracted the Koh-i-Noor from Shah Shuja for granting him asylum all these years! As Ranjit Singh declined passage to the British force through Punjab, the 'Army of the Indus' was assembled at Ferozepur and set off on 10 December 1838 for what came to be called the First Afghan War. Marching down along the Sutlej and through Sind, it went westwards up the Kachhi Plains, across the Bolan to

Quetta and Chaman, and then over the Khojak Pass into Afghanistan. The nine thousand five hundred British and Indian troops, comprising one regiment of the Queen's cavalry, two regiments of Company cavalry and nine regiments of infantry, along with six thousand men under Shah Shuja, had a 'tail' of thirty-eight thousand followers and thirty thousand pack animals.

As the column made ponderous progress, losing men and animals on the way, barring the route to Kabul was the strong fortress of Ghazni. It was captured on 23 July 1839 after its massive gates were duly mined and blown up. Conspicuous in this action was Subedar Devi Singh along with twelve Sappers from the Bengal Army and five from the Bombay Army. Devi Singh was awarded the Indian Order of Merit – the first gallantry medal of the Indian Army. The Sappers commemorate this event by incorporating the Ghazni fort in the badge on their caps.

Kabul fell on 07 August 1839, Shah Shuja was installed on the throne, and the bulk of the army withdrew. Dost Mohammad fled to take refuge with Nasrullah Khan, the Amir of Bokhara. Sir William McNaughton was appointed the Envoy and Minister, and Sir Alexander Burns as the Resident. What followed was an unmitigated disaster. The Afghan uprising began on 02 November 1841. The mob stormed the residency killing Burns and besieged the cantonment in the plain outside Kabul near the river. McNaughton was killed on 23 December while meeting some Afghan Chiefs to negotiate a withdrawal. Having been forced to withdraw, remnants of the seven hundred European and three thousand eight hundred strong Indian garrison, along with twelve thousand families and followers, marched out on 06 January 1842. Constantly sniped by the long-range 'jezails' and cut up en route, the remnants of the 44th Foot (Essex Regiment) made their last stand at Gandamak. Only one survivor, Dr Brydon, reached Jallalabad on 13 January 1842. He was also to survive the siege of Lucknow in 1857 and died fifteen years later.

> A little after noon on the 13th, one of the sentries, on that part of the wall that faced Gandamak and the road from Cabul, called aloud that he saw a mounted man in the distance... he was brought in bleeding and faint, and covered with wounds; grasping in his right hand the hilt and a small broken fragment of a sword which had

broken in the terrible conflict from which he had come.
—Account of a British officer in the Jallalabad Garrison,
January 1842

Jallalabad held out till 13 April 1842 when it was relieved by the 'Army of Retribution', the relievers marching in while the garrison band played the Scottish *Oh but ye've been a lang a' coming*. The Army of Retribution marched on to Kabul, entering the city on 15 September 1842. The great and spectacular Mughal *Char Chatta*, the covered bazaar of Kabul and one of the greatest buildings in Central Asia, was burnt to the ground, an event resented even today. The army withdrew to India on 12 October 1842 burning and destroying villages en route. Shah Shuja was murdered in April 1842. Akhbur Rehman, his successor, was poisoned in 1847 and Dost Mohammed was restored to the throne once again. The First Afghan War was a singular disaster in the annals of British-Indian military history, as well as the biggest disaster in the East till the loss of Malaya and surrender of Singapore to the Japanese a century later. The Afghan Church at Colaba, Bombay, was erected in 1852 as a memorial to the dead of the First Afghan War. Sita Ram, one of the participants and survivor having been taken prisoner, recorded in his memoirs *From Sepoy to Subedar*: 'If only the army had been commanded by the memsahibs all might have been well.' In 1025 AD Mahmud of Ghazni had carried away the gates of Somnath Temple to Ghazni. These gates were brought back by the Army of Retribution but were found as not being the original gates of Somnath and thence consigned to the Agra Fort.

Following the death of Ranjit Singh and the Anglo-Sikh Wars, the British annexed Punjab in 1849. The Russian Bear and the British Lion now had only the Afghan buffer in between, a buffer on the edge of empires. The frontier of British-India with Afghanistan – the North-West Frontier or simply the Frontier – was to be a constant factor with the British-Indian Army up to 1947.

Beyond the plains of the Indus lie the Suleiman Range, Hindu Kush – 'Hindu Killer' – and the Safed Koh. These mountainous regions formed the natural though loosely defined boundary between the Punjab and Afghanistan. Inhabited by the Pathans, an anglicized blanket term for Pakhtuns or Pashtuns, on both sides of the perceived border, it ran from Chitral, through Kohistan, Khyber, Tirah and Waziristan to Baluchistan. A harsh land spawns harsh people. The Pakhtun tribes like Afridis and Mahshuds inhabited specific areas and were in turn organised into *khels* – clans – under a *malik*. Fierce tribal loyalties and codes of conduct – *Pakhtunwali* or the way of the Pathan – prevailed, with no place for the statute or the rule book. Tribal councils or the *Jirga* settled all issues. *Melmastia* (hospitality) and *Nanawati* (asylum) was a sworn obligation to friend and foe alike. As the Pakhtun proverb goes 'A Pakhtun is at peace when he is at war'. *Zan, Zar* and *Zameen* (women, gold and land) were invariably the cause.

The spectre of a Russian advance into Afghanistan and moving onwards into British-India was the constant concern driving British policy towards Afghanistan. Monitoring Russian moves and intentions was the core of the Great Game.

*We spake of them all, but the last the most,*
*For I sought a word of a Russian post,*
*Of a shifty promise, an unsheathed sword*
*And a grey-coat guard on the Helmund ford.*
*Then Mahbub Ali lowered his eyes*
*In the fashion of one who is weaving lies.*
*Quoth he 'Of the Russians who can say?*
*When the night is gathering all is grey...'*
—Rudyard Kipling, *The Ballad of the King's Jest*

The harsh country, lack of any resources, scarcity of water and non-existent means of communication, all combined to make any military adventure into and beyond Afghanistan through the Frontier an extremely difficult proposition. It was said that 'too large an army would starve and too small annihilated'. The bogey of Russian expansion nevertheless fostered a concept of the 'Sepoy meeting the Cossack on the banks of the Oxus' rather than 'staying at home to receive the visit'. The Russian threat, therefore, lay not so much in its physical manifestation through the passes into the plains of British-India, as in its impact on the internal security of the Raj. Any Russian move would incite a popular rising, undermine the prestige of the

British and tie down a large number of troops. The internal security of British-India had to be secured through the security of the Frontier, and this remained an obsession till the end.

*Listen in the north, my boys, there's trouble in the wind;*
*Tramp o' Cossack hooves in front, grey great coats behind.*
*Trouble on the Frontier of a most amazin' kind ....*
—Rudyard Kipling, *Mutiny of the Mavericks*

Besides the Russian threat, the 'Frontier Problem' was essentially a question of how to protect the comparatively law-abiding tribes cultivating the fertile Indus valley from the predatory Pathans who inhabited the tangled hills beyond. The plains across the Indus were the 'administrated areas' and the country beyond up to the treaty boundary with Afghanistan, and across, constituted the tribal territory that was never fully controlled or administered and lived in 'ordered anarchy'. This working arrangement was a typically British comp-romise echoed in other far-flung areas like the North-East Frontier Agency. Following the First Afghan War, the British approach shifted from 'occupation' to buying out the tribes and 'punitive expeditions'.

The most direct link to the Frontier was the Grand Trunk Road along with the railway line which followed. Both crossed the gorge at Attock, where the Kabul and Indus rivers meet, through a fortified double-deck rail and road bridge completed in 1883, and onwards to Nowshera and beyond into the Yusafzai Hills through the Peshawar Valley and Peshawar – 'A city of a thousand and one sins', 'Paris of the Pathans' and 'The lynchpin of the North-West Frontier' – to Jamrud, Ali Masjid, the Khyber Pass and beyond to Landi Khana and the Afghan border at Torkham. Similarly, the Khojak Tunnel – the longest in India – was completed in 1891 to extend the Chaman railway to the Afghan border. The Amir called it 'a knife into my vitals'.

The disbanded Sikh soldiery after the First Anglo-Sikh War 1845-46 was formed into the Frontier Brigade in 1846. The addition of Punjab to John Company's possessions in 1849 brought about the formation of the Trans-Border Brigade in 1849. Both, along with The Guides raised in 1846, were amalgamated in 1851 into the Punjab

Irregular Frontier Force – the celebrated 'Piffers' – an Army under the orders of the Punjab Government, though militarily controlled by the Bengal Presidency Army from Calcutta, yet not under the orders of the C-in-C. It comprised five cavalry regiments, four mountain batteries, one garrison battery, four regiments of Sikh infantry, six regiments of Punjab infantry and one regiment of Gurkha infantry, besides the Corps of Guides. Kipling eulogised them in his *The Lost Legion*: 'All along the North-West Frontier of India there is spread a force whose duty is to shepherd the tribesmen... from one desolate post to another... ready to take the field at the shortest notice... their lives are as hard... and the papers never say anything about them'. The Sind Frontier Force, under the Commander in Chief Bombay, was also formed in 1846.

The Punjab Frontier Force was incorporated into the Indian Army and brought under the control of its C-in-C in 1886. The Presidency Armies were abolished and amalgamation commenced in 1893. Lord Kitchener became C-in-C India in November 1902 and set about effecting far-reaching reforms. The unification of the three Presidency Armies and The Punjab Frontier Force that began in 1880 was completed in 1905. All troops were now liable for service on the Frontier. Curzon, the Viceroy, had meanwhile detached the North-West Frontier from Punjab in 1901. The army was divided into four commands: Punjab including the Frontier, Bengal, Madras including Burma, and Bombay including Sind, Quetta and Aden. The Frontier Force on becoming part of the Indian Army was no longer a specialised force. What remains today in the Indian Army is the suffix Frontier Force (FF) with the 5th Gurkha Rifle (FF), 2 (Derajat) Field Battery (FF) and 4 (Hazara) Field Battery (FF) along with the distinctive spacing of the belt-runners five fingers from the buckle which owed its origin to carrying extra rifle charger clips in the belt equivalent to the width of the charger clip. Till it was finally abolished in 1990, the 5th Gurkha Rifles wore brown leather boots and belts, rather than the black of the Gurkha Brigade, which again owed its origin to the Frontier Force.

The Guides by themselves were another legendary force born on the Frontier, uniquely comprising both cavalry and infantry. They remained so till 1922 when they were bifurcated into the 10th Guides

Cavalry (FF) and the 5th Battalion 12th Frontier Force Regiment (Guides), later renumbered as 2nd Battalion 12th Frontier Force Regiment (Guides). Being 'Irregular' they were raised with funds generated through stoppages of pay of those who wished to join. The men were mercenaries in the best sense of the word and came from Punjab, Afghanistan, Nepal, Persia and Turkestan. Perhaps the most celebrated member being Dilawar Khan, a notorious bandit carrying a reward of two thousand rupees on his head. When offered amnesty to enrol for his knowledge of the country and people, he turned soldier and died as a Subedar. Setting off from Mardan on 13 May 1857 they marched to the Ridge outside Delhi, five hundred and eighty miles away, in twenty-six days. The regimental *bhisti* Jumma was immortalised by Kipling as *Gunga Din*. When the Guides were collectively awarded the Order of Merit (OM) in 1857, the men voted for the medal to go to Jumma. He was subsequently enrolled as a combatant and went on to win a Bar to the OM. But their greatest contribution to military lore and an addition to the English language was their 'Khaki' (from the Urdu *Khak* or dust) uniform. Since much of the Guides work was done in the mountains they were issued with sheepskin jackets (*Poshteen*) and the uniform dyed with mulberry juice that gave an authentic drab, mud-coloured effect. Others of the Frontier Force followed the example of the Guides.

The Frontier spawned other elites too. Amongst them was the mountain artillery. Capable of long marches with their guns and ammunition on pack animals, coming into action instantly on the narrowest of mountain-side ledges, often firing over open sights alongside the infantry, they were true Frontier professionals.

The Frontier environment also helped evolve the *Poshteen* – a long-sleeved knee-length sheep-skin overcoat which was an effective protection against the cold winds of the mountains. A cut version was the *Neemcha*. Another creation was the 'Gilgit Boots' – felt boots that came up to the knees to prevent snow ingress into the boots even while walking in deep snow. Both were effectively used by the Younghusband Expedition to Lhasa in 1903-04.

In 1863 the Yusafzai tribesmen North of Peshawar rose in revolt precipitating one of the regular punitive actions which came to be called the Ambela Campaign. The high-point of this campaign was the ferocious fighting for Eagles Nest and Crag Picket, which changed hands four to five times. It also earned the dubious distinction of extracting half as many casualties as were suffered over the entire fifty years stretch from 1849 to 1890 in as many expeditions.

Dost Mohammad died in 1863 and was succeeded by Sher Ali. The British were quick to sign a treaty with him to ward off the Russian threat. Simultaneously, the 'forward policy' was conceived and implemented, resulting in the establishment of Quetta in 1877 and active British involvement in the affairs of the Frontier.

Sher Ali, the Amir, having been forced to entertain a Russian delegation in 1878 while attempting to ward off accepting a British agent, was enough cause for the British to intervene once again. The Afghans wanted 'neither the sting nor the honey' of either. Sher Ali described himself as 'corn between the upper and lower millstone' and Viceroy Lytton called Sher Ali 'a savage with a touch of insanity' and contemptuously saw Afghanistan as 'an earthen pipkin between two iron pots'. The Afghans predicament is best summed up by Alfred Lyall in *The Amir's Soliloquy*:

*Shall I stretch my right hand to the Indus that England may fill it with gold?*
*Shall my left beckon aid from the Oxus? The Russian blows hot and blows cold*
*The Afghan is but grist in their mill, and the waters are moving fast,*
*Let the stone be the upper or nether, it grinds him to powder at last.*

The consequence of all this was the Second Afghan War. Three columns were assembled and marched into Afghanistan on 21 November 1878. The first column – Peshawar Valley Field Force – of sixteen thousand men and 48 guns went through the Khyber under General Samuel Browne, whose name endures as the designer of the Sam Browne belt, fighting its way after capturing Ali Masjid. The second column of 6300 and 18 guns – Kurram Valley Field Force – six thousand and six hundred went via the Kurram under General Roberts after capturing Peiwar Kotal, and the third of thirteen thousand men and 78 guns – Kandhar Field Force – under General Donald Stewart went through Quetta and Kandhar. A squadron of the 10th Hussars attempting to ford the Kabul River at night near Jalalabad on 31 March 1879 was swept away losing 47 men by drowning. Kipling recorded the incident in his poem *Ford o' Kabul River*:

*Kabul town's by Kabul river -*
*Blow the bugle, draw the sword -*
*There I lef' my mate for ever,*
*Wet an' drippin' by the ford ....*
*There's the river up and brimmin',*
*An' there's 'srf a squadron swimmin'....*

Kabul was occupied on 26 May 1879. Sher Ali had fled to Mazar-i-Sharif earlier where he died on 21 February 1879. Yakub Khan, who had succeeded his father as Amir, reluctantly signed the Treaty of Gandamak (the British troops called it the Condemned Treaty) on 26 May 1879 relinquishing Afghanistan's foreign policy to the British and accepting a British resident. Major Louis Cavagnari, a political officer who had negotiated the Treaty of Gandamak, was appointed resident. He, along with his assistant, a surgeon and an escort of twenty-five sabres and fifty bayonets of the Guides under a lieutenant reached Kabul on 24 July 1879 and set themselves up in the Bala Hissar, the citadel of Kabul.

On 03 September 1879, the Afghans struck. The resident and the entire escort, less three sowars who were away collecting fodder, one sepoy having gone out to purchase flour, and three other sepoys sent out as messengers, died fighting Afghan troops and tribesmen at the Bala Hissar in Kabul. This event was to become the inspiration for The Guides, just like the last stands by the French Foreign Legion at Cameron (in Mexico on 30 April 1863), and later the Sikh Regiment at Saraghari (on 12 September 1897). Yet another invasion followed. The North Afghanistan Field Force led by General Roberts and the South Afghanistan Field Force under General Donald Stewart occupied Afghanistan, entering Kabul on 07 October 1879.

The British set up camp at Sherpur outside Kabul. Yakub Khan was deposed and exiled to Dehradun where he introduced the famous *Basmati* rice to India. Abdur Rahman, a nephew of Sher Ali, was then installed as Amir. The Afghans true to style once again attacked the British. The South Afghanistan Field Force encountered the Durrani Afghans under Yakub Khan's brother, Ayub Khan, at Maiwand, north-west of Kandhar, on 27 July 1880, and it was routed with very heavy losses suffering 962 killed, including 21 officers. The remnants withdrew into the walled city of Kandhar only to be besieged. To the relief of Kandhar marched Roberts on 09 August 1880 – the famous march from Kabul to Kandhar. The relief column consisted of 9986 men, 7800 followers, 2800 ponies, 4500 mules and 950 donkeys. No wheeled transport of any kind was included. Averaging fifteen miles a day, the column covered the three hundred and thirteen miles in twenty-one days. Kandhar was relieved on 01 September 1880. The British force withdrew but retained control over the Khyber.

In April 1885, a military review of thirty thousand troops was held at Rawalpindi with the objective of impressing and awing the Afghans. It was reviewed by Viceroy Dufferin and Amir Abdur Rehman,

On 12 November 1893, the Durand Line was agreed to between Abdur Rahman the Amir and Sir Mortimer Durand, Foreign Secretary of India, and laid down as the limit of influence between Afghanistan and the North-West Frontier of British-India. It eliminated the tribal 'no-man's-land'. Demarcation commenced in 1894. Running from Chitral to the junction of India, Afghanistan and Iran, it cut through the ethnic homeland of a dozen major Pakhtun and Baloch tribes dividing them politically. It was marked with stone pillars over its eleven-hundred miles length. It remains contentious and scantly, if ever, accepted and respected by the Pathan tribes straddling it, or by the Afghanistan Government. The North-West Frontier Province was formed by Lord Curzon in 1903.

The Frontier, never out of the consciousness of the British home public, next caught their imagination with the siege of Chitral in 1895, which had all the ingredients of Victorian romanticism associated with the outposts of Empire. The four-hundred strong Indian Army and Kashmir Forces garrison at Chitral was primarily based to exclude the Russians. However, on the death of the Mehtar of Chitral in 1895, an uncle usurped the throne and laid siege to the fort. The men under Captain Townshend held out for forty-five days till relieved, winning much acclaim for Townshend. This was to influence him into another forty weeks siege during the First World War while commanding the 6th Indian Division at Kut el Amara in Iraq. Townshend surrendered on 29 April 1916 with 10061 Indian and British troops and 3248 followers.

At Maizar in 1897, the officers of a mountain battery, while fraternizing with the Pathans who feigned to be friendly, were set upon and killed. The gunners fought off the attacking Pathans winning nine Orders of Merit and giving birth to the Gunner tradition of not removing belts and side arms in the officers' mess.

In what was by now a recurring theme, in 1897 the 'Mullah of Swat' – nicknamed the 'Mad Mullah' – incited the frontier tribes to throw out the infidels. The Frontier erupted in revolt throughout Malakand and Tirah. Punitive expeditions followed. It took forty-thousand fighting men six months to restore order. The Malakand Field Force included the young Second Lieutenant Winston Churchill, as also the detachment of 36 Sikh Regiment that fought to the last at Saraghari on 12 September 1897 on the Samana Ridge. All twenty-one defenders died to a man, and each one was awarded the Order of Merit. There was also a unique award of the VC to Piper Findlater of the Gordon Highlanders, who, though shot in both legs, lay down near a rock and played on *The Cock o' the North* urging his battalion into the attack on the Dargai Heights on 20 October 1897.

In 1898, Curzon arrived as Viceroy and launched his new frontier policy. The Army was to withdraw from tribal territory and be replaced by irregular militia officered by British regulars. Routine frontier work now fell on the militia while the army frequently mounted expeditions from their cantonments to deal with recalcitrant tribes. The Frontier cantonments of Quetta, Wana, Razmak, Bannu, Kohat and others became familiar names to the old soldiers of the pre-Independence Indian Army.

After twenty years of relative calm, the Frontier erupted once again in 1919 into the Third Afghan War. About ninety-four thousand Martini-Henry breech-loading rifles, replaced by the .303 rifles, had found their way into Afghanistan and the Frontier through gun running from Muscat, arming the tribals. It extended the tribal fighting and sniping from four-hundred yards to a thousand yards. Habibullah, the Amir, influenced by the Turks, saw an opportunity in the war-weary British being caught up in the ongoing civil disturbances in India, including the Jallianwala Bagh incident in Punjab. He plotted to throw them out of the Frontier and seize Peshawar lost by the Pathans to Ranjit Singh in 1834. It took six months and seven-and-a-half lakh troops employing four-and-a-half lakh animals to restore order. It incited large-scale desertions from the frontier militias like the Khyber Rifles and Zhob Militia. Aerial bombing of Jallalabad and Kabul was also carried out. Hostilities came to an end with the Treaty of Peshawar, whereby the British accepted Afghan right to follow an independent foreign policy, and the Afghans accepted the Durand Line. The Third Afghan War virtually became an extension of World War I for the British and Indian Armies. War services on most memorials and general service medals, therefore, span and reflect the period 1914-1919.

The Frontier witnessed the invariable cycle of tribal revolt accompanied by kidnapping and looting, followed by a military expedition to subdue the tribes which included burning of villages and imposing collective fines, followed by relative peace till the tribes became restive again. The policy came to be known as 'butcher and bolt'. Use of force varied from a punitive foray to light aerial bombing raids and finally a column of up to a brigade. The 1930s saw the highest intensity of frontier expeditions and military activity with sophisticated weapons available to both sides. One famous action was the defence of Kila Hari on 05 April 1935 by a rifle company supported by a mountain artillery battery against thousands of Shamozais Pathans. The Royal Indian Air Force was first employed on the Frontier in 1937.

Frontier campaigning had been refined to a rigid art over the years. An advance into hostile territory was more likely up a river valley. As the column advanced, pickets would be put up ahead on the peaks and ridges dominating the valley and from which the Pathans sniped. After the column had passed the withdrawing pickets were invariably targeted. A badly picketed move meant casualties. One regiment in the thirties suffered eighty.

*A great and glorious thing it is*
*To learn, for seven years or so,*
*The Lord knows what of that and this,*

*Ere reckoned fit to face the foe --*
*The flying bullet down the Pass,*
*That whistles clear: "All flesh is grass."*
—Rudyard Kipling, *Arithmetic on the Frontier*

A rifle was a prized possession of a Pathan, who would go to great lengths to steal one, and nothing was more disgraceful for a soldier than to lose one. When an Afridi of The Guides deserted with two rifles in 1879, the commanding officer dismissed all seventeen Afridis serving in the unit, to be taken back only if they returned with the rifles. They came back with the rifles after two years. No man – dead or wounded – or a rifle was left behind. Punitive expeditions invariably imposed a collective fine of a certain number of rifles to be surrendered by the delinquent village or tribe.

The Pathan was a born marksman capable of precise hits with his rifle at a thousand yards. Consequently, all fortifications had the narrowest firing ports and no windows or doors on the outside. The Afghans found that the best results were achieved by picking off officers. To avoid being identified and picked-off, officers wore the same headgear as the men. The infantry similarly offered their headgear to the accompanying gunner party.

*A scrimmage in a border station –*
*A canter down some dark defile –*
*Two thousand pounds of education*
*Drops to a ten rupee jezail*
*The Crammers boast, the Squadron's pride*
*Shot like a rabbit in a ride!*
—Rudyard Kipling, *Arithmetic on the Frontier*

General Sir Andrew Skeen encapsulated the lessons and experience of the Frontier in his widely prescribed and read book *Passing It On* published in 1932: 'Probably no sign until that first burst of fire, and then the swift rush with knives, the stripping of the dead, and the unhurried mutilation of the infidels'. It was a sentiment echoed by Kipling in *The Young British Soldier*:

*When you're wounded and left on Afghanistan's plains,*
*And the women come out to cut up what remains,*
*Jest roll to your rifle and blow out your brains*
*An' go to your Gawd like a soldier,*
*So-oldier of the Queen!*

Notwithstanding the Indian Army's intense involvement with the Frontier which was primarily 'Pathan Country', it had no all-Pathan regiment until the Shahjehanpur Levy raised in 1858 was designated as the 40th Pathan Regiment in 1903. The only Pathan regiment was promptly named the 'Forty Thieves' and the commanding officer, very naturally, 'Ali Baba'! Flowing from their reputed proclivities, they were unfairly blamed for all undetected crimes in their station of posting. It caused some unease when their Pukhtun musicians played the regimental march on their *Srinai* and *Dhol*, for it was none other than *Zakhmi Dil* (Wounded Heart) – a very popular Pathan song: 'There's a boy across the river with a bottom like a peach, but alas, I cannot swim'. *Zakhmi Dil* was indeed popular with all troops who served on the Frontier. To their credit, the 40th Pathans also had a unique war memorial, perhaps the first one, after the Great War. A stone monolith depicting an upright .303 rifle cartridge was unveiled in 1919 at Attock overlooking the Indus. To the perverted frontier mind, it could mean anything! The 40th Pathans were merged as the 5th Battalion of the 14th Punjab Regiment in 1922, losing their all-Pathan character but retaining *Zakhmi Dil* as the regimental march.

The Frontier Mail ran from Bombay to Peshawar. The Frontier commitment forced the extension of the railway line from Peshawar to Landi Khana, the last railhead of the British-Indian Empire, through the Khyber Pass. Commenced in 1905, it was abandoned midway, then revived and finally completed on 03 November 1925. It was one of the most difficult and costly projects executed in India. The fifteen miles from Peshawar to Landi Khana entailed an expenditure of two million pound sterling, including the construction of thirty-four tunnels and ninety-two bridges or culverts. The tribesmen were encouraged not to oppose as it would make looting easier! 'Abandon hope all ye who enter here', inscribed on the fort gate at Landi Khana, summed up it being the last post in every sense of the word. Peshawar airfield, constructed later, ran diagonally across the railway line creating a unique rail-airfield level crossing.

Much as British officers, for reasons of impecuniosities, sought the Indian Army, the officers of the Indian Army sought service on the Frontier for similar reasons. Besides, it offered active service, independent command and the chance to win a gallantry award, even a VC in 'peacetime'. Just as Captain Andrew Scott won it fighting off armed Pathans who had entered the Quetta barracks on 26 July 1877, and Sepoy Isher Singh won it on 10 April 1921 beating an ambush in Waziristan. Then there was the lure of serving with exotic militia units like the Zhob Militia, Chitral Scouts or the Khyber Rifles. There were openings in the Indian Political Service which drew men from both the Indian Army and Indian Civil Service for the Frontier administration.

To add to the romance of the Frontier, there were such places like the *Kissa Khani* or the 'Story Tellers' Bazaar opposite Peshawar Cantonment. The pawn shops sold the auctioned personal effects of officers killed on the Frontier. *Kafilahs* from Bokhara and Samarkand brought exotic goods and languages to Peshawar. Here fused the Pashto and Dardi of Afghanistan with the Urdu and Punjabi of India, Central Asia with the Indian Subcontinent and the tribal with the modern. John Master called it 'a betwixt-and-between place, part India, part Central Asia'. Twenty-two miles south-west of Peshawar lies the town of Darra, famous then and now for offering authentic and functional copies of any weapon crafted in its home factories. The Khyber Pass, and indeed the Frontier, spawned its own mystique and romance, best narrated by Rudyard Kipling in *Ballad of the King's Jest*:

*'When spring time flushes the desert grass,*
*Our kafilas wind through the Khyber Pass.*
*Lean are the camels but fat the frails,*
*Light are the purses but heavy the bales,*
*As the snowbound trade of the North comes down,*
*To the market square of Peshawur town.*
*In a turquoise twilight, crisp and chill,*
*A kafila camped at the foot of the hill.....*
*And the tribesmen bellowed to hasten the food,*
*And the camp fires twinkled by Fort Jumrood.*

Over a century of involvement, the Indian Army mounted some two-hundred expeditions ranging from brigade-sized affairs to the '1919 War' involving seven-and-a-half lakh men. The political value of these military expeditions may have been questionable, but to the Indian Army, it provided an invaluable training ground; a field manoeuvre area and firing range where both sides used live ammunition. It enabled trying out new weapons and equipment: artillery star shells at Kabul in 1880, offensive air power in India in 1919 and the tank being first used during the Mohmand Operations of 1935 when the Vickers IIBs weighing eight tons were employed. Most importantly, battle drills and procedures were perfected for responding to the set battle situations – ambush, picketing of roads and so on.

Victoria's 'Little Wars' in far-flung corners of Empire were a staple in the newspapers and magazines at home. The Frontier figured prominently. Rudyard Kipling started writing about the Frontier in 1889 and there was scarcely an action or incident which did not find expression by him. Then there were Henry Newbolt and others. *Chums* was a widely read and popular magazine with the school boys. Adding to the romanticism were the war artists and soldiers who produced dramatised scenes of the action, later supplemented by photographs, featuring in the *Illustrated London News*. Even disasters were made glorious. It was Empire glorified in the name of 'The Widow of Windsor'. Churchill made his reputation less by military exploits and more by his writing *The Malakand Field Force*. World War I ended this era of military and imperial romanticism. The period between the World Wars brought the realities of industrialised fighting to the Frontier.

The Indian Army's affair with the Frontier ended with the partition of the subcontinent in 1947. The Frontier had dictated locating major cantonments along the road and rail trunk routes leading up to it. They all went to Pakistan. Nostalgia remains with books like MM Kaye's *Far Pavillions* and Paul Scott's *Jewel in the Crown* being made into BBC television series. Carved into the rock faces astride the road passing through the Khyber are the crests of regiments who had served there, including The Dorsetshire Regiment, whose regimental crest bears the inscription *Primus in Indis*, being the first regiment to serve in India. When the 1st Battalion The Somerset

Light Infantry, the last British battalion to leave India, marched through the Gateway of India, Bombay, to its waiting troopship, it carried the inscription 'Jellalabad' on its cap badge, having been part of the besieged garrison there in 1841-42.

> No man who has ever read a page of Indian history will ever prophesy about the Frontier.
>
> —Lord Curzon, *Viceroy of India (1899-1904)*

# A BIT OF COLOURED RIBBON

*'What is a medal worth to a soldier?'*
*'Worth! Everything! Glory is priceless'*
—Claude Melnotte

'A soldier will fight long and hard for a bit of coloured ribbon', said Napoleon, to the captain of *HMS Bellerophon,* transporting him to St. Helena in 1815. There is nothing as inconsequential as a strip of silk ribbon, with a suspended piece of metal, hanging on a soldier's chest, that generates so much pride, respect and motivation. The history of man abounds with deeds of valour. In the cause of God ... King ... or Country. Battles won or lost but deeds of unsurpassed heroism and bravery remembered. It was to honour and encourage indomitable courage that the tradition of gallantry awards and medals evolved.

Alexander the Great gave away small commemorative coin-like medallions to the veterans of victory at the Battle of Hydaspes (326 BC). Although some Roman medallions – pieces of metal struck with a design to commemorate a person, place or event – are known, it is widely accepted that the art of the medallion began in 1438 with the bronze medal of the Byzantine Emperor. However, individual gallantry awards in the form of jewelled pieces had been styled and awarded by kings and monarchs from about the 12th century onwards. Ranjit Singh of Punjab became the first Indian monarch to institute three gallantry medals, beginning with the Order of Ranjit Singh 1821. This bore a close resemblance to the French *Legion d' Houneer,* or the Legion of Honour, an obvious influence of the Frenchmen Allard and

Ventura at his court. The Indian princes continued to do so till 1947.

While motives are rarely simple, often mixed, and sometimes contradictory, a fundamental motive for soldiering in India has been, and remains, *Izzat*. Well aware of this power of *Izzat*, which induced their sepoys to gain for them the Indian Empire, the Honourable East India Company – HEIC or 'John Company' – founded two orders on 01 May 1837 for distinguished service. The first was the Order of Merit for Gallantry, later renamed as the Indian Order of Merit (IOM) on 17 April 1903. The other was the Order of British India, which rewarded long and distinguished service, and carried the title *Bahadur* prefixed with *Rai, Khan* or *Sardar* as appropriate. Anglo-Indians became eligible for the IOM from 20 February 1879. A lesser award established later was the Company's Meritorious Service Medal, superseded in 1888 by the Indian Meritorious Service Medal. Reckoned below the IOM, instituted in 1907, was the Indian Distinguished Service Medal (IDSM) for gallantry. Unlike some British awards which were restricted to officers only, the Indian awards were open to all ranks.

HEIC was the first 'government' in the world to introduce the practice of awarding a medal to all ranks for a campaign. This was, in due course, adopted universally, setting the trend for the General Service Medals which continues till today. The first, known as the Seringapattam Medal, was instituted in 1801 for the capture of Seringapattam in 1799. It has the fortress of Seringapattam engraved, with the sun in the sky shown as at one o'clock on 04 May 1799, the time of breaching the fortress wall. It was struck in gold, silver, bronze and tin, and awarded according to ranks, with a handful of gold medals for the very senior officers. Out of a total of 51,000 medals, some 30 gold and 45,000 tin medals were issued. A Seringapattam Medal is on display at the Indian Military Academy Museum, Dehra Dun. The last medal struck by the East India Company, before its dissolution by the Government of India Act of 02 August 1858, was the Indian Mutiny Medal 1857-59 with five clasps covering the major actions of the Mutiny. No man earned all five, and only a few received four clasps.

An 'Army in India' Medal was instituted on 14 April 1851 and made eligible for survivors of campaigns from 1803 to 1826. The India General Service Medal followed in 1854, encompassing campaigns from 1852 to 1895. Originally intended for the Burma War 1852-53, it was later styled as the India General Service Medal to obviate the need of giving medals for each campaign. The next India General Service Medal was instituted in 1895, and remained current till 1902, when the India General Service Medal 1908-35 was introduced, followed finally by the India General Service Medal 1936-39. All had clasps for notified campaigns.

Independent India introduced the General Service Medal 1947, which encompassed clasps for J&K 1947-48, Korea 1950-53, Goa 1961, the North-East Insurgencies of Naga and Mizo Hills, and the 1962 Indo-China war. Its dark red ribbon with thin green stripes was superseded by the Samanya Seva Medal 1965, notified in 1975 with retrospective effect, with clasps for Rann of Kutch 1965, Kargil 1965-66, Nathula 1967, and the current counter-insurgency operations in Tirap, Nagaland, Manipur and Mizoram. Concurrently, the Special Service Medal is the general service medal for other areas and operations.

Victory at Waterloo on 18 June 1815 prompted the British Army, for the first time, to issue a campaign medal – the Waterloo Medal – to all the participants irrespective of rank. It was the first standardised official British campaign medal, the next being Ghuznee 1839. The first coronation or jubilee medal for India was instituted by Queen Victoria in 1877 when she was proclaimed Empress of India or *Kaiser -i-Hind.*

Queen Victoria was intimately associated with instituting campaign and gallantry medals. Her reign saw more than a third of all medals issued before or since to the British and British Indian Army. These were much prized and sought after by officers and men alike. A recently arrived young private, marching to join the First Sikh War in December 1845, wrote how 'all our talk and hope was: Shall we be in time to get the *medal* ?' 'Scraps' on the Frontier being frequent, an award of clasp or medal was naturally restricted to the more serious and bigger affairs. The understanding was that when artillery was employed it generally translated into a clasp or a medal for the operation. The Chitral Relief Force in 1895 was accompanied by two guns of the Kashmir Mountain Battery. When the guns fired their first round at an enemy *sangar* the British officer went about shaking hands with the gunners saying that they had earned him a medal. They were awarded the India General Service Medal 1895 with its green and red striped ribbon and clasp 'Relief of Chitral 1895'. Nevertheless, there wasn't any defined system whether a medal or clasp would be issued. An action involving a thousand men may have got a medal while one with more than a lakh men employed may have got only a clasp to the general service medal. Gallantry and campaign medals are prized possessions of regiments and its members go to great lengths to subscribe and win auctions or buy them from collectors to restore them to the regiment.

While medals and decorations were primarily given for their intrinsic motivational value, the material benefits were not insignificant. The VC on its institution carried an annuity of £10, not an insubstantial amount at that time. Till it was dissolved, the HEIC paid up to twelve months *batta* (field allowance) with each campaign medal. The IOM conferred an allowance equal to the recipients pay at the time of the award, in addition to his pay or pension. By 1938, the Military Cross carried with it Rs 40 per month, besides substantial grants of land in the emerging canal colonies. Recipients were often selfless. Darwan Singh Negi, on being presented the VC, was asked by King George V if he wished for anything personally. Negi asked for a school for the children of his community at Karnaprayag. Similarly, Nand Singh, having been decorated with the VC and when asked so by the Maharaja of Patiala, requested that his village be exempted from the levy on irrigation water as it was hard on the poor villagers. Both requests were granted.

Apart from the medals and decorations instituted by governments, commanding officers of units too gave away medals for individual acts of bravery to their men. This was in keeping with the system of the day, where commissions were purchased, and regimental dress and accoutrements fashioned by the commanding officers, often through private means.

Drawing a distinction between campaigns within British territories and those conducted outside, special campaign medals were instituted for China 1842, the Frontier Campaigns in Afghanistan 1842-45, Gwalior 1843, the Anglo-Sikh Wars 1845-46 and 1848-49, China 1857-60, Abyssinia 1864, Afghanistan 1878-80 and Tibet

1903-04. The Sutlej Medal for the First Anglo-Sikh War 1845-46 was the first of such medals to be issued with clasps – one each for the battles of Mudki, Ferozeshah, Aliwal and Sabraon. It's ribbon colours were the reverse of the Waterloo Medal. Along with the Afghanistan 1878-80 Medal, another decoration was issued to those who took part in the famous march from Kabul to Kandhar under General Roberts. It was a five-pointed star made from bronze of the Afghan cannons taken at Kandhar on 01 September 1880.

Serving overseas in what were essentially British Expeditionary Forces, Indian troops became eligible to receive and were awarded, the British campaign medals for Egypt 1882-85, East Africa 1897-98, China 1900, South Africa 1899-1902, and East Africa and Somaliland 1902-04. Mahatma Gandhi too earned the South Africa Star while serving with the British Field Ambulance Corps. Indian troops deployed in Iraq and Persia between 1924 and 1929 received the British General Service Medal 1923.

The First World War, despite the unprecedented casualties and the most savage fighting, threw up just four medals for the combatants. Millions of people involved led to compulsions of economy. The 1914 Star, also called the Mons Star, was awarded for serving in France and Flanders between 05 August 1914 and 22 November 1914. It had a clasp with these dates inscribed to indicate the recipient as having been under enemy fire. As the period also saw the virtual extinction of the small regular British Army – 'The Old Contemptibles' – the medal is also referred to as 'The Old Contemptibles Medal'. The 1914-15 Star was awarded for service overseas, or on the NW Frontier of India, between 05 August 1914 and 31 December 1915, for those who had not received the 1914 Star. The Indian Corps of two divisions – 3 (Lahore) and 7 (Meerut) – and a cavalry brigade – 4 (Secundrabad) – was landed at Marseilles on 26 September 1914, and hurriedly pushed to the front. The infantry was withdrawn and sent to the Middle East in October 1915. Indian soldiers thus became eligible for one of the two medals. A cook of the 47th Sikh Regiment remarked to the Commander of the Indian Corps that they liked to cook close to the trenches otherwise the government may refuse to give them a medal and then in India they would be called the 'Marseille Wallahas' – those who served in the base and not the front lines.

The British War Medal was instituted for service between 05 August 1914 and 11 November 1918, and the Victory Medal for service between 1914 and 1919. The Victory Medal was never given alone, but always with the British War Medal.

One of the stars, along with the War Medal and the Victory Medal, was most widely earned, with virtually all servicemen, and civilians in any official capacity, receiving two or more of these. The three became popularly known as 'Pip, Squeak and Wilfred' after characters (a dog, a penguin and a rabbit) featured in a *Daily Mail* cartoon of the period. Another popular term described them as Tom, Dick and Harry. The pair of War and Victory Medals was similarly dubbed 'Mutt and Jeff'.

By 1916, the unprecedented scale of casualties wrought by the industrialised fighting had cast an all-pervasive sense of loss. The desire to remember and commemorate the war dead prompted the creation of a 'Next of Kin Memorial Plaque'. It took the shape of a circular bronze medallion, four and a half inches in diameter, with the figure of Britannia holding a trident and a lion in the foreground. The same imagery had been used on the Indian Mutiny Medal 1857-59. It carried the inscription 'He Died For Freedom And Honour' along its circumference and a raised rectangular panel on it was inscribed with the name of the deceased, without rank, to treat all the dead as equal. It was intended for the next of kin of all those who died 'on active service'. The soldiers dubbed it "The Dead Man's Penny'. Besides this, a scroll and a letter from King George V were sent to over thirteen and a half lakh recipients, a few of which can still be found with their descendants in Indian homes.

Up to World War I, the campaign medals for officers were struck in silver, and for the rank and file in bronze. Consequently, such silver medals are quite rare. Massed armies of the industrial age, and the corresponding compulsions of economy, made cupro-nickel the preferred material for medals.

The Germans, who were confident of a repeat victory as at Sedan in 1870 and the capture of Paris in 1871, had prior to the outbreak of war, struck and distributed for presentation to the troops a bronze medal inscribed 'Entry Of German Troops Into Paris' with the Eiffel Tower and the Arc de Triomphe below and the figures 1871-1914.

Unexpected Belgian resistance, and General Von Kluck's swing of his armies north of Paris to trap the French, made the medal redundant. Similarly, the British who were easily expecting to crush the Boer Rebellion, had the Queen's South Africa Medal struck and inscribed 1899-1900, but had to later alter it to 1899-1902.

Though awards for individual gallantry were long established, they became more formalised and universal in their application from the early 19th century onwards. As mentioned earlier, the first formal gallantry award for the Indian Army was the Order of Merit (OM) instituted in 1837, later renamed as the Indian Order of Merit (IOM). It predated the Victoria Cross (VC) by nineteen years, and the US Medal of Honour by twenty-four years. The IOM came to be known as the Indian soldiers' Victoria Cross since they did not become eligible for the VC until 1912. Initially, the IOM was not awarded posthumously, thus precluding recognition of many outstanding acts of bravery. Subedar Devi Singh of the Bengal Sappers won the first IOM for destroying the Kabul Gate of Ghazni Fort in 1839, during the advance to Kabul in the First Afghan War. The award of twenty-one IOMs to Havaldar Ishar Singh and his twenty fellow soldiers of the 36th Sikhs (now 4 Sikh), who died to a man defending the Saragarhi Post in the NW Frontier on 12 September 1897, is unparalleled. It was also the first time that a gallantry award was given posthumously. Subedar Kishanbir Nagarkoti of 1/5 Gurkha Rifles was awarded the IOM an unprecedented four times, the fourth bar being specially crafted of gold. The IOM was relegated by the Victoria Cross in 1912, and the last award of the IOM was gazetted on 25 September 1947.

Sepoy Usman Khan of the 57 Wilde's Rifles (now 9 Frontier Force, Pak Army) on being awarded the Indian Distinguished Service Medal on 26 October 1914 became the first Indian gallantry award winner of World War I.

The United States Medal of Honour, instituted in 1862, has been awarded to nearly three thousand four hundred individuals to date. It was awarded liberally up to 1927 when nine hundred and eleven medals were withdrawn as being undeserving. Till the First World War, it was the only US decoration for gallantry. Fourteen medals were awarded for gallantry during the Japanese attack on Pearl Harbour on

07 December 1941. Of the eighty-four awarded to the Marine Corps in World War II, twenty-seven were awarded on Iwo Jima in just one month's fighting. General Arthur MacArthur, and his son Douglas MacArthur, became the first father and son duo to win the medal. Some American Army and Navy awards differ in design though they have the same ribbon. The Purple Heart was instituted in 1782 for those wounded or killed in action. The purple-coloured heart-shaped medal was discontinued after the Civil War, but was revived in 1932. Audie Murphy was awarded the Medal of Honour, and practically every other American award for gallantry, besides French and Belgian awards. Becoming a Hollywood star after the war he acted in his own biographic film *To Hell And Back*.

The German *Eiserne Kreuz*, or the Iron Cross, was instituted by Frederick William III in 1813 for distinguished service in the Prussian War of Liberation, and first awarded on March 10, 1813. Revived by William I for the Franco-Prussian War of 1870, it was resurrected twice – in 1914 for World War I, and by Adolf Hitler on 01 September 1939, the day Germany invaded Poland. It reflected the cross worn by Teutonic knights of the fourteenth century. While the basic design remained constant – a Maltese Cross of cast iron edged with silver – the ribbon too has distinctive German colours – black edged with white. Originally it had three classes, but by World War II, it had expanded to eight grades. The Grand Cross of the Iron Cross was the highest grade and was awarded only once to *Generalfeldmarschall* Herman Goring. The Knights Cross with Golden Oak Leaves and Diamonds, the highest award for gallantry, was intended to be awarded only twelve times, and was again awarded only once to Hans Ulrich Rudel, a Stuka dive bomber pilot who flew over 3530 combat missions, sinking the Russian battleship *October Revolution*, destroying 519 tanks, besides bridges and armoured vehicles. He survived the war. As it is to be awarded only during war, it has not been awarded since 1945.

Pre-dating the Iron Cross, the French-sounding *Pour le Merite* (For Merit) was established by Frederick II in 1740. It depicted the Prussian Eagle surrounded by a blue enamelled scroll. It was the highest German military award till World War I. It was awarded to fighter pilots shooting down eight or more enemy aircraft. Max

Immelman became the first airman to receive it, and on account of his name and the colour of the medal, it came to be called the Blue Max. Immelman also pioneered the aerial combat manoeuvre called the Immelman Turn. He was shot down on 18 June 1916. Blue Max went into disuse in 1935 and was eclipsed by the Iron Cross in World War II. It was later revived purely as a civilian award for outstanding achievements in the sciences or arts. The insignia is returned on the death of the person awarded.

The Cross of Saint George, the highest Russian award with four classes, was initially established by Imperial Russia in February 1807 by decree of Emperor Alexander I. Abolished after the Russian Revolution of 1917, the Order of Glory replaced it during the Soviet Era. The fall of the Soviet Union in 1991 led to the Cross of Saint George being reinstated. The highest Soviet award, the Hero of the Soviet Union, is now designated as Hero of the Russian Federation.

Japan's exclusive and long-standing military award, Order of the Golden Kite, had seven classes with eligibility by rank. It stood abolished in 1947.

Victoria Cross, the most exalted British decoration for bravery, though instituted in 1856, was applicable from the year 1837, that being the year of accession of Queen Victoria to the throne. She herself chose the words *For Valour* inscribed on the medal. Crafted from the bronze of Russian guns captured at Sebastopol during the Crimean War, the VC was awarded to Captain John Wood of 20 Bombay Infantry (now 2 Rajputana Rifles) at Reshire in Persia in 1856, thus becoming the first VC of the Indian Army.

A proclamation at the Coronation Durbar at Delhi in 1911 made Indian soldiers eligible for the VC. Between 1912 and 1947, forty VCs were awarded to Indian soldiers, and twelve to British officers of the Indian Army. Sepoy Khudadad Khan of the 129 Baluch Regiment (now 11 Baluch, Pak Army) earned the distinction of being the first Indian to win it on 31 October 1914 at Hollebeke, Belgium. A small memorial marks the scene of his action. Though Darwan Singh Negi and Khudadad Khan won the VC for actions on the same day, however, Khudadad Khan's award was gazetted earlier. Eleven VCs were won by Indians in World War I. Second Lieutenant (later Lieutenant General) PS Bhagat became the first Indian officer to win it in 1941 in

Eritrea, Africa. Amongst the VCs awarded to Indian soldiers during World War II, Havaldar (later Honorary Captain) Umrao Singh of the 4 (Hazara) Mountain Battery carried the unique distinction of being the only Gunner VC in the British Commonwealth and Empire. He was the last surviving Indian VC and passed away on 21 November 2005. On retiring in 1965 he was offered £ 32,000 for his VC which he declined saying it would stain the honour of those who fell in battle besides him. Jemadar Mir Dast of the 55th Cooke's Rifles (now 7 Frontier Force Pak Army) was the sole Indian to win both the VC and the IOM. His brother Mir Mast was awarded the IDSM, but deserted to the Germans, whereupon the award was withdrawn.

Six hundred and twenty-six VCs were awarded during World War I, and a hundred and eighty one during World War II. Three recipients were awarded the medal twice, or bars to the original award, including Colonel Arthur Martin Leake in the Boer War and World War I, Captain Noel Chavasse in World War I, and Captain Charles Upham of New Zealand in World War II. The 1st Battalion Lancashire Fusiliers landing at Gallipoli on the morning of 25 April 1915 lost eleven officers and six hundred and ninety-eight men before the beach was captured. Six VCs went to those nominated by the survivors through secret ballot. The battalion earning the sobriquet of 'Six Before Breakfast'. Eleven were awarded for the defence of Rorke's Drift on 22 January 1879. A total of one thousand, three hundred and fifty-eight have been awarded to date. Field Marshal Roberts and his son Lieutenant Roberts both won the VC, with the son becoming the first posthumous winner.

To maintain the exclusivity of the VC, the Distinguished Service Order (DSO) came about from 1866 onwards and was given to officers performing exceptional service in the field. From 1917, it was awarded for acts of gallantry in the face of the enemy, with the precondition that the recipient should have been mentioned in despatches earlier. The Indian equivalent of the DSO was the Indian Distinguished Service Medal (IDSM) from 1907 onwards. Instituted from 31 December 1914, the Military Cross was awarded for distinguished service in action and given to captains, subalterns, warrant officers and Indian Viceroy Commissioned Officers. Its equivalent for the other ranks was the Military Medal.

Military horses, mules and even dogs were sometimes decorated with campaign and gallantry medals. Field Marshal Roberts's charger *Vonolel* was decorated by the Queen with the Afghan Medal 1878-80 with four clasps, the Kandhar Star 1880 and the Jubilee Medal 1887. The mules and horses would wear the medal ribbons on the brow band of the parade head collar. *Bobbie*, a dog, accompanied the 66th Regiment (Berkshire Regiment) to Afghanistan, and was present at the Battle of Maiwind on 27 July 1880 where the Regiment suffered two hundred eighty-eight killed. The survivors, along with Bobbie, were personally presented the Afghan Medal 1878-80 by Queen Victoria. A dog accompanying the Chitral Relief Force in 1895 was awarded the DSO for bravery.

Commemorative awards like the Coronation Medals were also given away from time to time. The last such British and first Indian commemorative medal was the Independence Medal 1947. It was followed up with silver and golden jubilee editions in 1972 and 1997 respectively.

The three-hundred-years old St Pauls Cathedral, London, has a tablet commemorating the services of the Indian Army from 1749 to 1947. Engraved on the tablet are the Star of India, Order of the Indian Empire, Victoria Cross, Order of British India, Indian Distinguished Service Medal and the Indian Order of Merit.

Hawai Sepoy Kartar Singh Tonque, a Wapati aircraft gunner, was Mentioned in Despatches during operations in Waziristan in 1937, and thus became the first awardee of the Indian Air Force. Lieutenant Indra Lal Roy was awarded the Distinguished Flying Cross in September 1918, flying with the Royal Flying Corps on the Western Front.

Effective since 27 October 1947, the Sainya Seva Medal, or the Service Medal, is the longest enduring Indian medal for non operational service under field conditions, and has nine clasps to date, commencing with Clasp J&K. Its universal application for all field areas in the country has earned it the nickname of the 'Kit Issue Medal'!

Instituting and conferring awards post-Independence came with some technical hurdles. British awards were not acceptable and could not be invoked. Indian awards were finalised in 1948, however, they had to await institution till 26 January 1950, when India became a republic. The Indian awards were then made effective from 15 August 1947. The Adjutant General asked Mrs Savitri Khanolkar, who had a deep knowledge and understanding of Indian languages and mythology, to design Independent India's awards. Little did she know that the very first winner of the Param Vir Chakra (PVC) would be her daughter's brother-in-law.

Patterns of Indian gallantry awards came to be largely fashioned on the British awards, though the engravings on the medals have a decidedly Indian theme. The Param Vir Chakra has the *Vajra* (thunderbolt) which Indian mythology ascribes to Rishi Dadhichi, who sacrificed his life to reclaim the heavens for the *Devas* from the *Asuras,* and donated his thigh bone to Indra, the king of gods, to make the awesome *Vajra.* The will power of Dadhichi made the *Vajra* and the one who wielded it invincible. Like the VC, the PVC ribbon is crimson. Ashok Chakra, corresponding to the George Cross, stood for gallantry other than in the face of the enemy. Sena Medal, Nao Sena Medal and the Vayu Sena Medals were introduced in 1960.

Brigadier Rajinder Singh of the J&K State Forces, killed while fighting the invaders near Uri in J&K on 25 October 1947, was conferred the Maha Vir Chakra (MVC). That became the first award for gallantry of Independent India. Major Somnath Sharma won the first PVC posthumously on 03 November 1947. Warrant Officer Dev Raj Singh became the first recipient of the Ashok Chakra for chasing and capturing Nathu Ram Godse after Gandhi's assassination.

Though not mandated by any rule or regulation, it is customary to salute an individual with the VC or PVC irrespective of his or one's own rank.

Winston Churchill to a Victoria Cross winner in World War II:

> 'You must feel very humble and awkward in my presence'.
> 'Yes, sir,' replied the soldier.
> 'Then you can imagine how humble and awkward I feel in yours,' replied Churchill.

Unlike other armies, embellishments on medal ribbons are rare on British and Indian awards. The VC and PVC both have a miniature cross and chakra respectively on their ribbons. A second-time award, or 'Bar' to any award, has a rosette, and now a chakra, on the ribbon. Being 'Mentioned in Despatches' entitled one to a bronze oak leaf on the campaign ribbon; it is now a bronze lotus leaf. Mention in Dispatches owes its origin to the mention of gallant or distinguished conduct of individual officers in the commander's reports or dispatches from the field. Till the introduction of gallantry medals, this was the only recognition of distinguished conduct. After the Battle of Meeane on 17 February 1843, privates, both European and Indian were for the first time mentioned in such dispatches. With the introduction of gallantry medals, and those mentioned but not awarded one, were formally notified as 'Mentioned in Dispatches'.

One of the rare non-gallantry or distinguished service embellishments was the figure 1 or 8 on the North Africa Star of World War II for the members of the 1st and 8th Armies.

Campaign medals and stars were instituted for various theatres of the Second World War, unlike World War I. The colours of the ribbons had a symbolic connect with the theatre, and these were said to have been personally designed by King George VI, just as those for World War I were designed by King George V. The 1939-45 Star, the India Medal and the Burma Star were the ones mostly earned by the Indian Army.

The Siachen Medal very appropriately depicts an infantry soldier and an Air Observation Post (now Army Aviation) Cheetah helicopter against the background of snow-capped peaks straddling a glacier. A fitting tribute to the foot soldiers and the helicopter pilots who put them there and sustain them. The ribbon has a white band in the centre with granite grey bands on either side, symbolizing the snow and the granite moraine of the glacier emanating from the Karakoram – meaning Black Gravel.

Instituted in 1973, the Prakaram Padak – Wound Medal – for armed forces personnel wounded as a result of direct enemy action or during counter-insurgency operations, was made effective retrospectively from 15 August 1947. It is not awarded posthumously. The red and white ribbon is the soldier's true and ultimate badge of honour.

As medals increased, their weight made them cumbersome to wear, and by the beginning of the last century, ribbons alone began to be worn. 'Full Dress' with medals was replaced by 'Service Dress' with ribbons. 'Full Medals' were now worn on ceremonial occasions only. Order of precedence of medals was laid down in 1912. Medals worn suspended from the ribbon are called 'Swing Style', and those mounted on a plate with the ribbon also on the plate in the background as 'Court Style'. Old soldiers with medals on their mufti, and the son wearing his father's medals on the right side of his chest are a fading tradition in our milieu. Nonetheless, be-medalled veterans marching down Rajpath on Republic Day, and the famous portrait of Havaldar Chelu Ram's son with the VC, along with his widow and father, shall remain enduring images.

Spinks and Sons, the royal medallion makers of London, are amongst the oldest and have the distinction of crafting the largest number of medals. 210 VCs are displayed in the Imperial War Museum, London. The finest medal collection in the country, though sadly neglected, is housed in the Moti Bagh Palace Museum of the erstwhile Maharajas of Patiala.

*From the graven earth furnaced to molt,*
*Thus the seed of a medal's birth*
*From a smelters forge hammer and mould,*
*Baptised in blood from the enemy's gorge*
*For the fearless and the brave adorned breasts*
*and for the warriors laid in their earthen graves.*
—Major Alok Singh Kler

## BRITISH-INDIAN ARMY ORDERS, DECORATIONS, CAMPAIGN MEDALS AND STARS

### MILITARY DECORATIONS AND ORDERS:

Victoria Cross (VC)
George Cross (GC)
Distinguished Service Order (DSO)
Order of Merit (OM)
Indian Order of Merit (IOM)
Distinguished Service Cross (DSC)
Military Cross (MC)
George Medal (GM)
Indian Distinguished Service Medal (IDSM)

Distinguished Service Medal (DSM)
Military Medal (MM)

Knight of the Order of the Garter (KG)
Knight Grand Cross of the Order of the Bath (GCB)
Knight of the Order of the Bath (KCB)
Companion of the Order of the Bath (CB)
Knight Grand Cross of the Order of the British Empire (GBE)
Knight of the Order of the British Empire (KBE)
Commander of the Order of the British Empire (CBE)
Officers of the Order of the British Empire (OBE)
Members of the Order of the British Empire (MBE)
Order of British India (OBI)
British Empire Medal (BEM)
Grand Commander of the Order of the Star of India (GCSI)
Knight Commander of the Order of the Star of India (KCSI)
Companion of the Order of the Star of India (CSI)
Knight Grand Commander of the Order of the Indian Empire (GCIE)
Knight Commander of the Order of the Indian Empire (KCIE)
Companion of the Order of the Indian Empire (CIE)

## CORONATION AND JUBILEE MEDALS:

Queen Victoria Empress of India Medal 1877
Queen Victoria Golden Jubilee Medal 1887
Queen Victoria Diamond Jubilee Medal 1897
King Edward VII Coronation Meal 1902
King George V Coronation Medal 1911 (Civil / Military and Police)
King George V Silver Jubilee Medal 1935
King George VI Coronation Medal 1937
Delhi Durbar 1903
Delhi Durbar 1911

## CAMPAIGN MEDALS AND STARS:

Morighyr Mutiny Medal 1766
West of India and Guzerat (Deccan Medal) 1778-84
Carnatic 1780-84
Mysore 1790-92
Ceylon 1795-96
Seringapattam Medal 1799
Egypt 1801
Army of India Medal 1803-26 : 21 clasps
Roderigues Bourbon Mauratius 1809-10
Java 1811

Nepaul 1814-16 : 21 clasps
First War in Burma 1824-26 : 21 clasps
Ghuznee Medal 1839
Afghanistan Medal 1842 (Kandhar, Ghazni, Kabul)
Jellalabad 1842
Khelat-i-Ghilzie 1842
China 1840-42
Scinde 1842 : 3 variations
Gwalior Star 1843 : 2 variations
Sutlej Campaign 1845-46 : 4 variations and 4 clasps
Punjab Campaign 1848-49 : 3 clasps
India General Service Medal 1852-95 : 24 clasps
Indian Mutiny 1857-58 : 5 clasps
China 1857-60 : 5 clasps
Abyssinia 1867-68
Ashanti Medal 1873-74
Afghanistan 1878-80 : 6 clasps
Kabul-Kandahar Star 1880
Egypt 1882-89 : 13 clasps
Khedives Star 1882-91 : 1 clasp
Sudan 1896-98
India General Service Medal 1895-1902: 7 clasps
China 1900 : 3 clasps
East and Central Africa Medal 1897-99 : 4 clasps
South Africa Medal 1899-1902
African General Service Medal 1902 : 35 clasps
Thibet 1903-04 : 1 clasp
India General Service Medal 1908-35 : 12 clasps
The 1914 Star : 1 clasp
The 1914-15 Star
The British War Medal
The Victory Medal
General Service Medal 1918 : 4 variations
India General Service Medal 1936-39 : 2 clasps
1939-45 Star
Africa Star : 2 clasps
Pacific Star with Clasp Burma
Burma Star with Clasp Pacific
Italy Star
France and Germany Star
Defence Medal
War Medal 1939-45
India Service Medal
General Service Medal 1947
India Independence Medal 1947

## EFFICIENCY AND LONG SERVICE DECORATIONS AND MEDALS:

Meritorious Service Medal (King George V)
Long Service Good Conduct Medal (Military)
Indian Long Service and Good Conduct Medal (For Europeans of Indian Army)
Indian Meritorious Service Medal (For Europeans of Indian Army)
Volunteer Officers Decoration
Volunteer Long Service Medal
Efficiency Decoration
Territorial Decoration

# UMBALLA TO AMBALA

*Cities and Thrones and Powers, Stand in Time's eye,*
*Almost as long as flowers, which daily die:*
*But, as new buds put forth, to glad new men,*
*Out of the spent and unconsidered Earth the Cities rise again.*

The field of Panipat witnessed three epic battles which decided the fate of Hindustan. On the route from the mountain passes in the North-West, through which the invaders came to Panipat and Delhi, lay 'Umballa' – a natural staging post along the traditional invasion route. When British conquests took them North-Westwards, its strategic location become the sine qua non of its military importance.

The origin of Ambala is shrouded in antiquity but it apparently owes its name to *Amb* (mango) *Wala* (of) – the fruit growing in abundance in the Shivalik foothills.

By the late 18th century, as British influence and domination marched inland from Calcutta, they controlled such large areas of India that a new military strategy was evolved based on the need for rapid response and deployment of troops and artillery. This had profound consequences for settlement patterns and for the actual form and layout of urban areas. The concentration of troops in city centres was replaced by separate camps – or cantonments – on the periphery of the main cities. From 1800 onwards, real military power resided in the tree-lined avenues and neatly clipped compounds of these sub-urban settlements, rather than in the formidable bastions of the city forts, which were reduced to mere symbols of imperial power.

The concept of the cantonment arose from the Moghul practice of governance. Sir Thomas Roe had noted as early as 1616 that on tour, the royal camp covered an area of twenty square miles, and that it was organised like a town with regular streets where each nobleman or tradesman had his allotted place, topographically and socially. Being aliens to the local systems, the British, where it did not conflict with their commercial interests, simply adapted the established pattern of life and institutions to their own ends. In any case, it suited the hierarchical nature of English society equally well, if not better, than Moghul India. In reality, the cantonment was a refined and permanent Moghul military camp. Cantonments added substantially to the local economy, and still do.

The plans of British cantonments followed a common pattern in the layout of their constituent parts. Generally, they lay five or six miles from the city which they guarded. Between city and cantonment were placed the lines of the Indian regiments. This careful segregation of the Indian lines was far more common after 1857 and was intended to avoid billeting Indian troops within the European quarter or too near the native population. The gap between city and cantonment was deliberately maintained. A road was often built through it, later a railway line too. The layout was inevitably dictated by functionality, and the grid streets aligned in strict symmetry. Segregation was all pervasive. Officers were separated from other ranks, married-quarters from barracks, British troops from Indian, artillery from cavalry, elephants and camels from oxen and horses. The general had a fine big house in the middle of the camp, and at the end of each regimental barrack-block, a house for the sergeant-major. Ambala was no exception and was typical on all counts – down to the segregation of plots, by rank, for burial in the cemetery!

As the British moved West from the Hoogly, military cantonments followed – Barrackpore and Danapur in 1765, Bareilly and Kanpur in 1811. Ambala was established in 1825 and developed as a cantonment from 1843. Central to the chain of these military stations and extending all the way from Barrackpore to the North-West Frontier (in fact from Chittagong to Kabul) was the Grand Trunk Road, otherwise known as the Grand Military Road, laid out by Sher Shah Suri much before the arrival of the British, but renovated and maintained by them after 1839 under James Thomason.

The original alignment passed through the present-day airfield where an old Mughal arched bridge still survives. Passing through Ambala, the 'Road of Hindustan' and the cantonment complemented each other, just as it complemented other cantonments along its entire length, being the backbone of British dominion in northern India. Peshawar was linked to Calcutta by telegraph through Ambala in 1856. When the railway network began being laid from 1860, the first major line was aligned and ran parallel to the Grand Trunk Road. The Delhi-Ambala broad-gauge line was extended to Kalka on 03 January 1891. Kipling loved it and immortalized both the road and Umballa in *Kim*, and his poem *Route Marchin* echoed this sentiment:

*We're marchin' on relief over Injia's sunny plains,*
*A little front o' Christmas-time an' just be'ind the Rains;*
*Ho! Get away, you bullock-man, you've 'eard the bugle blowed,*
*There's a regiment a-comin' down the Grand Trunk Road....*
*So 'ark an' 'eed you rookies, which is always grumblin' sore,*
*There's worser things than marchin' from Umballa to Cawn-pore.*

The growing Sikh empire under Ranjit Singh, with its military capability and predatory forays up to the Yamuna, fuelled British apprehensions and brought about the Treaty of Amritsar on 25 April 1809, mutually restricting the eastern limit of the Sikh State to the Satluj River. From Karnal, then the western-most cantonment, the British military presence was stepped-up to Ambala and Sirhind. Sirhind was abandoned in the closing years of the nineteenth century due to extreme paucity of water making it impossible to maintain a large contingent of cavalry. The Sirhind garrison was relocated to Ambala expanding it into one of the biggest cantonments in North India. The Sirhind Brigade retained its name, though relocated at Ambala, and in 1914 it went to war as the Sirhind Brigade. The Sirhind Club, which also moved to Ambala, was registered as such with the Registrar of Companies in Britain and was obliged to retain the name.

Between 1815 and 1947 the British created over 80 hill-stations. Shimla was established between 1827 and 1831 and become the summer capital in 1864: 'Abode of the Little Tin Gods'. The annual move of the Government from Calcutta to Shimla resulted in Ambala becoming the rail-head base, 1077 miles from Calcutta, till the branch line was extended to Kalka in 1891, and the unique mountain-rail driven up to Shimla on 09 November 1903. The lure of the cool of Shimla was a lasting obsession for those serving at Ambala.

*If down here I chance to die, solemnly I beg you take*
*All that is left of "I" to the Hills for old sake's sake.*
*Pack me very thoroughly in the ice that used to slake*
*Pegs I drank when I was dry - this observe for old sake's sake.*
*To the railway station hie, there a single ticket take*
*For Umballa - goods train - I shall not mind delay or shake.*
*I shall rest contentedly spite of clamour coolies make,*
*Thus in state and dignity send me up for old sake's sake.*

Captain Robert Napier, a sapper officer who had helped in planning Darjeeling Cantonment, was moved to Ambala in 1842 to plan the cantonment. Construction of permanent barracks commenced in 1843, and till recently, housed the Mechanized Battalion and the Golden-Lion Canteen in the King Edward (KE) Lines area. The canteen barrack was originally the theatre and 'Supper and Temperance Room'. The adjoining present-day Local Audit Officer's office was commissioned as the Sergeants Mess in 1870, and a 50-bed section hospital which rose in 1859, is now a barrack opposite the Recruiting Office. The Military Hospital came up in 1855. 1 Allenby Lines – the Artillery Division Officer's Mess – was the first mess building and was constructed in 1843. The original Rest Camp Barracks are today the Canteen Stores Depot.

The area presently called the Allenby Lines was the *Kali Paltan* or 'Native Troops' Lines of the British Cantonment at Ambala. It was named as the Allenby Lines after the Great War 1914-18 in honour of Field Marshal Allenby who commanded the British Eastern Expeditionary Force (EEF) in the Palestine Campaign of World War I. The EEF was predominantly composed of Indian troops including the 7th (Meerut) Division, which had amongst others, the Sirhind Brigade and cavalry from Ambala. The EEF achieved fame in the battles of Megiddo and Jordan Valley, the Capture of Gaza, Jerusalem and

Damascus and the cavalry charge by the 15 Indian Imperial Service Cavalry Brigade for the capture of Haifa on 23 September 1918. Allenby was the 90th British Field Marshal.

At the turn of the nineteenth century, the Allenby Lines housed the Indian Infantry, the KE Lines the British Infantry, the area occupied by the Air Force today the British Cavalry, and the Panipat Lines the Artillery. The BI (British Infantry) Bazaar adjoined the Sirhind Club. The BC (British Cavalry) Bazaar was located on the Staff Road near Indira Chowk and the RA (Royal Artillery) Bazaar North of the Panipat Lines. The bazaars survive, though expanded and merged, and their nomenclature lost, except for the *Topkhana*. The Cemetery and the Race Course, used as a convoy ground today, lie on the outskirts adjoining the road to Yamunanagar. JD Cunningham, an eminent historian who wrote *History of the Sikhs,* was buried at Ambala in 1851.

An enduring legacy is that of the buildings housing the Corps Headquarters. Originally built for the Headquarters of the Ambala Brigade and the Garrison Engineer in 1846, they successively accommodated the headquarters of 'Ambala Brigade Area', 4 Infantry Division, Punjab Haryana and Himachal Pradesh Area, 1 Armoured Division and now the 2 Corps. Constructed at a cost of Rs 4,706 in 1846, Rs 9,802 was spent to undo the storm damage in 1947. An extensive renovation was carried out recently, and these will endure as heritage buildings of Ambala Cantt.

A garrison church for spiritual solace and as a focal point for regular European congregation was mandatory in every cantonment. Although Roman Catholic and non-conformist chapels existed, the grandeur was inevitably that of the Church of England. Architecturally, English Gothic imported straight from 'home' prevailed. Amongst the most imposing churches were the ones at Peshawar, Nagpur and Ambala. St John's Church at Ambala was designed by Captain Atkinson and consecrated in 1857. It was Hereford Cathedral transplanted at Ambala. The all-brick structure was bombed out, along with a part of the Sirhind Club, by the Pak Air Force on 18 Sep 1965 while attacking Ambala airfield. The Sirhind Club was restored through grants by the Punjab Government and voluntary contributions by workers of Indian Ordnance Factories. The church lies in ruins though its imposing spires still stand.

The 'Bungalow' – another adapted British creation – was ideal as tropical housing developed in India and exported all over the world. The plan everywhere was similar with minor changes. The house would have a colonnaded portico where carriages could embark and disembark residents and guests in sunshine or rain. It would also be encircled by a wide colonnaded veranda to keep the sunlight from falling on the walls of the rooms. Over time, part of this would be enclosed to form a study or office. The drawing room was positioned behind the portico with the dining room behind and the bedrooms flanking them on either side. A high roof attempted to beat the heat. Kitchens were located away from the house in a separate outhouse. The bungalow compound was extensive – 15 times the area of the house was considered proper proportion in 1925 for officers! The last major construction in Luytens New Delhi followed this pattern.

Like the bungalow, the troop's barracks too adopted a pattern. Generally linear and double storied on a five-step raised plinth all around to keep the rain and snakes out, they too had verandas on both sides and were aligned to present the short-side to the sun, giving an impression of being un-military-like, as well as out-of-line and symmetry with the layout grid.

Today the bungalows survive in Ambala predominantly on the Mall Road – some dilapidated and decaying, while some in a surprisingly good state of repair. Most of the barracks still serve the original purpose.

*The mouldering rooms are now as they stood*
*Nearly a century and half ago,*
*The well is there and the creaking stair*
*And the roof beams rotting slow,*
*The lawns and compound filled with fun and sound*
*Are turned to wild green ground.*

The Flag Staff House and the adjoining Angora Farm were constructed in 1908-1909 as 'Captains Quarters for 2 Single Officers'. Modifications and additions have completely altered the original though the core remains the same. The MES Inspection Bungalow, built in 1871 at a cost of Rs 4982, is one of the few bungalows which has remained unaltered, serving its original purpose till date.

The other typical entity separate from the bungalow was the club. With the British military outpost moving forward from Karnal to Sirhind, a service officers club was established and registered as the Sirhind Club. When Sirhind was abandoned, the garrison relocated to Ambala, and the club retained its name as it had been registered as such, as mentioned previously. The present club building was constructed in 1891 and opened on 07 May of the same year.

The golf course was laid out in the 1880s and affiliated to the Sirhind Club. The sporting passions of the day being polo, pig-sticking and tennis, it barely survived and was practically defunct by 1947 when it was regularly auctioned to cattle graziers to keep the grass down. It flourishes today as a 6085 yards par 72 course.

Troops from the Ambala garrison were to 'march to the sound of guns' whenever the trumpets called. The ill-fated 'Army of the Indus', mustered at Ferozepur in 1838 for intervention in Afghanistan, drew contingents from Ambala. Hardinge, an old soldier, became the Governor-General in July 1844. War and acquisition of Punjab was his driving motive. Beginning from January 1845, he ordered the forward deployment of troops and guns to Ferozepur, Ludhiana and Ambala. The Ambala garrison of 4,133 soldiers and 24 guns in January 1845 was thus increased to 12,972 men and 32 guns by December 1845. The *casus belli* came on 11/12 December 1845 when the Sikhs crossed the Sutlej. Hardinge had arrived at Ambala on 03 December 1845 and placed himself subordinate to General Gough to participate in the campaign. The artillery train and cavalry from Ambala and Meerut, along with the British troops from the hills, set out for the 'Sutlej Campaign' on 12 December 1845 for their first encounter at Mudki on 18 December. Inevitably, Ambala contributed to the Punjab Movable Column and Delhi Field Force in 1857, the Second Afghan War in 1878 and World War I as part of the 7th (Meerut) Division.

In the beginning of 1857, musketry depots were established at Dum-Dum (Calcutta), Ambala and Sialkot to train detachments from all units in the use of the new Enfield Rifle and its cartridges. The discontent fuelled by the impending introduction of these cartridges prompted the widespread and mysterious burning of all unguarded structures at Agra, Ambala and Sialkot. The incidents at Ambala were particularly severe and a reward of Rs 1,000 was announced to help nab the initiators. The 'Devils Wind' was soon to blow over North India. The resentment and distrust generated by the new cartridges had its influence on the Ambala garrison too. However, the presence of 2,290 European troops to 2,890 Indians prevented any open outbreak of violence. The 5th and 60th Native Infantry Regiments stationed at Ambala were nevertheless disbanded. With the outbreak of the rebellion at Meerut on 10 May 1857, the C-in-C, General Anson came down from Shimla, arriving at Ambala on 15 May, and held his first council of war. General Anson and three other senior officers present during the meeting soon died of cholera on the outskirts of Ambala. The fifth, Colonel Chester, the Adjutant General, was killed fighting. It was, therefore, never known what was discussed and decided at Ambala. British troops stationed in the hills were assembled at Ambala and marched off to the relief of Delhi. The Punjab Movable Column assembled at Wazirabad on 25 May and consisting of two field batteries, a cavalry regiment and a British and an Indian Battalion marched through Lahore, Amritsar and Jullundur, arriving at Ambala on 05 August 1857 en route to Delhi. The Delhi Field Force had been constituted earlier with troops from Meerut and Ambala and had taken up positions on the Ridge outside Delhi.

The turmoil of 1857 caused the transfer of power from the East India Company to the Crown on 01 November 1858. Lord Canning, the last Governor-General, become the first Viceroy and immediately set forth on a policy promoting reconciliation which quickly earned him the nickname 'Clemency' Canning. Setting out on a tour of northern India and holding grand durbars en route at Kanpur, Lucknow and Agra, the fourth durbar was held at Ambala on 19 January 1860. It was a spectacle meant to impress. The Viceroy's Camp required 150 large tents carried on 80 elephants, 500 camels and 500 bullocks. 100 bullock carts were used for transporting equipment while 527 coolies carried the glass windows for the tents and 100 *bhistis* sprayed the camp streets to keep the dust down. On the line of march, the camp extended 24 miles on the road.

Sher Ali, the Amir of Afghanistan, was similarly hosted to a grand durbar at Ambala in 1869.

Kitchener, who was C-in-C Indian Army from 1902 to 1909, initiated wide-ranging reforms which indirectly propped Ambala to its heydays in the 1920s and 1930s. Observing that the Army was scattered 'all higgledy-piggledy over the country without any system or reason', he formed the Army into nine divisions grouped in two commands; Northern and Southern. Each was oriented to a portion of the NW Frontier. Ambala lay on the Northern axis astride the rail and road artery leading to the Khyber. The Northern Army consisted of the 1st (Peshawar), 2nd (Rawalpindi), 3rd (Lahore), 7th (Meerut) and 8th (Lucknow) Divisions. The Sirhind Brigade located at Ambala formed part of the 7th (Meerut) Division. The Sirhind Brigade – comprising the 1st Highland Light Infantry, 1/1 GR, 1/4 GR and 125 Rifles (today 5 Rajputana Rifles) set sail for France in 1914 as part of the Meerut Division, which along with the Lahore Division, formed the Indian Corps. The 9th Hodsons Horse (which with the 10th Lancers formed the Hodsons Horse in 1922) mobilised from Ambala with the Ambala Cavalry Brigade and set sail for France in October 1914. It returned to Ambala on 01 January 1921 after serving in France and with Allenby in Palestine and setting a record for the longest overseas service in the Great War and after.

Kitchener's reform shifted the emphasis on recruitment predominantly to North India, and training centres were established accordingly. The Corps of Sikh Pioneers (the forerunner of the Sikh Light Infantry) Centre was established at Ambala in 1922, till it was merged in 1941 with the Sikh Light Infantry Centre at Bareilly, co-located with the Jat Regiment Centre. The Sikh Regiment Centre at Nowshera in the NWFP was shifted to Ambala in August 1947, and then in March 1952, it moved to Meerut. The Mountain Artillery Training Centre (MATC) was also situated at Ambala, in the present day Panipat Lines, having moved from Lucknow in 1928. The Royal Artillery Station Mess was one of the oldest Gunner Station Mess in India and was the custodian of the entire Indian Mountain Artillery heritage silver and a very complete and interesting set of records. Both the Centre and the Mess went to Pakistan in 1947. The only surviving relics of the MATC are the Gurudwara (constructed in 1930 through a voluntary contribution by all mountain batteries), two Vickers 3.5 Inch Rifled Muzzle Loading Howitzers (cast in 1879 and now placed outside the Flag Staff House) and the Breech Loading 60 pounder (outside the Sub-Area Headquarters). The foundation stone of the present Station Artillery Mess, lately converted to the Corps Headquarter Mess, was laid by Lieutenant General KP Candeth in 1972. Except for Ambala and Dehra Dun, all other mountain artillery stations were in the NW Frontier, with the mountain batteries being turned over from Ambala. The first and the last Veterans Reunion of the erstwhile Indian Mountain Artillery was held at Ambala in March 1933. Coincidentally, honouring the Gunner legacy, an Artillery Division commenced raising at Ambala on 01 May 1997.

Ambala, the large and long famous station was, during its heyday, the cantonment of a horse artillery, cavalry and an infantry brigade along with pioneers. It fell from its greatness in the 1930s owing to the drying of water supply, which also impacted fodder for the horses. This was attributed to an earthquake in 1908 in the Shivalik foothills injuring and altering the water-bearing strata. The removal of mounted troops become imperative thereafter. Ambala continues to live by its water scarce reputation, though lately, the problem has been alleviated. A unique and an elaborate network of covered brick-water channels with siphons and aqueducts still survives, though no longer in use, its death knell being sounded by water scarcity and the coming of cast-iron and galvanized-iron pipes. Covered wells sunk in the compounds provided drinking water. Mostly filled over or dry, they can today be seen in all old compounds. One such covered well, with an exquisite cast-iron ornamentation, is located in the Military Hospital area.

Till the static and operational functions of formations were bifurcated at the outbreak of World War II, the Brigades controlled 'Areas' and the Divisions 'Districts'. The Ambala Brigade Area encompassed the districts of Karnal, Ambala and Sirhind. On bifurcation, the Ambala Sub-Area came about. This was merged with the Punjab Haryana and Himachal Pradesh Area in 1991 and re-designated as the PH & HP (Independent) Sub Area in 1999. The present-day Corps Headquarters buildings were first constructed as the 'Brigade Area Headquarters'.

Post India's partition, Ambala became the home of the famous 4 Infantry Division. In the prevailing ambiguity about the Army's role and place in the decade following Independence, 4 Infantry Division under Major General BM Kaul undertook construction of accommodation as part of *Operation Amar*. A total of 100 married and 50 single-officers quarters, 162 Junior Commissioned Officers married-quarters and 727 Other Rank married-quarters were constructed. The Prime Minister and the Defence Minister inaugurated them on their completion. While the Division was busy mixing cement with sand, 'Hindi-Chini Bhai-Bhai' induced fraternization welcomed a visiting high-powered Chinese military delegation under Marshal Yeh Chiang-Ying. The delegation was shown a firepower demonstration by 4 Artillery Brigade in support of a battalion attack by 14 Punjab at the Naraingarh Ranges in 1958. Ironically, 4 Infantry Division was moved in November-December 1959 to the North-East as the Chinese threat manifested itself, and was to meet its tryst with infamy at Sela in 1962.

Regrouped and rejuvenated, 4 Infantry Division redeemed its honour at Khem Karan and Asal Uttar when it moved from Ambala into battle on 04 September 1965. On 19 August 1965, 6 Mountain Division had been concentrated at Ambala from Bareilly and was similarly committed in the Sialkot Sector. 29 Infantry Brigade Group from Ambala headed for Dera Baba Nanak. As in the days of yore, the Western Command Headquarters were moved down from Shimla and established at Ambala in September 1965.

With the advent of powered flight and the coming of military aviation, Ambala pioneered its introduction in India in 1919. The first military aviation flight took place from the polo ground – later turned into the airfield. Headquarter Royal Air Force India Command was formed here in 1920 and moved to Delhi/Shimla in 1922. No 1 (Army Cooperation) Squadron of the RIAF formed in 1935 at Drigh Road, Karachi and equipped with Wapiti fighters (nicknamed 'Wat-a-pity') was moved to its permanent location at Ambala in 1938, making Ambala the cradle of the fledgling RIAF. That year also saw the establishment of the Air Force Station Headquarter on 01 April. At the outbreak of World War II it was the sole IAF Squadron and was moved to Burma from Ambala on 01 February 1943.

During the war, the Technical Training School and the Service Flying Training School were established on 23 October 1940. The latter imparting both elementary flying training and advanced training for flying instructors. These were upgraded to Air Force Academy in 1949 before moving to Secundrabad in 1951. The Flying Instructors Training School similarly moved to Tambram (Madras) in 1953. The bulk of the senior pilots of the IAF earned their 'wings' at Ambala. The Air Force Station was to have more 'firsts' to its credit. The first Distinguished Flying Cross awardees of the IAF – Engineer and Majumdar – were decorated here at an investiture in 1942. Group Captain Arjan Singh assumed command of the station on 15 August 1947. On 04 November 1948, three Vampire jet fighters arrived at Ambala to equip No 7 Squadron making the IAF the first Asian Air Arm to operate jets. No 7 Squadron had been raised at Ambala in February 1943. When the Gnat was introduced into service, No 2 Squadron was re-equipped with Gnats at Ambala in early 1962. No 14 Squadron was the first to be equipped with Jaguars in UK and arrived at Ambala in July 1979.

On 15 August 1947, aircraft from Ambala, after a fly-past over Ambala, flew on to Delhi for a similar fly-past. Appropriately, the IAF first went into action from Ambala when Spitfires from the Advanced Flying School were flown to Srinagar on 30 October 1947. The crowning glory came in 1971. Gnats from No 18 Squadron at Ambala flying detachments at Srinagar earned the IAFs first and only PVC in Flying Officer NS Sekhon. Entering the gate of the Air Force Station, a pillar proclaims 'Ambala – Pioneers of Military Aviation', a sobriquet richly deserved.

Unknown to the casual traveller on the Grand Trunk Road or Sher Shah Suri Marg, the sprawling Ambala cantonment straddling the road combines a vast panorama of military history – glorious and sad. To a discerning eye, its bricks and stones speak of its heritage. And what of the future?

*On ruins which still speak of the past*
*The stranger now treads the ground,*
*But the purpose remains all the same*
*To soldier to the trumpet's sound.*

(All verses adapted from Rudyard Kipling)

# PARATROOPING TO DACCA

## As narrated by Brigadier Tejinder Singh

Regimental and family affiliations run deep in the Indian Army. My father, Brigadier Sucha Singh VrC, MC was an exceptional paratrooper of the Maratha Light Infantry Regiment. He had commanded 2 Para (Maratha), then 1 Para (Punjab) and raised 51 Parachute Brigade at Gwalior. On being commissioned on 21 December 1969 from the Indian Military Academy, Dehra Dun, I opted for Bombay Sappers recruiting Maratha troops and volunteered for parachute duties. On completion of the Young Officers Course, I was posted to 411 Parachute Field Company, Bombay Sappers, as part of 50 Parachute Brigade.

50 Parachute Brigade was mobilised sometime in February 1971 to counter the Naxalbari insurgency that had overtaken Bengal at that time, and this deployment morphed into the operational deployment for *Operation Cactus Lily* in East Pakistan. 411 Parachute Field Company moved for the operation in July 1971. An airborne assault had been planned as part of the operations in East Pakistan.

The Parachute Brigade was commanded by Brigadier Mathew Thomas who had been a subaltern in 2 Para when my father was the commanding officer. He earmarked 2 Para, his own battalion, for the airborne assault and also insisted that the honour of commanding the Engineer Platoon, forming part of the Battalion Group, should go to me, being the son of a former commanding officer of the battalion. 2 Para was located in the Botanical Gardens in Calcutta while we were located at Barrackpore and moved to the Botanical gardens to marry up with 2 Para on outbreak of hostilities. On commencement of operations, the objective given to the battalion was to capture the bridge on the Poongli River intact, thereby isolating the strong points of Jamalpur and Mymensingh from Dacca.

Aerial photos of the target area confirmed the presence of bunkers on both sides of the bridge. Since the only immediate engineering task was neutralisation of the demolition charges on the bridge, the platoon was disposed of in four sections. The first section, with D company, had an independent task to deny a ferry crossing about four km downstream. A section each was tasked with stops placed about one km North and South of the main position, and the last section was in reserve with platoon headquarter. These sections were to be concentrated should the need for any engineering task emerge.

We moved out from the Botanical Gardens into Quarantine on Night 10/11 December 1971. However, the evening before the move, the Platoon JCO, Naib Subedar Nawaji Bagal, informed me that two of our personnel were missing. This jolt from the blue caused me to activate the entire platoon in search of the two. Sappers Jagdale and Parte, the defaulters, were located in a ditch, dead drunk. I had rather radical views about such behaviour during operations and decided it called for summary punishment in the form of shooting to death for cowardice. Mercifully, my JCO persuaded me to withhold the sentence on the grounds that it would be better to take action in the operational area once we were deployed. This was as sane an advice by an experienced old soldier to an over-eager youngster as has ever been given, because the punishment never took place. However, Sapper Jagdale, who was my jeep driver, was removed from the position and Sapper Sadhu Singh took over.

Practically the entire transport aircraft fleet of the IAF was mobilised for the para-drop of the battalion group on 11 December 1971. C119 Packets were positioned at Dum-Dum and the Dakotas at Kalaikunda. We took off in the afternoon from Dum-Dum, from where all heavy drop equipment like guns and jeeps were loaded onto the Packets. The drop took place at 1630 hrs, approximately 3 to 4 km from the objective. Three things come to my mind as I look back. First, the air dispatchers went about distributing chocolate to us in a welcome change to normal procedure. Second, unlike in practice jumps, the Dropping Zone (DZ) was strewn with left-over parachutes of the Heavy Drop and previous sticks. And third, we were dropped at 700 feet, so one was on the ground rather quickly. Villagers gathered around the Drop Zone informed us that the Pakistani officers had already evacuated the Jamalpur and Mymensingh garrisons. So the subsequent Pakistani elements that ran into our position were basically JCO and NCO-led parties withdrawing to Dacca.

The objective was captured without any opposition, and I immediately confirmed that no demolition charges were in place, nor were the bunkers booby-trapped. By now it was past last light, and I was standing on the bridge along with an Observation Post Officer of 17 Para Field Regiment, when we observed vehicles approaching from the North, the direction of Mymensingh, at full speed with headlights on. The Gun Position Officer at the DZ confirmed on the artillery radio net that none of our vehicles had left the DZ and that these were enemy vehicles. While other vehicles stopped well short of our position, one vehicle drove on into the battalion defended area. It was hit and stopped by a Rocket-Propelled Grenade and overturned. This was an enemy engineer team coming to prepare the bridge for demolition. One officer and 15 enemy sappers were captured alive, besides others who were killed on the spot. Explosives in the vehicle caught fire and burnt the whole night.

A little after midnight I was called to Battalion Headquarter where the CO, Lieutenant Colonel KS Pannu, anticipating a counter-attack wanted mines to be laid. Since no mines had been received from the DZ, I offered to take out a patrol to the DZ and get them. This done, I began laying mines around first light with my reserve section. While doing so, I noticed an enemy party advancing towards us. I, therefore, pulled the section out and proceeded to the bridge which was at a considerable elevation. The enemy personnel coming towards us moved over the minefield and we saw one individual being blown up by a mine. Thereafter, in the ensuing firefight and artillery shelling, this enemy party was neutralised. Sometime later, a large body of about 50 troops was observed trying to outflank our position and cross the river in order to retreat to Dacca. Two Medium Machine Guns (MMGs) positioned opposite their crossing point waited till they were all in the open sand banks of the river and neutralised them. Watching all this action from the vantage point of the bridge was a surreal experience.

I was then asked to go out as part of a patrol to try to recover as many enemy vehicles as possible out of the lot that had stopped short of our position the previous night and had survived the strafing by our fighter aircraft earlier in the morning. While most vehicles had been destroyed and were deserted, there were some enemy personnel still with the vehicles and a firefight ensued. I shot one individual at close quarters, and after the rest had been silenced, I took his steel helmet and replaced my turban with it. It had his name *Ziafat* written in ballpoint-ink on the inside strap of the helmet. I got hold of a brand new Isuzu truck and drove it into the battalion area.

The link up by 1 Maratha Light Infantry took place around mid-day on 12 December 1971. The leading platoon commander was my course mate Second Lieutenant BK Ponwar. While inspecting the bodies of Pak soldiers killed the previous night, I found one youngster whose pay-book showed that he had just joined the Pak Army and had drawn only one payment. We also found a boot, with the toe blown off, belonging to the individual who had stepped on our mines. I quickly recovered the mines we had laid since I did not want to be left behind when the Battalion Group started the move southwards towards Dacca. We moved to Tangail proper on 13 December 1971.

On Night 15/16 December 1971 we advanced towards Dacca and stopped at a suburb of Dacca named Mirpur where the battalion firmed in. In the morning, I had gone to the forward company to assess any mine-laying requirement and was sitting with the company commander, Major JS Sethi, eating a breakfast of eggs, when a jeep driven by the Adjutant 2 Para, Captain Nirbhay Sharma, flying a white flag, approached us from the rear. He stopped to inform us that he had been tasked by Major General Nagra to take a note over to the Pakistani lines advising them to surrender to avoid unnecessary blood-shed. Both Major Sethi and I decided to join the mission and jumped onto the jeep.

We drove into the very forbidding looking Pakistani forward defences without a shot being fired at us or being challenged. After we had gone about a hundred yards, an NCO carrying a Light-Machine Gun (LMG) stopped us. He was highly excited and shivering, consequently, was instantly obeyed by all of us. He effectively took us all as POWs. An officer then appeared and took us to the Pak Battalion Headquarter. We were treated courteously and information of our arrival was transmitted to the sector commander, a Major General, who promptly arrived on the scene in a shiny black Buick. After reading the note, he ordered our weapons, equipment and vehicle restored and we moved along with him towards 2 Para for him to parley with General Nakra. A Pakistani Lieutenant had jumped into our jeep just as we were underway and was sitting with his legs outside the jeep. About halfway back, an LMG from 2 Para opened fire, and we were caught on the elevated road-bund, unable to take any cover. Major Sethi took a burst on his left knee and lost his leg. The Pakistani officer, a shot on his heel. I was hit on the head and I thought that the bullet had ricocheted off my helmet. In fact, the bullet had pierced the helmet on the left side, burnt the scarf I had wrapped around my head under the helmet, and exited at the back of the head. I narrowly missed becoming the only person in history to have been killed by his own father's battalion! Needless to say, the helmet is a prized souvenir.

Thereafter, the move into Dacca was a free-for-all, with cheering crowds heralding our entry to the cries of *Joy Bangla.* Since I was mobile in my jeep, unlike the rest of the battalion, I was able to move ahead and take down the nearest Pakistani Flag. I then entered Dacca International Hotel. There I was stopped by some persons of the international press who stated that this was neutral territory and hence out of bounds to both militaries. I responded that this provision was null and void now since there was only one side left. This led to much mirth and backslapping. A photograph of us driving into Dacca, with me at the wheel and Naib Subedar Nawaji Bagal in the co-driver seat, appeared in the *Illustrated Weekly of India* and also in the *Newsweek* magazine captioned 'Indian troops entering Dacca'.

Intelligence reports received before we emplaned for the jump had indicated that there were seven F-86 Sabre Jets still intact with the Pak Air Force, but these were unable to take off since the runway was heavily damaged due to our bombing. I, therefore, headed straight for the airfield to locate these assets. I found the Officers Mess on the airfield totally flattened with only the Officers Mess sign board standing. I then went to inspect the bomb damage to the runway and the dispersal area and found the fighters in their blast pens. I got into the cockpit of the nearest fighter and tried my utmost to have it start up, but failed in the effort.

For the surrender ceremony the next day, 2 Para was detailed to provide the guard of honour. I, however, was free to move around as I pleased. I drove into the ceremony area just after Lieutenant General AAK Niazi arrived. My immediate impulse was to remove the flag from his vehicle. Soldierly ethics prevailed, and considering that it would be an insult to a senior commander, enemy notwithstanding, I refrained from doing so. I have regretted this decision ever since as, after the surrender ceremony when I saw that vehicle again, it had been stripped clean by somebody else.

During the day there was much movement of troops of both armies. Our troops used one side of the road while the Pak Army moved on the other side, with Military Police of both armies co-ordinating the movement. I took this opportunity for some sightseeing around Dacca with as many of my platoon as could fit into my jeep and trailer. This was made easy as the Mukti Bahini had taken over all fuel pumps in Dacca, and one could just drive in for a free fill-up anytime. At one point a Pak Havildar saw us and said, "Sahib, if we had officers like you and we were the troops, no army on earth could defeat us". This remark coming from the enemy was worth more than all other compliments.

We de-inducted to Tangail on 18 December 1971 and the next day moved by road to New Bongaigaon. The Para Brigade had moved west to the Fazilka Sector in Punjab. 411 Para Field Company was located at Gidderbaha, near Malout, where we married up with the unit.

# THE CHEETAH

The border war fought with China in 1962 highlighted the need for a light utility helicopter which could operate at high altitudes as the performance of the existing piston-engine helicopters fell drastically with increasing altitude. France had produced the Alouette III with a powerful gas-turbine engine capable of such performance. The first lot was acquired and its licensed production commenced in the country in the late sixties. It also brought about a transition from light fixed-wing aircraft like the Auster, to helicopters, for Air Observation Post (AOP) duties – which entailed direction of artillery fire by the pilot at targets unobservable from the ground. The Army thus got the Alouette III as their observation platform.

The Alouette was revolutionary for its time. It had a gas-turbine engine running at 33,500 revolutions per minute. An automatic fuel-control governor ensured appropriate fuel injection and, therefore, power output, depending on the operating requirements related with the pitch of the rotor blades. Plus, it relieved the pilot from the traditional throttle, making it a delight to fly. But in the extreme altitudes of our Northern Borders even the Alouette had its limitations. Something with a better performance was required, and that machine evolved by mating the best of Alouette II and Alouette III.

While the Alouette II had a light-weight tubular airframe, the Alouette III had a powerful Artouse III engine. When this engine was mounted on the former, an extraordinary helicopter took shape – named the Lama by its French manufacturers and the Cheetah by the

Indian Army. Proving to be an all-time great, it could lift its own weight, or another Cheetah, under-slung and operate at extreme high altitudes due to its excellent weight-to-power ratio. Inducted first into the Army AOP Units and later into the Air Force, its manoeuvrability and unrestricted view in all directions from the cockpit, made it an ideal observation platform.

The Lama first flew on 17 March 1969. During demonstration flights in India, it landed and took off at a record 24,600 feet. In 1972, a French test pilot climbed to a peak height of 40,800 feet, where the engine flamed out due to lack of oxygen. He set another record for the longest autorotation – the equivalent of a 'glide' by a helicopter – and landed! Just as a mule is a cross between a mare and a donkey, so was the Lama between an Alouette II and Alouette III, hence nicknamed as the 'Mule of the Air'. And like the mule, the Lama is also a load-carrying pack-animal in the high altitudes of its native South American mountains.

In one of the first high-altitude rescue operations by the Cheetah, I flew as co-pilot to evacuate two critically ill climbers from about 18,000 feet on 24-25 August 1976. They were part of a French expedition to Kanchenchunga. On 20 October 1976, while carrying out a sortie in North Sikkim, I and my co-pilot took off from a helipad at 16,400 feet to return to our base at Bagdogra. In the normal course, we would have lost height gradually along the Teesta River Valley, but that day we decided to climb to exploit and experience the Cheetah's capability. After about 30 minutes we had attained 26,800 feet. We were abreast of and practically at the same height as Kanchenchunga. The Cheetah was still climbing at about 200 feet per minute. Lacking adequate oxygen for breathing, and facing very strong winds, we called it quits! The Cheetah had taken us where even eagles do not dare.

On 13 April 1984, Cheetah helicopters of the Indian Army AOP landed troops at Sia La and Bilafond La on the Saltoro Ridge, west of the Siachen Glacier, at a height of 20,000 feet, thus pre-empting Pakistani plans to occupy and claim the area as part of Pakistan Occupied Kashmir. It signalled the launch of *Operation Meghdoot,* made possible and sustained by the Cheetah helicopters, which added another distinction in their superlative operational history.

One of the most outstanding actions of *Operation Meghdoot* was the capture of Qaid Post (later named Bana Post). It was occupied by Pak troops in March / April 1987, enabling them to interdict all helicopter movement, and consequently, critical logistic support, into the Northern Glacier. The final assault to dislodge the enemy was launched on 25/26 June 1987. The 60 strong attacking force, backed by over 100 support troops, finally put six men on the objective. It also involved approximately 300 sorties over hundreds of hours of Cheetah helicopter flying to prepare for the assault. The impossible made possible by the Cheetahs!

All Cheetah pilots will recall some incident when its superb performance enabled them to beat the elements and get out of an otherwise hopeless situation.

The Indian Cheetah went extinct in the wild in the 1930s. As the Indian military looks for a replacement and gets one, the military Cheetah would have served for 50 years. Even after it fades away, old aviators will remember it as an outstanding machine in the league of the world's greatest aircraft.

# KHAKI

The Persian *khak* or dust gave birth to the word *khaki* – the colour of dust. Khaki became a universal form of military dress, and later on, a casual style of trousers. It all began with the Anglo-Sikh Wars – the last great military engagement in the establishment of the British Indian Empire.

After the First Anglo-Sikh War 1845-46, Henry Lawrence was appointed as Resident at the Court of Lahore, and the Agent to the Governor-General for affairs of Punjab and the North-West Frontier. He chose two young officers – Lumsden and Hodson – as political assistants. Settlement and administration of the wild land of Trans Indus, the area between the Indus and the mountain frontier with Afghanistan, with the focal point being Peshawar, required obvious and serious attention. There being no troops of the East India Company except at Lahore, a military force was required. Such a force would require a specialized body to guide the troops in the field as well as collect intelligence. Thus was born the idea of a Corps of Guides. The new 'Irregular' Corps, being outside the military system and customs of the Army, was to be uniquely composed of horse cavalry and foot infantry. Its uniform was also a matter of discretion for its commandant.

Henry Lawrence chose Harry Lumsden as the Commandant and William Hodson as Second-in-Command for raising the Corps of Guides on 14 December 1846. As the Guides work was primarily amongst the tribesmen, and the men too were recruited from amongst them, they were conveniently dressed in the local attire of white handspun cotton pyjamas, smock and turban. These were soon found to be too conspicuous in the arid, rock strewn, barren terrain of the frontier. Lumsden and Hodson then improvised a more suitable colour. As a first attempt at camouflage, the clothing was dyed with the extract of the local mazari palm. This produced a grayish colour; however, the mazari extract could not dye the leather sheepskin jerkins or *poshteens.* The alternative found was mulberry juice which produced a drab yellowish shade. This was the first colour resembling what ultimately evolved into khaki. Other dyeing agents employed were *Multani Mitti* or Fullers Earth, tea and coffee.

The drab coloured uniform soon found favour with other irregular units raised for service on the Frontier. It then came into use elsewhere instead of the scarlet and white European pattern uniform of the regular army. All units raised for service during 1857-58 adopted khaki as their field service uniform, including the British units at the Siege of Delhi in 1857. The first British unit to do so was the 52nd Foot – later the Oxfordshire and Buckinghamshire Infantry. Khaki as a universal uniform was discarded in 1858, then formally reintroduced in 1861, only to be discarded again in 1864.

The Indian Army first went to Africa for the Abyssinia Campaign of 1867-68. This was also the first major campaign when troops wore khaki. Drawing lessons from the disastrous First Afghan War of 1839-42, all troops employed in the Second Afghan War of 1878-80 used white drill locally dyed khaki. At the conclusion of this war, khaki became the official service uniform of the British Indian Army. Produced under local unit arrangements, a wide variety of shades came into service, until a uniform mill-dyed khaki was produced and patented in England in the late 1880s, the dye being imported from Germany. The official history of the Guides records the regimental dying of their uniforms as:

> The clothing of the Guides was dyed by men regimentally employed, each soldier contributing 1/4 anna per mensem from his pay. This arrangement was maintained until early in the twentieth century, for quite twenty years after the general adoption of fast-dyed khaki clothing; and its abolition was agreed to with reluctance, as in addition to the khaki uniform the dyers used to dye the brightly

coloured *pagris* so popular among certain classes of Indians when wearing plain clothes.

While the British Army favoured grey field service uniforms, the Indian Army found khaki as the most practical. During the campaign in Egypt in 1880-82 the British Army too found khaki to be more appropriate and adopted it for their service uniform. It was well and truly established by the time of the Boer War in 1899. At the end of the war, British troops came to be referred to as 'Khakis', and as elections were held thereafter, all elections seeking to capitalize on a recent military victory were referred to as 'Khaki Elections'.

The United States Army adopted khaki during the Spanish American War of 1898, with the United States Navy and Marine Corps doing so thereafter. British service dress was fully and finally changed to khaki in 1902 along with all colonial armies. The Japanese followed in 1905. By World War I all belligerents had adopted khaki, albeit with some variations in the shade. By World War II it was universal.

Khaki being so readily available and adaptable, it became the standard for all uniformed services in India and other British colonies. Besides the Army, it found favour with the police, para-military, postal services and practically all government bodies. Colonial civil servants too adopted the khaki bush shirt and shorts, eminently suited for the climate and perhaps adding a touch of official authority to their appearance. The police today are synonymous with khaki.

At the outbreak of World War II, the Indian Army had adopted khaki as universal for all dresses, however, the need for camouflage in the jungles of Malaya and Burma dictated adoption of the more amenable 'Olive Green'. At the end of the war, with large stocks available, the olive green became the standard colour of uniform of the Indian Army. Yet the Service Dress or SD remained khaki. This gave way to the dark green service dress in the late 1980s. The only piece remaining khaki is the winter-wear woollen Angola Shirt, which too should change to olive green. The Air Force similarly changed from khaki to blues in the 1980s.

Just as utility-driven military attire – the Trench Coat, Cardigan, Jodhpurs and the Beret – became popular with the fashion world, the trousers known as 'Khakis' became popular following World War II. These were initially war surplus military issue uniforms. Today, it refers to the fabric and style of trousers based on the original military model rather than the colour.

Of the two who started it all, Lumsden became a Lieutenant General in 1875 and retired thereafter. He died in 1896. Hodson raised the Hodson's Horse in 1857, an irregular cavalry unit which today forms part of the Indian Army as an armoured regiment. Hodson was killed in action on 09 March 1858 at Lucknow. The Guides bifurcated into cavalry and infantry in 1922. The 10th Guides Cavalry went to Pakistan in 1947, while The Guides Infantry ultimately became the 2nd Battalion Frontier Force Regiment (Guides), Pakistan Army.

# LEGACY OF THE GREAT WAR

'The War to End All Wars' or 'The Great War For Civilisation' did not achieve what the belligerents or its protagonists imagined. Neither did it end 'Before Christmas', as the British expected, nor 'Before the Leaves Fall', as per the German objectives. In due course, it very appropriately came to be labelled as the First World War, as it could not prevent the Second World War.

The Great War was dominated by technological developments of the barbed wire, heavy and massed artillery, magazine-filled rapid-fire rifles and belt-fed machine guns. All contributed towards the butchers work. The industrialised fighting changed the very nature of war. For the record, about 70 million military personnel were mobilized and 16.5 million killed. Of the million horses employed, only 60,000 survived. India provided 1,73,000 horses, mules and camels for the war and recruited 14,40,437 men, sent 13,81,050 for service overseas, of which 74,187 officers and men were killed and another 70,000 wounded. 13,516 names are inscribed on the India Gate Memorial, New Delhi completed in 1933. India bore the cost of these men, besides an outright contribution of £100 million towards the overall war effort.

*They went with songs to the battle, they were young,*
*Straight of limb, true of eye, steady and aglow.*
*They were staunch to the end against odds uncounted,*
*They fell with their faces to the foe.*
—Laurence Binyon, *For the Fallen*

Harry Patch, the last surviving Tommy of the trenches of the Western Front, died on 25 July 2009 aged 111 years, 1 month, 1 week and 1 day.

While the larger issues of empire, colonialism, class and its effect on an entire generation impacted the world at large, The Great War also left some memorable terms and phrases on the military and everyday lexicon which endure till today. Even vernacular languages felt the effect.

So when the German warship *Emden,* prowling in the Bay of Bengal, shelled Madras harbour and the city on 22 September 1914, causing panic and mass evacuation of the population, it brought the war to India before the Indian troops went into action on the Western Front. The Tamils, evidently impressed with the demonstrated German capability, coined a new word – *emden* meaning 'an enterprising, resourceful and meticulous person'.

Massive armies pitted against each other had a large number of senior officers visible much more now than before. The gold braid on their caps led to them being called 'brass hats' or simply 'brass'.

By 1914, artillery systems evolved into rapid-firing breech-loading guns with a hydraulic recoil system. The range of firing increased considerably, well beyond the contact distances of infantry, and the shell had an explosive filling with a fuse to detonate it on impact. The industrial revolution enabled mass production of both the gun and ammunition. Employment of massed artillery delivering fire from well behind the front line was inevitable. The Somme offensive beginning 01 July 1916 on a 17-mile front was preceded by one week of round-the-clock preparatory bombardment. When the offensive began, the British suffered 57,470 casualties, including 19,240 dead, on the first day itself. The Paschendale Offensive on 17 July 1917 was preceded by 15 days of bombardment. As the targets were not visible from the gun positions for directing the fire of the guns, observers were hoisted in baskets attached to tethered balloons to observe and direct the preparatory bombardment in depth. Hoisting of such observer balloons signalled the opening of an offensive. This gave birth to the phrase 'when the balloon goes up', meaning when the action or hostilities start. It is still used to indicate or refer to the commencement of operations. Such massed artillery employed as a barrage of fire also introduced 'barrage' as a prefix for anything done overwhelmingly and rapidly – for example, a barrage of questions, or abuse.

The Battle of Somme also highlighted problems of coordination between the lifting of artillery fire and the infantry assault immediately thereafter. Keeping time with the available pocket watches was cumbersome. This prompted the large-scale introduction of wristwatches with luminous dials to enable the infantry to time the assault with the artillery fire in the darkness of the trenches.

Amongst the German artillery, the 77 mm field gun was more worrisome than the heavier guns and howitzers, because its high-velocity shell travelled faster than the speed of sound and was heard 'whizzing' and exploding before the 'bang' of it being fired could be heard, thus giving no warning of its coming. Soon labelled the 'whizz-bang' by the soldiers in the trenches, the slang came to be used for anything quick and effective. The British Tommy dubbed the pre-printed letter-cards provided for sending home 'whizz-bangs' as these had phrases like 'I am well', 'I am in hospital' etc and he simply cut out the non-applicable words and sent them. Today it applies to anything noisy, speedy, efficient or having a stunning effect, like a hard-hitting alcoholic drink or a drug, a competent engineer or a workman, or even a useful mechanical device.

Attempts to break through the static trench line defences involved massed infantry attacks. The soldiers would climb out from the top of their trenches to assault the enemy, giving rise to the phrase 'going over the top'. As it resulted in horrendous, and in hindsight, needless casualties, it is today used to describe anything outlandish or irrational as 'over the top'. Attacking troops were signalled to 'go over the top' by whistles blown by the commanders, much like the commencement of a game of football, giving birth to the phrase 'kick-off' – implying to commence or start an event.

*Lines of grey, muttering faces, masked with fear,*
*They leave their trenches, going over the top,*
*While time ticks blank and busy on their wrists,*
*And hope, with furtive eyes and grappling fists,*
*Flounders in the mud, O Jesus, make it stop.*
—Siegfried Sassoon, *Attack*

Military aviation was still in its infancy in 1914. It started with reconnaissance and graduated to dropping of small bombs over enemy lines. The crew, carrying rifles and revolvers, would fire at enemy planes at close quarters. Soon a machine gun was fixed on the aircraft and aerial combat between aircraft became a reality. Tactics like diving at the enemy with the sun at the back, tighter circles to get behind the enemy and so on resulted in a melee of weaving, twisting and turning of aircraft in the sky, which the ground troops quickly dubbed as 'dogfights'. This term for aerial combat endures in the jet age.

By the time of the Crimean War in 1850, soldiers were equipped with thick, heavy serge greatcoats to ward off the cold, notwithstanding the restricted agility imposed by their bulk. World War I brought them into the trenches where mud, rain, snow and extreme cold combined to add to the greatcoats weight with layers of caked mud. Burberry of England had produced closely woven cloth – Gabardine – in early 1900 which was water-repellent and much more practical than rubberised-cloth for rain capes. The trenches of World War I prompted combining the gabardine rain cape with a warm inner-lining as a substitute for both the greatcoat and the rubberised rain cape. Designed primarily for officers, shoulder straps were added for epaulettes and a belt to give it a military appearance. A double-breasted, fully buttoned front in khaki or beige colour made it compatible with a military uniform. The soldiers called it 'trench-coat'. Having seen widespread use during the war, it caught the public attention when Hollywood characters were shown wearing it in post-war movies. Today the trench-coat has transited from the trenches to the fashion ramps.

An unglamorous offshoot of the trenches was the 'trench foot'. Prolonged exposure of feet to wet, cold and unhygienic conditions prevailing in the trenches resulted in poor blood supply to the feet, leading to infection and gangrene, necessitating amputation. Hence, the medical condition of feet caused by exposure to extreme cold and moisture is today referred to as trench foot.

Indians had for long referred to England as *Bilait.* It gained wider currency when Indian troops landed in France in 1914. Going 'Home' or to England was, and is, frequently referred to as 'Blighty'.

An Indian soldier wrote home from the Western Front:

*And so the war is raging by sky and land and sea*
*And underneath the water, five kings are fighting three*
*The cannon roar like thunder, the bullets fly like rain*
*And only the hurt, the maimed and blind will ever see home again.*
—Shrabani Basu, *For King And Another Country*

Full understanding and acceptance of psychological conditions resulting from 'shell shock' and 'battle fatigue' were to come later. Cowardice, especially 'cowardice in the face of the enemy', was the generally accepted reason for any physical failing, for which military law prescribed the death penalty. During World War I, 3080 British soldiers were awarded the death sentence, of which 346 were carried out – 240 being for deserting posts under fire. On reaching a breaking point under battlefield stress, some resorted to self-inflicted injuries to get away. Others hoped for a 'Blighty Wound' – serious enough to be sent to England for long treatment yet not life-threatening. If self-inflicted, it was called the 'Blighty Touch'. Colonel Bruce Seaton, commanding the Indian Hospital at Brighton, examined 1000 Indian troops to ascertain if any of them were self-inflicted. In a secret report, he concluded that there was no evidence to suggest self-wounding among the Indian soldiers. The most common practice among British troops was to put a bullet in the foot. The metaphor 'shoot oneself in the foot' coalesced into implying unintentional harming of one's interests whilst in the process of trying to damage someone else or to demonstrate gross incompetence or ineptitude. People shoot themselves in the foot in all walks of life today!

The Indian Expeditionary Force to France was the first major deployment across *Kala Pani*. The multiple castes, religion, ethnic variations and food preferences of Indian troops on the Western Front, compounded by the prevailing field conditions, inevitably resulted in a logistics nightmare. Meat being the most complex to handle, a solution was found by delivering sheep and goat live which were slaughtered under unit arrangements as per religious and customary sensibilities. This came to be referred to as 'Meat On Hoof' or MOH. The term and practice of supplying MOH is still used in the Indian Army, especially in remote areas of deployment.

Equipping and clothing millions of soldiers was a major effort by itself. All means to exercise economy were employed. Amongst them was sorting through discarded clothing collected from the battlefields or hospital units. Anything usable or repairable was re-issued, and the rest sent home to be recycled. The label 'Pure New Wool' came to indicate that an apparel had been made from non-recycled fibre and, therefore, had no association with the wounded and the dead. Today the label confirms non-recycled wool.

Before the war, officers were expected to have a private income and paid for their uniforms and kit. With heavy casualties, officers had to be found from the lower social classes or promoted from the ranks placing a heavy financial demand on them for their uniforms and kit. It soon became imperative to offset this expenditure. An outfit grant or allowance was thus introduced which exists to this day.

Paperwork never ceases in the army – reports, strength returns, casualty statements, ammunition available or expended and so on. The trenches of World War I were no exception with regular piles of instructions. The soldiers called it 'bum fodder' or 'bumf' – the only use apparent to them. The term endures, especially in the military, to refer to any voluminous piece of written papers with very little inherent substance.

Loss of limbs was as commonplace as loss of life. Those who lost all four had to be carried in a basket giving birth to the term 'basket case' – someone or something totally dependent on help or aid.

*In Flanders fields the poppies blow*
*Between the crosses, row on row,*
*That mark our place; and in the sky,*
*The larks, still bravely singing, fly*
*Scarce heard amid the guns below.*

John McCrae's *In Flanders Field* came to associate poppies with the war dead. Poppy wreaths are today symbolically laid on war memorials. Some countries like Canada have a poppy imprinted on the car number plate to signify the owner as a veteran.

With millions dead and many whose remains were not found or could not be identified, memorials to the 'Unknown Soldier' were erected to remember and pay homage to them. Today they are prominent landmarks in most capitals of the world.

The war produced some outstanding poetry and prose, mostly by young men who saw the horrors first-hand in the trenches. Some are universally inscribed on memorials and cemeteries till today. The fourth stanza of Laurence Binyon's *For The Fallen,* published in *The Times* on 21 September 1914, has come to be the universal 'Ode Of Remembrance' read at most commemorations:

*They shall not grow old, as we that are left grow old,*
*Age shall not weary them, nor the years condemn.*
*At the going down of the sun and in the morning*
*We shall remember them.*

The Second World War was to generate its own 'Block Busters'*.

---

* *A heavy aerial bomb capable of destroying a whole block of buildings.*

# FROM PESHAWAR TO ZOJILA

## With 11 Field Regiment (Zojila) in J&K: 1947-48

## As narrated by Major General Lachman Singh Lehal PVSM, VrC

On 20 February 1947, the British Government announced its intention to transfer power not later than June 1948. Lord Mountbatten, the new Viceroy and a man in a hurry, arrived on 22 March. On 03 June, he announced that the partition of India into the Dominions of India and Pakistan would occur by 15 August. My unit was located at Peshawar and on 12 August, my British Commanding Officer (CO) told me that he was sending me on two months annual leave during which I would be posted to a unit of the Indian Dominion. Parting from my battery of Punjabi Musalmans was an emotional affair with moist eyes as the train left Rawalpindi on 13 August. When the Boundary Award was announced belatedly on 16 August, mayhem followed.

As I did not get my posting till the first week of October, I decided to visit the Sub-Area Headquarters at Jullundur Cantt. They advised me to report to the Mountain Artillery Centre at Ambala Cantt. On arrival, I was allotted a tent in the compound of the Haig Lines Officers Mess. The next day, I was advised to proceed to Army Headquarter (HQ), Delhi, who in turn posted me to 8 Field Regiment at Ranchi. On reporting to the unit location, I discovered that it was the "advance party" as the main regiment was still in Pakistan. Lieutenant Colonel Anup Singh Kalha, who was a Kings Commissioned Indian Officer (KCIO), had also arrived to join the same regiment. On 22

October Pakistan-backed tribals invaded Kashmir. On 27 October Indian troops landed in Srinagar and two days later Kalha and I were ordered to report to Artillery Directorate, Army HQ at the earliest for a special assignment. On arrival, Kalha was posted as Commander Artillery, JAK Force, in the rank of Colonel, while I was posted to 11 Field Regiment at Pune. I reported there to Lieutenant Colonel SJ Sathe, the first Indian CO of the Regiment, and he instructed me to leave for Pathankot the next day as the Officer Commanding Advance Party. En route we were asked to detrain at Ambala as all rail moves beyond had been suspended. After about a week, we were squeezed into a composite military special to Pathankot carrying ordnance stores and leave parties for units in J&K. We reached Pathankot the next day. The Regiment had not beaten us and arrived a few days later.

In the officers mess set up in the Dak Bungalow, I realized that the officers were strangers to each other as most of us had been posted from all over. Further, the men were strangers to the officers. The troops came from South India, and none of us knew any South-Indian language. The CO now informed me that I was to command Alfa Troop of 30 Field Battery.

During the strict and harsh war-time training and exposure to actual war in Burma, I had imbibed the essential ingredients of artillery fire. The sole function of an Observation Post (OP) officer was to bring timely and accurate fire on the enemy. This was only possible if the vehicles moved the guns and ammunition to the gun areas in time by day or night, and the wireless and line communications between the OP and guns worked without fail. I located my troop Viceroy Commissioned Officer (VCO) and in a mix of Hindustani and English conveyed to him that I would inspect the vehicles, signal equipment and guns starting at 9 am next morning. It was late afternoon when I finished with the guns and their tools.

Next morning we left the camp at sunrise, crossed the Ravi over the boat bridge and bumped along the pitted *katcha* road to Jammu. At Jammu, we were guided by a Military Police(MP) Dispatch Rider (DR) to the Royal Stables, even as darkness descended on this very cold early winter night. My orders to fill-up vehicle tanks with petrol, and report vehicle defects needing repairs, got a sullen reception from my VCO and the *jawans* who wanted a mug of hot tea, a hot meal and a warm bed after a long and tiring day. However, the next morning I sensed an attitudinal change in the men, as they saw that all vehicles and guns of our battery had reached Jammu before dinner while a number of vehicles of the Regiment were still to join us.

By midday we learnt that our CO had been promoted as the Commander Artillery JAK Force. Colonel Kalha had been posted as Brigadier Artillery Southern Command at Pune. The Regiment and B Troop left for Srinagar next morning leaving Battery HQ and my troop at Jammu. We received orders to report to 1 Patiala at Akhnur. Lieutenant Colonel Bikram Dev Singh, DSO, MBE, CO 1 Patiala, gave his orders in the evening of 09 December for the capture of Chhamb on 11 December. His plan of attack was to deploy a company after last light of 10 December at Chapreal on the east of Manawar Tawi to guard his rear and right flank against enemy interference. Two companies were to cross the Tawi after midnight 10/11 December north of Mandiala while one company and a troop armoured cars under Major Sukhdeo Singh, MC, the Second-in-Command, were to demonstrate a frontal attack on Chhamb from the direction of Palanwala. The CO with the defence platoon and sniper section was to move East of the Tawi in line with the advance of the two companies.

My troop deployed west of Palanwala after last light 10 December while I joined the battalion. After midnight I, along with my OP party, moved with the CO. After about one hour, I found that my men, carrying heavy wireless batteries were finding it difficult to keep pace with the CO's party. With a sense of embarrassment, I sought some porters to carry my wireless batteries. The CO grunted in annoyance and asked, "How many porters do you need?" I asked for two, and he gave me the three civilian porters who were carrying reserves of mortar and machine-gun ammunition and digging tools.

After daylight, the wireless silence was broken by the two companies to report that they were in Mandiala area. About 9 am we heard a few stray shots South of Mandiala followed by a report that two enemy snipers had been killed. At about 10.30 am, a couple of rifle shots, from a grassy area about 400 yards from us, went over our heads. The sniper section deployed around us while the defence platoon probed towards the source of the firing. After a few minutes, we saw a man on a pony galloping away from us. The sniper on our right missed from a kneeling position. The CO let out an abuse at the sniper whose second shot felled the man while the horse galloped off to disappear in the scrub and high grass. Wireless silence having been broken, the CO assumed a tight control over the companies on the move towards Chhamb. The companies advancing from Mandiala were now involved in a firefight with the enemy in Chhamb. The CO ordered Major Shamsher Singh, the right company commander, to cut off the enemy by capture of the area behind Chhamb village. The company was held up by heavy Light-Machine-Gun (LMG) and rifle fire and I was asked to engage the enemy. On seeing the first ranging round Shamsher spoke excitedly on his wireless set in Punjabi, "*Gola dushman di gichy te laga, isi jagah fire karo*" (the shell has hit the nape of the enemy, fire at the same spot). It was planned to bombard the objective for five minutes "on call" from Shamsher. On my suggestion, it was agreed that a smoke shell be fired from one gun to indicate the end of the fire plan. As the fire plan started and the assault company moved forward under the artillery covering fire, the CO ordered his Second-in-Command to attack the enemy in Chhamb village with vigour and bold use of the armoured cars. Some shells, on hitting the treetops, produced an air-burst effect over the enemy trenches demoralising him. Soon a very light signal indicated the capture of the objective.

My party waded across the Tawi behind the CO. As we climbed the Tawi bank, we could see the armoured cars and the company climbing it too. Then we heard a loud explosion followed by a wireless broadcast by the armoured car VCO, "*Saale top khana ne apna hi armoured car barbad kar dia*". The CO changed direction to the scene of the explosion where we discovered that an anti-tank mine on the track had blown the rear tyre of the armoured car. The pioneer platoon was summoned but a 3-tonner was blown up on another mine before the pioneers arrived to clear the remaining two mines.

The CO climbed the double-storey burnt house of Honorary Captain Bhola Singh, a retired Gunner VCO, and gave out the deployment orders to his companies, guns and machine-guns from the window of the first floor of the house. I still remember the attack on Chhamb as a model of a battalion attack under the effective control of the CO.

On 14 December, as we were getting into the evening "stand to" positions, a hail of bullets flew over our heads from a patch of tall grass about 500 yards in front of my OP. I could see a lot of movement in the area. Firing two ranging rounds, I ordered, "Charge I, 900, nine rounds gunfire, search 100 sweep 3 degrees". The area along the edge of the tall grass was covered in thick dust through which I could see flashes of shell bursts. After some initial yelling and shouting by the enemy, a death-like silence descended on the scene, while we stayed in our "stand to" positions. Soon bullets began flying again over our heads while we waited with grenades in our hands to face an enemy charge. Strict orders were given that no one would fire without the certainty of a kill. We also became aware that a large number of the enemy had assembled in front of us on the other side of the village street. This erupted into a battle of abuse in rich Punjabi, accompanied by an occasional burst of fire from the enemy side. The artillery guns kept silent as the enemy was too close to our defences. At about 4 am, silence descended once again on the scene as the enemy disengaged and disappeared toward the Pak border.

Just as we were settling down to the 'Battle of Abuse', I was told by the Battery Commander (BC), Major Bhupindra Singh, that a vehicle with full lights was approaching the gun area from the direction of Palanwala. As it came near, it started switching the lights off and on while driving towards Chhamb. The BC, in the meantime, was walking around the gun area with a stick in his hand to chase the gunners out of the slit trenches to their action position on the guns. As the vehicle emerged out of the Tawi, a loaded gun was laid on it to fire on the orders of the BC. It turned out to be Jhanda, the Battery Captain, who was bringing artillery ammunition from Jammu. He had heard the gunfire in the evening while at Palanwala and had decided to reach the gun area with the ammunition to ensure that the guns did not go short of ammunition during the battle.

Next afternoon, displeasure of the General Officer Commanding (GOC) was conveyed to us for 'wasteful expenditure of ammunition', but we had won the confidence of all ranks of the battalion. At about 9 am I walked back to the gun position about 500 yards behind my OP. As I approached Number 3 gun, the detachment showed me two .303 bullets embedded in the gun shield. Their looks and body language showed the pride of battle-tested soldiers. We had become a team of veterans.

Two days later, we were invited to the Patiala Officers Mess dug-out for dinner. Maharaja Hari Singh had sent a case of Black Dog whisky to show his appreciation to the battalion of a brother prince. Spirits were high after a few Patiala pegs and the CO spoke to me, "You did well by asking me for porters". Bhupi mentioned that some babu in Delhi had disallowed an officers mess in the peace establishment of a battery and we had been eating from the men's *langar.* The CO generously offered membership of 1 Patiala Officers Mess to us whenever and wherever we were together in any location.

On 24 December, we received news of the fall of Jhangar, with heavy loss of men, weapons, vehicles and armoured cars. A platoon of 1 Mahar kept on firing at the attackers till they were cut to pieces on their machine-guns. The setback at Jhangar infused a new spirit amongst us to defeat the enemy at all costs in the coming battles.

On being relieved by a battery of 16 Field Regiment in Chhamb, we rejoined our B Troop in Naushera on 01 January 1948 to form a battery. By now, the lashkars in large numbers were aggressively poised around Naushera. 'Z' Brigade had been assembled in the T Junction area of roads Jammu-Naushera-Jhangar and Rajouri-Naushera. On 03 January I went as Forward Observation Officer (FOO) with 3 Maratha LI (Para), commanded by Lieutenant Colonel Rawind Singh Grewal, MC, a veteran of great repute. He told me that his task was to clear the enemy from Bhajnoa feature and he expected me to give him the necessary fire support. He mentioned that he practiced command from the front and expected me to maintain physical contact with him. I informed him that I had been sanctioned only five rounds per gun from my troop for the day's operations. The advance, in full view of the enemy at Bhajnoa, started after first light. When we were about 1200 yards from the base of Bhajnoa Hill, two enemy machine-guns opened fire on us. The advance continued with bullets flying high over our heads. I, with my OP party, followed Rawind at the tail of the leading company which entered a nala about 800 yards from the objective. The bullets were now flying closer overhead. After a brief pause in the nala in which I registered a target indicated to me by Rawind, he ordered the company to advance on a broad front. As he was emerging out of the nala behind the company, a machine-gun burst hit Rawind in the leg. The leading troops raced back to the safety of the nala where Raiwind, in pain, told the Company Commander to keep the enemy engaged in a controlled firefight. He forbade any talk of his wounds on the wireless and instructed me to report to Major Belliappa, his Second-in-Command, to help him with artillery support. Soon after my reporting to him, Belliappa decided to pull the battalion back after evacuating the commanding officer. On observing our withdrawal, the enemy became more aggressive. I asked for more ammunition which was not agreed to. As we fell back, I could see the enemy in small groups running forward to new positions to keep our withdrawing troops under fire. I resorted to firing smoke to cover our withdrawal and exceeded my authorized quota of ammunition. My explanation that I had understood the restriction on ammunition to apply to High Explosive (HE) only was found unacceptable, but was tolerated as a pardonable misinterpretation under the circumstances.

Next, I was told to set up an OP on the Gorkha Hill, occupied by 1/9 GR under Lieutenant Colonel KL Atal. The OP provided excellent observation of the area up to Bhajnoa, Naushera and the Naushera-Jhangar Valley. A couple of days later, at about 9 am, I saw an unbelievable sight of about 1000 men, about 2500 yards from my OP, in a well-dispersed formation advancing towards us. I opened fire with my troop without much effect on their advance. The spread of shells covered only a small portion of the enemy advance. The enemy went to the ground where the shells landed while the rest of the line continued to advance. At this stage, I was told to stop firing to preserve ammunition and to keep reporting the progress of the enemy advance. A little later, I was told to be prepared to indicate the target to aircraft expected to be in the area in about 20 minutes. Before the aircraft came on the scene, I saw the enemy entering a nala. I indicated the nala area with the help of a smoke shell to the aircraft circling overhead, who strafed and bombed the enemy in the nala. There was no further movement of the enemy during the day and he fell back during the night.

Z Brigade was moved back to Akhnur leaving 3 Maratha LI (Para) and 5 (Bombay) Mountain Battery in Naushera. Now began a period of hectic activity to dominate the no-mans-land by raids, aggressive patrolling and occupation of tactical features to improve the defensive layout of Naushera. Kangota and Tain Dhar were occupied, and the defences were strengthened with barbed wire, anti-personnel mines, bunkers/sangars and registration of Defensive Fires (DFs). Lines were laid to all defended localities.

Brigadier Usman, the Brigade Commander, now instituted a series of measures to raise the morale and patriotic spirit of all ranks. The daily evening conference was conducted in Hindustani and *Jai Hind* became the form of salutation. All officers, not committed on operational duty, were expected to attend the daily evening conference where the day's activities were analysed and next day's tasks allotted. Usman emphasized that the enemy was gradually closing in and was building up for a major attack on Naushera. An enemy success here would not only give the invaders a feeling of superiority over the Indian soldiers but whet his appetite for grabbing more. He emphasized that the coming Battle of Naushera had a national dimension and was a historic challenge to our generation of soldiers. It would be the first major battle of free India and we had to live up to the great reputation of the Indian Army.

In the third week of January, Lieutenant General Cariappa paid a flying visit to Naushera in an Air OP Auster aircraft. He instructed Usman to secure Kot feature to add to the security of Naushera. Kot-Pathradi area was estimated to be held by about 500 ex-State Force soldiers armed with Medium-Machine-Guns (MMG) and 3-inch mortars, in additions to small-arms. With Kot in enemy hands, the enemy could close in with Naushera defences from the direction of the Tawi and threaten the guns by infiltrating into the built-up area of Naushera town in conjunction with a massive attack along the Southern, Western and Northern perimeter of Naushera.

Usman planned a two battalion silent attack on Kot-Pathradi area. About five days before D-Day, registration was carried out by firing one round at first light on Kot, Pathradi and other targets. Ponies were assembled in Naushera and careful leaks given out to indicate an attack towards Jhangar while armoured cars led forays towards Jhangar. A strict wireless silence was observed.

2/2 Punjab was to capture Kot by advancing along Rajauri road to Pt 3227 and Kot. 3 Maratha LI (Para) was to simultaneously attack

Pathradi-Uperla-Dhandesar from the direction of Rajil. I followed Usman's party as the FOO with the brigade reserve. Everything seemed to go well. 2/2 Punjab fired the success signal around 7 am on the capture of Pt 3227. The next company moved through Kot village without searching the houses scattered astride the ridge-line. Wireless silence had been broken after the success signal. On hearing the progress report from CO 2/2 Punjab, Usman spoke in a jovial tone, "End of exercise. Time for breakfast". Suddenly there was a lot of confused firing about 500 yards ahead of us. The enemy, ensconced inside the houses in the wintry morning, was shocked to see Punjabis walking on the ridge-line on top of them. Realising their predicament, they assembled in the misty morning, fixed bayonets and firing their weapons charged at the advancing company from its southern flank, killing seven and wounding four. Shocked by the sudden charge, the Punjabis ran back towards Pt 3227. Usman ordered the brigade reserve to form-up about 300 yards behind him. Two aircraft appeared on the scene as pre-arranged. Usman felt that in view of the confused situation the use of aircraft or artillery for softening the objective was not advisable for fear of killing or wounding our own men who might be in the objective area. The Punjabis, in the meantime, had regrouped and resumed a methodical advance. The final objective was captured within an hour. 3 Maratha LI (Para) had an even bitter struggle but had cleared the enemy from the area of Pathradi-Uperla-Dandesar.

Night of 5/6 February was uneventful. Unknown to us, the enemy had closed-in along our extensive perimeter with commendable stealth. The raiders had achieved a tactical surprise and launched a simultaneous attack along the length of the perimeter at first light. 3 Maratha LI (Para), with a section of mountain artillery, had left for road opening just before "Stand to", while 1 Rajput had extended its front by taking over the area of 3 Maratha LI (Para), thus thinning the defences along the Western Perimeter of Naushera. Tain Dhar and Kot were heavily mortared after which hundreds of raiders charged forward under covering fire from LMGs and showers of grenades. With rifles, swords and knives in their hands, wave after wave jumped over the barbed wire and through bursting mines. Within minutes, calls for defensive fire started pouring in from all the pickets. The lines and wireless communications were soon jammed. Lieutenant Colonel

Mohinder Singh, MC, CO 22 Mountain Regiment, set up an ad hoc "Fire Direction Centre" in the Brigade HQ to allot priorities and coordinated the calls for fire. Major Bhupinder Singh, BC 30 Field Battery, complied with the allotted priorities by firing battery, troop, a section or a single gun.

Tain Dhar, the Brigade Vital Ground, was held by a platoon of 27 men of 1 Rajput. It saw the bitterest fighting. The enemy tried to swamp the picket by determined rushes despite the fire of LMGs, rifles and grenades. A section of 3-inch mortars, deployed behind the picket, soon expended all its ammunition. 30 Field Battery now resorted to direct firing over open sights on the right and left shoulders of Tain Dhar to check the enemy attacking from the flanks. On the return of the section of 5 (Bombay) Mountain Battery, the 3.7-inch howitzers blasted the enemy along the forward slopes of Tain Dhar.

Brigadier Usman, realizing the gravity of the situation, ordered the company of 3 Rajput, under Major Gurdial Singh, sited half-way up the hill, to reinforce the picket or recapture it, if already lost. While Gurdial moved with his company at a forced pace, the enemy was attacking desperately to close in with the defenders through the minefield over the bodies of their dead and wounded. The reinforcing company reached the top only to find one survivor, who was keeping the enemy at bay with his rifle fire. The sudden appearance of the company caused the attackers to panic who broke off and ran down the hill.

Within minutes of the start of firing on Tain Dhar, I was ordered to occupy the OP at the Western Perimeter in the area of the Brigade Officers Mess. The perimeter, as mentioned earlier, was thinly held. While walking up to the OP, I could hear firing all around on the hills. On arrival, I ordered a direct line to be laid between my OP and the guns about 500 yards behind. Amazingly, the Western perimeter was relatively peaceful with only an occasional burst of LMG fire by some nervous person in the trenches and the restrained response from the enemy side. About 10 am, I got instructions from Lieutenant Colonel Mohindar Singh that 3 Maratha LI (Para) would be attacking Radian feature on my right shortly and I should provide fire support to them by observation in keeping with their progress.

I shifted my OP from the ground to a corner of the parapet on the roof of the mess building and asked my OP assistant and the signallers to stay in the trench underneath to avoid detection of the OP. From my new perch, I had an excellent view of the ground in front of me. I watched the Marathas forming up and noticed that the firing had increased considerably. The bullets were now flying all over the mess building but I was so involved in the developing battle and my role in it that I was not conscious of the danger. I was absorbed in the cheery sight of the Marathas, with fixed bayonets, advancing towards Radian feature. A few minutes later, I saw the unforgettable scene of hundreds of the enemy getting up from behind rocks and out of the *sarkanda* in the *nala* in front of me like frightened partridges. With bullets flying all over, I saw the Maratha's steady advance with some firing on the move and a few kneeling down to fire on the enemy on their front. The fleeing rabble presented a dream target before me and I went for fire for effect with the battery. I saw some of them fall while others ran in different directions. I changed to air burst ammunition. With some rounds falling ahead of them, I saw a big group running in a circle. They were paralysed with fear, leaderless and followed anyone who took the lead. Soon they dispersed into small groups, and chased by artillery fire, they disappeared into the numerous *nalas* in the area. The aircraft came on the scene and played havoc with the hiding enemy raining rockets and cannon fire.

Despite our successes at Tain Dhar and the Western Perimeter, the firing on most of the pickets continued till after midnight. Our local patrols on 07 February morning reported that the enemy had disappeared leaving a large number of dead. By midday 07 February, it slowly dawned on us that we had won a great victory. Usman was undoubtedly the Hero of Naushera. The Official History of J&K Operations 1947-48 records that "The battle of Naushera was par excellence a gunner's battle". 30 Field Battery and the section of 5 (Bombay) Mountain Battery formed the gunner element. The History also comments on the contribution of the OP along the Western Perimeter. It is a matter of pride that not even one of our localities fell to the enemy. Naik Jadunath Singh of 1 Rajput was awarded the PVC posthumously for the defence of Tain Dhar.

The obvious next step now was the recapture of Jhangar. 19 Infantry Brigade, under Brigadier Yadunath Singh, was inducted into

Naushera by 17 February. The month of February was spent in securing the Beripattan-Naushera lines of communications and pushing the enemy away from Naushera. On 22 February, 19 Brigade, with 30 Field Battery in support, destroyed the enemy base at Kalal village in Sadabad Gap along the old Moghul Route. During the disengagement in the evening, Lieutenant Colonel IJS Butalia, CO 4 Dogra was killed. On hearing the news, Lieutenant Colonel Kulwant Singh Dhillon, CO, 1 Kumaon, went back with two of his companies and brought back the body. The next day 30 Field Battery fired an eight-gun salute at the enemy in Kalal area when the pyre of Colonel Butalia was lit.

During March, operations for the capture of Kaman Ghosha and Ambli Dhar were successfully completed. On 05 March, I joined 1 Rajput for the attack on Katora Khori Bumps. 1 Rajput planned to capture it by a silent attack at night. I had registered the first Bump soon after the capture of Kaman Gosha. After a slow march along a very narrow track, we halted in a small open patch and waited for dawn to identify our objective. In the morning twilight, we could see the silhouette of our objective. The leading company was ordered to capture the objective by a silent attack. As the company moved up the slopes on a two-platoon front, I saw the men falling and rolling down the hill before I heard the LMG fire. The CO and I ran behind a nearby spur. Both sides now engaged each other in a small-arms fire-fight while I registered the objective as a battery target. Under covering fire from the battery, the two company attack succeeded against stiff opposition. 1 Rajput losses amounted to 10 *jawans* killed, while the company commander, two VCOs and 29 *jawans* were wounded. Next day I was ordered to report back to Naushera where I learnt that the offensive for the capture of Jhangar was in the offing.

The plan was to advance along Ambli Dhar-Gaikot Forest-Jhangar with 19 Brigade. 50 Para Brigade was to simultaneously advance along Kothi Dhar-Pir Thil Nakka-Jhangar, while 7 Cavalry column was to advance along the track Naushera-Jhangar, in line with the advance of 50 Para Brigade. 7 (Bengal) Mountain Battery, 30 Field Battery, Troop 16 Field Regiment and Troop 37 (Coorg) Anti-Tank Regiment (4.2-inch mortars) were grouped together to support both brigades. This was the largest artillery concentration to date in the J&K operations. I was the FOO with 3 Maratha LI (Para) which was the lead battalion of the Para Brigade with the task to secure Pir Thil Naka.

It was uncertain whether the enemy was holding Pir Thil Naka as patrols had given contradictory reports. On 15 March, Lieutenant Colonel Virk, DSO issued orders for a two-company-up advance against the central portion of Pir Thil Naka Ridge through the intervening valley. I was with the left company commander, Major Chopra. With the eight-inches high wheat in the terraced fields, we headed for the small village of Kea on a raised ground in the middle of the valley. We descended into the valley hoping to meet no opposition. As the leading platoon entered Kea, the enemy opened up with LMG, rifle and mortar fire. Chopra and I, followed by our wireless parties, ran to different corners of a dilapidated mud-hut to seek shelter. I opened fire on the ridge in front to keep the enemy's head down and prevent them from bringing down aimed fire. A firefight started as our *jawans* found cover behind bunds and boulders. I now thought of establishing physical contact with Chopra and found that he had been killed by a bullet in his head. With the enemy in prepared defences in the pine trees on the ridge, he had the advantage of observation over our troops in the open valley. We had no choice but to stick it out until night by adjusting our positions under cover of HE and smoke from the guns and mortars. Virk, in the meantime, had deployed MMGs, LMGs and brigaded infantry mortars to cover our withdrawal after dusk. The withdrawal, including the dead and wounded, was conducted safely after dark under cover of artillery, MMG and LMG fire. Virk decided to hold on to the captured ground on the precept of 'Ground once gained must not be lost'. The benefits of holding the ground became obvious next day as it provided an excellent view of the objectives and was used for giving orders for the attack by the brigade and subordinate commanders.

The plan was to attack frontally at first light on 17 March with 1 Patiala on the left and 3 Maratha LI (Para) on the right. While the artillery and brigaded mortars registered the targets, the IAF softened the objective area on 16 March. The IAF also planned to fly two fighter-bombers over the objective area on 17 March from 8 am onwards. I was FOO with Major Sucha Singh, MC, a Burma veteran and dare-devil company commander. On his insistence that we maintain physical contact then onwards, we shared a shallow trench for the night as a sleeping bay. We moved forward to the Forming Up Place (FUP) at 4 am and crouched together silently about 300 yards below our objective. As the artillery opened fire on our objective at 7.30 am for five minutes, we moved forward as close to the fire as safety permitted. As the guns switched fire to the 1 Patiala objective for a five-minute bombardment, 4.2-inch mortars fired 200 yards ahead of the Maratha objective as a deterrent to any reinforcements or counter-attack. The fire plan included one gun of 30 Battery to fire smoke to add to the fog of war. As soon as the artillery fire lifted in front of our company, we climbed up the steep slippery slope over boulders on all fours and assaulted the enemy, shouting the Maratha war-cry 'Shree Chhatrapati Shivaji Maharaj Ki Jai'. There was hardly any resistance as the enemy had withdrawn. Pir Thil Nakka was secured by 8 am and Virk decided to exploit the situation by sending a company with me as the FOO to secure Susloti Dhar, which too was secured by 1 pm without any opposition. The enemy was on the run.

In the evening I was told to go forward with 3 Rajput who had been ordered to continue the advance during the night. At about 4 am on 18 March, there was a brief spurt of automatic small-arms fire in front of us and a few mortar bombs landed in our area. After a short exchange of fire, 3 Rajput waited for daylight to make the next move. Virk appeared on the scene as it was getting light. His battalion had been ordered to lead the advance. He had heard no firing as he walked about two miles to our position. With the intuitive skill of a natural soldier and with an eye for the ground, he announced that there was no enemy in front of us. He told me to join him in 3 Maratha LI (Para) advance to Jhangar. We met no opposition, except a few long distance rifle shots, as we approached the massive and dominating feature of Matlassi.

At about 10 am, Usman issued orders for a two-battalion simultaneous attack with 3 Maratha LI (Para) on the left and 1 Patiala on the right. We were now out of the field gun range as the road was mined and landslides had rendered it unfit for vehicular traffic. I came on the wireless network of 7 (Bengal) Mountain Battery which was on call to both the FOOs with the battalions. Except for a few long-range LMG bursts there wasn't any opposition. The Marathas reported the capture of Matlassi at about 3 pm while 1 Patiala captured their objective a few minutes later.

It was a full moon night with good visibility all round and a cold breeze whistling through the trees. Someone produced a drum whose beat soon had the men doing the Bhangra and singing Punjabi folk songs and ditties. Some rum produced by a resourceful comrade added cheer to the victory celebrations.

The operations on 50 Para Brigade front were progressing well while 19 Infantry Brigade on the Ambli Dhar Ridge was keeping in line with the advance on the left ridge.

In the fourth week of March, 30 Field Battery returned to Naushera on being relieved by a battery of 16 Field Regiment. There were rumours that 19 Brigade had been tasked to capture Rajouri and Brigadier Yadunath Singh had asked for our battery. On 06 April, 19 Brigade received orders for the capture of Rajouri. It was known that about 500 ex-J&K State Force personnel with MMGs and 3-inch mortars were holding Barwali Ridge and Mal area astride the road Naushera-Rajouri in front of Chingas. The 48-km fair weather road to Rajouri had thickly wooded hills in the west and Naushera-Tawi in the east. Local information indicated that the road between Naushera and Chingas had been mined and had a number of road-blocks. To assist the advance of 19 Brigade, Central India Horse (CIH) less two squadrons and 5 Jat were allotted to the brigade.

4 Dogra led the advance to capture Barwali in the early morning of 08 April and the first attack around midday was stalled against strong opposition. Yadunath ordered 1 Kumaon under Lieutenant Colonel Kulwant Singh Dhillon to move forward, in case required. About 3.30 pm, 4 Dogra fired the success signal and Yadunath, along with CO 16 Field Regiment and BC 30 Field Battery, moved up to cheer up the battalion. When the party was about 800 yards from the top, they were fired upon from their right. Yadunath, waving his white handkerchief shouted '*Apna Commander Sahib Hai*'. The intensity of fire increased with the bullets flying closer overhead. Someone in the party shouted *Dushman*, and everyone including Yadunath ran down the hill through thorny bushes and stumbling over boulders. The party halted on seeing CO 1 Kumaon who reported the capture of Barwali Ridge. Under persistent pressure from 4 Dogra, 5 Jat and 1 Kumaon,

the enemy resistance on the west of the road collapsed and Chingas was captured by 10 April evening. During this operation, Second Lieutenant RR Rane of the Engineers cleared mines and road-blocks under incessant enemy fire despite being wounded so that guns, tanks and vehicles could move forward to support the advance. He was awarded the PVC for this gallant action.

On 12 April, 1 Kumaon with my party and squadron CIH waded through the Tawi over boulders and through deep water to reach Rajouri by dusk. The town was cleared the next day.

On 02 May 1948, we were ordered to report to Jammu for a special task and to move on 05 May, the next road opening day. Late in the evening of 04 May we were told that Commander 19 Brigade had specially come to Naushera to see us off. He did not wish to disturb our move arrangements and wished to take our salute at the Naushera Traffic Control Point (TCP) as we drove past him. It was decided that Major Bhupindra Singh would receive the Brigadier at 6 am at the TCP and the battery would drive past in vehicles with the co-driver saluting. Next morning, as we drove past the Commander, an envelope containing a cyclostyled letter in Roman Hindustani for each member of the vehicle was handed over to the co-driver. It was a personal letter for every man in the Battery under Brigadier Yadunath Singh's signature expressing his appreciation of the outstanding contribution of the Battery during the operations in Naushera, Jhangar and Rajauri and wishing us well for the coming summer offensive in the Valley.

On arrival at Jammu the Brigade Major (BM) Artillery invited the BC and me for dinner in his room. He explained to us the urgency of reaching Srinagar within two days to avoid delaying the Summer Offensive. Arrangements had been made to fly the BC to Srinagar next morning so that he could tie up the tasks of the battery in the coming operation. The BM had no road map and told us that Srinagar was about 200 miles from Jammu. We were the first to cross the Jammu TCP for Srinagar on 07 May. I led the convoy with Captain Jhanda Singh bringing up the rear. It was a slow move on the hilly road. We were stopped in the late evening about two miles short of Ramban by an MP Subedar who told us to line up on the left of the road as the bridge on the Chenab was closed for repairs. We learnt that the bridge was expected to be opened to traffic at 7 am.

With a mix of persistence, cajolery and importance of our operational role we won the acquiescence of the Engineer Captain and the MP Subedar to let us be the first to cross the bridge, provided we lined up on the road with our leading vehicle about 200 yards short of the bridge before 6.30 am. We were on the move as agreed and were across the bridge one vehicle at a time. Thereafter we made good progress. At about 3 pm I was stopped by an MP Major at Banihal TCP. To his query as to my destination, I told him in all innocence that I intended to stop as close as possible to Srinagar short of the Banihal Pass! I drove ahead in the warm sunshine and was soon going up the hill. About an hour later alarm bells started ringing as it was getting cold in cotton Olive-Greens and a jersey, and my gun-towers could be heard struggling up the hill in first gear. On looking back, I could see the convoy spread out along the winding road with wide gaps between vehicles. I knew by now that I had to get across the Pass before I stopped. It became very chilly as soon as the sun set. Finally, I found a slightly wider bend in the road about 100 miles from Srinagar and stopped there for the night.

Early next morning I was woken up by my orderly with a hot mug of tea and the news that "General Sahib and Nehruji had been held up by Havildar Abu Bakr's gun at the Banihal Pass". I immediately went about finding out what it was all about. The engine of Havildar Abu Bakar's gun-towing vehicle had stopped (*garam ho gaya*) in the middle of the road. Having failed to start it, Abu Bakr decided to wait for help. After about an hour the detachment was alerted by a hooting siren followed by a pilot jeep halting close behind the gun. The MPs jumped out of the jeep shouting at the gunners to clear the way. Hearing the loud shouting by the MPs General Thimayya got out of his car and asked Abu Bakr, "What is the matter with your vehicle and where is your officer?" Abu Bakr explained his predicament, and the General instructed the MP VCO to gather men from his party to push the vehicle to a side. Soon about a dozen men along with the gun detachment were pushing the vehicle. General Thimayya also joined the men and the Prime Minister also came out of the car to push the vehicle. With so many hands and the command from Abu Bakr "All To-gether...Heave" the gun was soon pushed to a side. While the detachment assembled near the gun-tower, Thimayya and Nehru shook hands with the men and patted them before leaving. We reached Srinagar. On arrival the next day, I found Major Bhupinder Singh who told us that air flights to Srinagar had been suspended due to bad weather since we left Jammu and he had decided to come by road. We narrated our 'encounter' with the Prime Minister and General Thimayya and he told me, 'No wonder the MP at Banihal did not let me cross the TCP yesterday afternoon'. The MP Major was bitter that his kind consideration to permit the Gunners to go 'just a little ahead of the TCP' had caused problems for the Prime Minister.

As we came down from the mountains, the Valley with its lush green fields, the tall majestic poplar trees and the dust-free breeze was heavenly. We were pleasantly surprised to get a regular supply of fresh meat, vegetables, milk and fruit in our rations, unlike the Jammu Sector where we lived on tinned carrot, powdered milk and *dal.*

Thimayya's plan for the summer offensive to capture Domel was to attack with 161 Infantry Brigade under Brigadier Sen along Uri-Chakoti-Domel axis. 163 Brigade under Brigadier Harbaksh Singh was to advance along Handwara-Tithwal axis a couple of days before D-Day to divert the maximum enemy from Muzaffarabad to face this threat. 77 Para Brigade was to hold Uri and be in reserve.

After about four days of our arrival in Uri, I went as an FOO with Sawai Man Guards whose task was to check the enemy dispositions on the Salamabad feature. The enemy engaged us with MMG, LMG and 3-inch mortar fire. As we tried to disengage and withdraw in the evening to Uri, the enemy followed us in small parties within a mile of the perimeter.

On 18 May, we learnt that D-day was 20 May. While 163 Brigade made progress towards Tithwal, 161 Brigade's offensive towards Chakothi, launched with great expectations, failed to take off. 2 Dogra failed to clear Salamabad, and 6 Raj Rif had to be used to clear the enemy from this feature. Sen's plan was to launch a mobile thrust with Squadron 7 Cavalry, Company 7 Sikh in tracked Armoured Personnel Carriers (APC) and an Assault Engineer Company under Lieutenant Colonel Rajinder Singh 'Sparrow' towards Chakothi, as soon as Salamabad feature was secured. At about 11 am on 21 May I was told to report to CO 7 Cavalry in area Milestone 64 as the FOO with the Mobile Column. On arrival I learnt that there were two road-blocks a couple of miles ahead and the advance could not start till these were cleared and bridges put across. It was finally decided that 7 Sikh should lead the advance on foot with me as the FOO. We were ordered to advance straight away and to continue the advance throughout the night. I transferred my wireless set and other items onto two ponies which were allotted to me. The advance started. Around midnight we came under fire from Urusa feature. After daylight 7 Sikh secured Urusa Ridge after I fired a few rounds on it without any response from the enemy. I now discovered that I was with two companies of 7 Sikh, while the rest of the battalion, including the CO, had stayed back with the Mobile Column. Anyway, we resumed the advance and secured the lower heights of Kopra Hill. Further attempts met with stiff resistance from Kopra Top. We dug down on the lower ridge which gave us an excellent view of the Chakothi plain. Our attempts to secure Pt 7315 did not succeed, and we were suffering casualties from sniper fire at the hands of the enemy on the jungle-covered top. We were told that the Pakistan Army was now facing us. A desperate attempt by the two companies of 7 Sikh, still under Major Bant Singh, with artillery support from 11 Field Regiment and Patiala Mountain Battery, managed to capture Pt 7315 on 25 May. I was recalled to Uri in the second week of June to find that a new CO, Lieutenant Colonel Gyan Singh, had taken over.

While the above operations were going on, 4 Kumaon operating along the Mahura-Kazinag-Pandu axis had made spectacular progress by capturing Chhota Kazinag on 22 May and Pandu on 25 May. Pandu was the highest feature in the area and provided good observation on Road Domel-Chikothi. Similarly, Pir Kanthi and Ledi Gali were secured by our troops by 29 June with the guns firing super charge to reach the targets. 32 Field Battery had occupied a gun position in Urusa area to support these operations. There was no other suitable place for deploying more guns ahead of Uri.

July saw the Pakistan Army on the offensive in J&K. On 03 July we received the sad news of Usman's death due to artillery shelling in Jhangar. The UN had now sent a commission to the sub-continent to resolve the conflict in J&K. The Indian Army was instructed not to undertake any fresh offensive due to the arrival of the commission while Pakistan made the best of the opportunity for improving its defensive posture. On 07 July, 1 Patiala was forced to fall back to Baltal along the Zoji La axis. 30 Field Battery was moved to Sonamarg-Baltal area by the middle of July in support of 1 Patiala. In the Tithwal Sector, our troops were pushed back across the Kishen Ganga by 08 July. In Ladakh, the raiders had reached Tharu, about 13 km from Leh, by the middle of July. Pandu was lost on 23 July. The enemy now had observation over the gun position at Urusa and also the road Uri-Chakothi. Consequent to the shelling of our gun position at Urusa, it was decided to pull the guns back to Uri.

Planning now started in earnest to open the land routes to Leh and Poonch. It was obvious that priority should be given to open the Srinagar-Kargil-Leh axis in time to provision the Kargil and Leh garrisons before the Zoji La closed. HQ 77 Para Brigade under Brigadier KL Atal was accordingly moved to Baltal on 10 July 1948.

Zoji La was planned to be captured by a frontal attack after cutting off the enemy by a left outflanking move by two battalions via Sonamarg-Bot Kulan Ganj Pass. 1/5 GR (FF) led the advance from Sonamarg before dawn on 03 September. As the leading troops approached the pass in the afternoon of 04 September, they came under fire from an enemy platoon and MMGs. The pass was captured by first light 06 September, by which time the main attack to clear the enemy in the Zoji La had already failed. Seeing little advantage in pressing the attack along Bot Kulan Ganj the troops were ordered to return to Sonamarg.

The main brigade attack for the capture of Zoji La was to be launched by the 5 (Royal) Maratha LI under Lieutenant Colonel Adam, with 1 Patiala providing a firm base from their existing dispositions. It involved a frontal attack at first light on 05 September. I was detailed to be the FOO. The plan was to move into the area of the pass during the night and under cover of a timed 30 minutes fire plan by the battery, two companies were to capture Mukund Ridge. The CO with two reserve companies decided to stay in the Pass about 1000 yards from the foot of Mukund Ridge. He wanted me to stay with him to be available for any changes in the fire plan and in case he had to launch an attack with his reserve. After his orders on 04 September afternoon, I tried to convince him that the fire plan should be 'On Call' and not timed to retain flexibility on H-hour. I also tried to put across to him that the rate of advance in the hills, in my experience, was much slower than in the plains and the hills of Jammu. He told me that I did not know his Royal Maratha warriors and their capabilities in the mountains.

The fire plan started on time while it was still dark. In the increasing visibility, I could see the line of our forward troops moving nearly half-way up the hill when the fire plan came to an end. I had no choice but to extend the firing. We could now see our troops near the top of Mukund Ridge. There had been no reaction from the enemy. Suddenly we heard a lot of firing in the objective area. We could see men running into positions on the crest from the enemy side while our line paused. Then we saw our men walking down and breaking into a run towards the bottom of the Ridge. At this stage, two aircraft appeared on the scene and started strafing the enemy on the crest of the hill which helped the withdrawing troops to rush down somewhat safely. The CO with the reserve companies was too far back to do anything. The attack had failed, not only because of the enemy on Mukund Ridge but also due to the enemy from the Machine Gun Hill and Chabutra opening up a devastating MMG and LMG fire on our troops as they climbed to the crest line.

It was now decided to launch an attack to capture Mukund Ridge with 5 (Royal) Maratha LI and Chabutra with 3 Jat simultaneously. J&K Mountain Battery was deployed in addition to 30 Field Battery. I was the FOO with 5 (Royal) Maratha LI while Captain Dutta of the J&K Mountain Battery was the FOO with 3 Jat. The frontal attack on Mukund Ridge and Chabutra on night 13/14 September met the same fate with Captain Dutta being killed. I was wounded.

As the outflanking moves and frontal attacks had failed, the only hope was to employ tanks to achieve a breakthrough. Failure to open the road to Kargil and Leh before the closing of Zoji La in the winters would entail the loss of Ladakh, especially in view of the UN Commission's arrival and the likelihood of a cease-fire before next summer. The use of tanks was a desperate gamble in a desperate situation which paid off.

I was evacuated and with that, the J&K Operations ended for me. At the Military Hospital, Delhi I found Major Sucha Singh, MC, who too had been wounded in action. The Indian Army went on to force the Zoji La and relieve Leh. The cease-fire and the Karachi Agreement followed.

Postscript:

The narrator was awarded the Vir Chakra for his role in the defence of Tain Dhar-Naushera. As GOC 20 Mountain Division he accepted the surrender of Pakistan 16 Infantry Division at Bogra (Bangla Desh) in December 1971.

11 Field Regiment was awarded the Honour Title 'Zojila'.

# ANOTHER TIME ANOTHER PLACE

'Sir, the Eye Ell has landed', reported my staff officer one morning in the winter of 2005. It had been snowing intermittently for about a week. All activities had come to a standstill. Now that the skies had cleared, an IL-76 heavy-lift transport aircraft of the Indian Air Force had landed at Leh bringing in fresh supplies, mail, newspapers, essential stores and men returning from leave or newly posted in. Aircraft are the only physical link of snowbound Ladakh with the outside world in winters. It had carried out one more mission, just as other aircraft had been doing for nearly five decades to the remotest corners of the country.

A year earlier, I had similarly arrived at Leh on a freezing frosty winter morning to begin my tenure. As the giant IL-76 touches down, the reverse thrust of the four engines to check the speed sends a shudder through the aircraft and a roar piercing the early morning quiet of the still asleep town. The aircraft quickly decelerates and comes to a halt near the end of the short runway. It thereafter taxis to the parking bay. The rear cargo clam-doors open sending a gush of piercing cold dry air into the warm interior of the aircraft. Unlike the earlier transport aircraft, this aircraft is pressurized and internally heated. The outside temperature is minus-fourteen degrees Celsius. Out pour over 200 men returning from leave, training courses or being inducted on posting to Ladakh. The aircraft will return with those proceeding on leave or on completion of their tenure.

*****

Forty years earlier, at another time and another place, the monsoons had withdrawn and there was a nip in the early morning air. The sky was crystal clear, having been washed of suspended dust and smoke. In the pre-dawn darkness enveloping Bagdogra Airfield stood a four-engine AN-12 transport aircraft being readied for supply dropping in North Sikkim. The loading of packages to be dropped was complete. We entered the cockpit through the hatch below the nose. The aircraft started up and took off. It was still dark, and a very faint hint of daybreak was visible on the eastern horizon. We climbed steadily, and soon the vast stretch of bluish-white snow-covered Himalayas was visible from end-to-end. Following the Teesta River Valley, we were soon astride Kanchenjunga (The Five Treasures of the Great Snows) when the first rays of the sun broke over its summit appearing to set it on fire.

Gradually, the entire Kanchenjunga massif was awash in the deep golden-orange sunlight. As the sun rose it turned into pure gold, then yellow, and then in an instant, pure white. With the valley still in darkness, it appeared to float in the air. It was sheer magic as if the gods had used a giant brush to unfold the colour spectacle. What the tourists flock to see from Tiger Hill at Darjeeling, we had witnessed in company with the angels.

In the words of John Gillespie Magee's *High Flight*:

*Oh ! I have slipped the surly bonds of earth,*
*And danced the skies on laughter-silvered wings;*
*Up, up the long, delirious, burning blue ...*
*Where never lark or even eagle flew —*
*Put out my hand, and touched the face of God.*

After the mesmerizing spectacle, we were back to business and the crew in the aircraft became active as the drop zone was approaching. The dropping crew secured themselves with safety leads attached to the aircraft's interior. The rear doors opened with a rush of ice-cold air. The hook securing the load platforms was released. All was ready for the drop. Hearing the aircraft engines, the troops on the ground had lit a smoke-candle to indicate the wind direction in the drop zone at 16,000 feet.

As the aircraft came over the drop zone, at a signal from the navigator, the pilot pulled up sharply. With a grinding roar, the platforms with the packages slid over rollers from the open doors at the rear and the parachutes snapped open. The aircraft, having suddenly become lighter by a few tons, rapidly gained altitude. The pilot immediately initiated a tight turn as a few kilometres beyond was the Chinese-controlled Tibetan border. As the aircraft turned, we could see the loads landing and their parachutes collapsing. The troops on the ground were now entering the drop zone to retrieve the loads. The odd ones which landed in a minefield would be lost.

We were now heading back with the aircraft steadily losing height. By now the sun was well up in the sky, and as we came abreast the Kanchenjunga, it was glistening pure white in the company of Everest, Makulu and Lhotse. A short while later we landed. Twenty years later, I was the Commanding Officer of an Artillery Regiment near where the air-drop had taken place on that morning. By now a road had been constructed and there was no more supply dropping from the air.

*****

A few months later, but at the same place, we had completed a surveillance sortie over Nathula in a helicopter and then landed at Kalimpong to refuel. A young Gurkha soldier on duty at the helipad asked me if we would come the next day. He said he was proceeding on leave and would be thrilled to hitch a ride. I said we will for his sake.

The next day dawned with inclement weather. All flying was on hold. As the day progressed the weather improved slowly, and by 11 am it was marginal, just about permissible for flying. All helicopters had to clear the hills by 12 o'clock to avoid the turbulence which built up by that time. Time was running out. It would be touch and go. I asked the commanding officer if I could undertake the sortie. He was understandably reluctant. Then I told him that our credibility was at stake as I had promised a Gurkha rifleman that I would come. He cleared the sortie, the only one that day.

We took off and landed at Kalimpong. The man was waiting dressed smartly in his best uniform. His entire platoon was also there to see him off. With smiles all round we took off with perhaps my most cherished passenger on board.

*****

Moving to another time and another place, we had been chasing militants in the far corner of Manipur near the Myanmar border. Three of them had broken the cordon thrown by a Gurkha Battalion. Quick as rabbits, they had jumped into a nearby *nala* and attempted to get away. A Gurkha trooper had given chase. The insurgents suddenly turned around and opened fire. Not to be deterred, the trooper had returned the fire, and drawing his *khukri,* had leapt on them. In the ensuing mêlée, two insurgents were killed while the third, though wounded, escaped. The Gurkha trooper was also wounded.

A week later, about thirty odd men filed into an AN-32 transport aircraft at Tulihal Airfield, Imphal. I was also on board proceeding on leave. When all was ready, an ambulance drew up and a stretcher with a wounded soldier was carried aboard. It was the Gurkha trooper being evacuated to Delhi for specialized medical treatment. Recognizing me, he pulled himself to attention lying on the stretcher and gave out the customary salutation '*Ram Ram Sahib*'.

*****

This time the place was Daulat Beg Oldi (where *Daulat* – rich, *Beg* – great, *Oldi* – died) at the foot of the Karakoram (place of black gravel) Pass and the origin of the Shyok River (Shyok – sorrow, Shyok River – River of Death) in the extreme north-east corner of Ladakh. It had been a contentious place in the border fighting of 1962. A gravel airstrip had been constructed there at 17,000 feet which had fallen into disuse due to fissures in the surface. In 2004, we were keen to reactivate it. A physical assessment of the effort required to reactivate it called for a visit.

We took off from Leh in a Cheetah helicopter. Having climbed to 19,000 feet we hopped across the Ladakh Range and into the Shyok River Valley. Following the river due east, we took a sharp northwards turn and headed towards the Karakoram Pass. After about another hour of flying against very strong and gusty winds, we arrived over DBO, as Daulat Beg Oldi is commonly referred to. We landed and set about examining the strip, with the helicopter engine kept running at these altitudes to prevent failure of re-starting in the rarefied air. Assessment done, we retraced our path back to Leh. The strip was repaired over the next couple of months.

A trial landing by an AN-32 aircraft was carried out in 2006, and in the highest traditions of the Indian Air Force, the Air Officer Commanding-in-Chief of the Western Air Command was on board, just as General Thimmaya had been on the first landing at Leh in 1948.

*****

Another day, and for the last time, I was on board an IL-76 bound for Thoise from Chandigarh. It was a few days before I would hang my uniform. I was paying a farewell visit to my Regiment deployed in the Siachen Glacier.

The IL-76 entered the Shyok River Valley and began to descend. With high mountains on both sides and the airfield aligned along the river bed, the airfield has a unidirectional approach and take off. Once committed to land, there is no option to go around. The aircraft landed. The next day I was on my return trip to Chandigarh.

*****

Having hung my uniform and retired to Chandigarh, my day starts with the early morning sound of jet-engines overhead as the aircraft head for Leh and Thoise. Another day and another time!

# VEXILLUM IN THE WIND

*A moth-eaten rag on a worm-eaten pole*
*It does not look likely to stir a man's soul,*
*'Tis the deeds that were done 'neath the moth-eaten rag,*
*When the pole was a staff, and the rag was a flag.*
—Edward Hamley

Vexillum, the Latin for a square flag or a banner, coined the term *Vexillology* – the study of flags. These coloured symbols or signs of groups or clans marked the position of the clan leader or chief. On the battlefield they indicated the location of the commander or a fortification and served as the rallying point or focus of attention. With the evolution of trained and organised armies, maintaining formation on the battlefield became critical. Flags helped achieve it and reinforced their importance. The distinctive colour of such flags evolved into these being referred to as 'Colours'.

Generally attributed to ancient India and China, they are also found in accounts of early Egypt, Greece and Rome. On Indian battlefields, besides flags, the elaborately decked-out king's elephant served the same purpose. Ancient Indian flags were generally elongated triangles in shape. Royal Mughal flags had a yak's tail attached to the flagstaff, a practice carried from Central Asia. In contrast, Roman soldiers carried a square flag hung from a horizontal bar affixed to a staff.

Flags are now generally rectangular with the standard ratio of the hoist to fly being 2:3. Classified by their shape and function, the Standards are strips of cloth tapering gradually towards the fly and ending in two points. Banners, on the other hand, are strictly square in shape and usually carry the 'Coat of Arms'. A Guidon is like a Standard, but rounded at the end, or with a swallowtail and two rounded ends. Pennants are small triangular flags carried on a lance. Streamers, now reduced to pennants, were long tapering flags of great length used on ships.

With long-standing organised military structures and units coming into being, it became customary for the sovereign to present flags or 'colours' to units, as a symbol or object of sovereign authority and to evoke allegiance and to motivate and inspire the men. These flags were usually referred to as the 'Kings Colours'. They acquired utmost reverence and respect which endures today. Elaborately embroidered, honours won on the battlefield were emblazoned on the colours. Besides the sovereign's colours, regimental colours carrying their insignia or crest served the purpose of embodying the collective spirit, identity, traditions and honour of the unit.

Being associated with valour, dedication and allegiance, the flag in due course became an object of respect and veneration, as also a symbol of identity – cultural, civilization, national and sovereign.

Loss of colours amounted to unmitigated disgrace. In 55 BC, when a Roman force invading England showed a reluctance to go ashore in the face of the enemy, the soldier carrying the Eagle (colours) jumped ashore, taunting others to stay on board if they wished to see their Eagle captured. They followed to the last man. When the colours fell, it signalled the death of the commander, or some serious injury, invariably causing great confusion.

A battalion had a 'stand of colours' consisting of the King's or Queen's, and Regimental Colours. Both were carried on parade or battlefield by the junior-most ensigns. If he was wounded, the next junior ensign took over. On being honoured to carry the colours for the first time, an ensign stood champagne to all officers in what was called 'wetting the colours'. Colours were standardised to 6 feet 6 inches by 6 feet and were carried on a 9 foot 10 inches staff. Quite naturally, the colour party was a prominent target on the battlefield. A special honour bestowed to very few regiments was the right to march through the City of London, or nominated city, with 'bayonets fixed, colours flying and drums beating' without any official permission.

When the British-Indian Army garrison at Kabul was forced to withdraw on 06 January 1842, it was cut up en route with the remnants largely belonging to the 44th Foot Regiment making the last stand at Gandamak near Jallalabad on the morning of 13 January. To prevent the colours falling into Afghan hands, a captain tied the colours around his waist. The Afghans spared his life and took him prisoner assuming the elaborately embroidered silk waistband to signify a man of importance and therefore a suitable hostage.

Three colours – those of HMs 24th Regiment of Foot, 25th and 45th Bengal Native Infantry – were lost to the Sikhs at Chilianwala on 13 January 1849. The loss of colours of the 24th Regiment again at Isandhlwana in Africa on 22 January 1879, though recovered later, and the 66th Regiment at Maiwand in Afghanistan on 27 July 1880, indicated that they had no place on the modern battlefield. The colours were last carried on the battlefield at the Battle of Laing's Neck-Majuba Hill during the Anglo-Boer War on 27 February 1881.

Colours are still presented and carried on ceremonial occasions with due respect, veneration and honour. The 16th Light Cavalry, the oldest armoured regiment of the Indian Army, was raised in 1776 by the Nawab of Arcot. Its glorious history of rallying even as their commander fell was symbolically recognized in 1922 when the Prince of Wales presented the Regiment with two Standards. This honour was extended by Independent India when the President presented the regiment two colours on its 200th Anniversary in 1976.

While the colours served as the rallying point for the infantry and cavalry, the artilleryman rallied around his gun: served and defended to the last, but never abandoned. The artillery thus does not have colours, the guns are its colours.

The Royal Indian Navy was first presented colours on 09 December 1935. After India became an independent republic, thirty-three Kings Colours of the Indian Army and Navy were laid up in Chetwode Hall of the Indian Military Academy, Dehradun on 25 January 1950. Seventeen Indian State Forces colours were similarly laid up on 06 April 1956 when the state forces merged with the Indian Army. It symbolized the end of an era and of duty faithfully performed under these flags. The Indian Navy was the first to receive the Presidents colours on 27 May 1951 in a packed Brabourne Stadium, Bombay.

The old navy colours laid out at the Indian Military Academy were returned to the Navy on 16 May 1989 and are kept at the Naval Academy. The Indian Air Force received them on 01 April 1954.

Given the significance and respect accorded to the colours, it is a historic occasion in the life of a unit to be presented colours, usually by the President of India otherwise by the Army Chief. Another inspiring ceremony – the 'Trooping of Colours' – takes place when the colours are trooped or paraded ceremonially in front of the soldiers. It owes its origin to the times when the colours were trooped to enable the soldiers to recognise them as their rallying point in the midst of battle.

Of the many legendary tales associated with flags is one about the 31 Native Infantry Regiment and Bhuratpur. Following the victorious Central Indian Campaign, Lord Lake laid siege to the Jat stronghold of Bhuratpur towards the end of 1804. Commencing on 09 January 1805 three assaults were made on the fortress but were repulsed. The fourth assault took place on 21 February 1805. The 31 Native Infantry secured a lodgement and planted their colours on the bastion within the breach. But their position being untenable, they were ordered to withdraw. On 24 February 1805, Lake marched away, without capturing Bhuratpur and having suffered 446 killed and 2479 wounded. The colours planted in the breach had been shot up and tattered and were to be replaced. But on the night before the new colours were to be presented, the old colours had simply disappeared. On 18 January 1826 Bhuratpur was captured by Lord Combermere. The 31 Native Infantry was again present there. When their colours were planted on the fort, tied alongside were the old tattered colours. The regiment had secretly preserved them and now redeemed their honour. They were presented with an Honorary Standard inscribed 'Lake and Victory' and authorized an extra Jemadar (a modern day Naib Subedar) for bearing the additional colour. The successor battalion, 4 Guards (1 Rajput) is entitled to an additional Naib Subedar till today.

*You cannot choose your battlefield,*
*God does that for you;*
*But you can plant a standard*
*Where a standard never flew.*
—The Colours

Progressing from being symbols of the sovereign, flags logically evolved as symbols of sovereignty. All nations have flags and they invariably evoke strong sentiments and emotions of identification, pride and patriotism. The Danish flag instituted in 1219 is considered to be the oldest. To keep the flag 'flying' and 'plant' the flag as a symbol of victory are universal expressions today.

The 1775 rebellion by thirteen of the twenty British North-American colonies inspired the American flag, first stitched by Betsy Rose, later adopted as the US flag. The flag had thirteen alternating red and white stripes with thirteen stars in the canton. The Star-Spangled Banner – the US national anthem – was inspired by the US flag. Francis Scott Key, held prisoner on board the *HMS Minden*, witnessed the all-night bombardment of Fort McHenry at Baltimore by the ship which, incidentally, was constructed at the Bombay Docks. At daylight, the American flag still flew over the fort. Deeply moved, Key sat down and composed the poem *The Defence of Fort McHenry*, which later became the national anthem as *The Star Spangled Banner* in 1931.

Soviet troops stormed Berlin in the closing stages of World War II, and planted the red banner with the hammer and sickle on the German parliament building, the Reichstag, on 02 May 1945. Their photograph became famous as a symbol of Soviet victory over Nazi Germany. Interestingly, the photographer, Yevgeny Khaldei, improvised the flag from a red tablecloth with a hurriedly stitched hammer and sickle! On 07 May 2007, the Russians enacted a federal law whereby the Victory Banner to be used for all celebrations of the Soviet Victory Day was to be a replica of the flag with the hammer and sickle raised on the Reichstag.

Another photograph by Joe Rosenthal of the US Marines hoisting the stars-and-stripes on Mount Suribachi, Iwo Jima in the Pacific on 23 February 1945 became one of the most celebrated images of the war, later inspiring the US Marines War Memorial, Washington DC. Less well known is that at both places flags had been hoisted earlier, and the hoisting was recreated for the photographs, with a larger flag at Mount Suribachi. The six American flag raisers at Iwo Jima hadn't participated in the fighting till then. The son of the last survivor of these flag raisers later scripted the movie *Flags of Our Fathers.*

When the Allies liberated Paris on 25 August 1944, a French soldier climbed up the Eiffel Tower to plant the French tricolour atop it where the Nazi flag had flown for five years. The event is commemorated by a plaque affixed in the viewing gallery on the uppermost floor of the tower. Similarly, the Indian tricolour planted atop the Haji Pir Pass after its capture in 1965, and images of Indian troops atop captured peaks with the tricolour in Kargil in 1999, are acclaimed photographs. A corresponding symbol of defeat was the picture of General Percival walking with the Union Jack towards the Japanese to offer the surrender of Singapore along with over a lakh troops on 15 February 1942.

The symbolism associated with flags can be quite extraordinary. In 1857, during the siege of the Residency at Lucknow, the defenders kept the Union Jack flying day and night as a gesture of defiance. When the siege was lifted, and the Residency relieved, the flag was kept flying round the clock thereafter. It became the only place in the British Empire where the Union Jack was not lowered at night. Ninety years later, on the night of 13/14 August, the local British commander had the flag lowered finally, and the flag plinth demolished and plastered, so that free India's flag could not be flown the next day. The flag lowered from the Residency and the one from Fort William, Calcutta are displayed in Windsor Castle Museum.

General MacArthur accepted the formal surrender of the Japanese on 02 September 1945 aboard the *USS Missouri* – flagship of the 3rd US Fleet anchored in Tokyo Bay. He had the flag flown by Admiral Perry in Tokyo Bay in 1853 displayed on the surrender deck in a glass case. However, a popular myth is that the flag that flew over the Capitol in Washington when the Japanese attacked Pearl Harbour on 07 December 1941, crippling the American Fleet and initiating them into the war, was the one flown on that occasion. Symbolically, Generals Percival and Wainwright, both Japanese prisoners of war, were present at that surrender.

Invariably, the most memorable ceremony whenever countries gained freedom from colonialism, was the lowering of the colonial power's flag and hoisting of the national flag. One of the most common cries of Indian nationalists fighting for independence was '*Chalo Dilli*', with the intent of flying the Indian flag atop the Red Fort. On the morning of 15 August 1947, the tricolour was first hoisted on the Constituent Assembly (Parliament) building and in the afternoon at Prince's Park near India Gate. As a goodwill gesture the Union Jack was not lowered publicly before hoisting the tricolour. Prime Minister Nehru then hoisted the national flag at the Red Fort. That flag is today preserved in the Officers Mess of Headquarters Delhi Area.

The Indian national flag was designed by Pingali Venkayya from Machilipatnam and was adopted by a resolution at the AICC Karachi meeting in 1931. It was officially adopted as the national flag of India by the Constituent Assembly on 22 July 1947.

The colours and emblems on flags are invariably representative of something of significance and importance. Cavalry lancers fly red and white pennants on their lances as a tribute to their country of origin Poland, the red and white being their national colours since 1230. Most Islamic states have a crescent moon incorporated in their flag, considered to be a sacred symbol by the Assyrians from the 9th Century BC. Their colours are also from amongst the traditional red, white, green and black. Most European flags use the Christian cross which was much used during the crusades.

In keeping with the British practice of a 'Sovereign's Flag' being distinct from the national flag, India too adopted separate flags for the President and its state Governors after its independence. The Viceroy's flag was succeeded by the Governor General's flag from 1947 to 1950, and the President's flag from 26 January 1950. The flag was divided into four rectangles of dark blue and saffron, superimposed with the Ashoka Lions, an elephant, a scale and a vase with a lotus flower. It flew atop the Rashtrapati Bhavan till 15 August 1971 after which it was abolished. These symbols are imposed on the four corners of the President's Banner presented to the President's Body Guard.

Switzerland and Vatican City are the only states to have square flags while Mozambique has a Kalashnikov assault rifle (AK 47) on its flag. Sixty four of the almost two hundred national flags carry a religious symbol, including India's Dharam Chakra. Nepal is the only country not to have a quadrilateral flag but in the shape of two combined right angled pennants superimposed with the symbols of the sun and moon.

The Kachchwaha Rajputs of Jaipur, having established close ties with the Moguls, served as leading generals in the Mogul armies. Man Singh served with Akbar and Jehangir, and Jai Singh with Aurangzeb. Man Singh as *Subedar* (Governor) of Kabul in 1586 faced five rebellious chieftains who he defeated with the help of his clansmen from Jaipur. The five colours of the rebels were formed into a five-coloured flag *'Panchranga'*, which remains the state flag of Jaipur till today. Aurangzeb bestowed the title of *Sawai*, meaning one and a quarter, on Jai Singh. To this day the flag atop the city palace at Jaipur has another quarter sized one flown with it. The Nizam of Hyderabad was fed with a *Kulcha* by a holy man, consequently, the *Kulcha* was adopted on the flag of the Nizams.

From the legendary skull and bones black 'Jolly Roger' flown by pirates on the high seas to the white ensign flown by 'men-o-war', the association of flags with maritime activity is another interesting facet of their use. When the English ships confronted the Spanish Armada in 1588, they had two great advantages – greater speed and heavier armament. This enabled them to keep their distance while they fought. The greater distance at which sea battles now started generated the need for simple distinctive flags for recognition. Thus England's flag, the cross of St. George, evolved into the white ensign. Ensigns of the British type are almost universal today.

The Indian Navy retained the red cross of St. George till 15 August 2001, when it was removed and the Naval Crest imposed on the white background. The new ensign was not distinct enough to facilitate recognition, and the original purpose of recognition soon prevailed. The red cross of St. George was reintroduced on 25 April 2004 with the state emblem Ashoka Lions in golden yellow superimposed on the intersection of the cross in the centre.

Ships use signalling flags to spell messages by using a standardised colour and design code. When Nelson asked his signal officer, John Pasco, to hoist a rather longish message goading his men to do their duty before the Battle of Trafalgar on 21 October 1805, the lack of capacity to do so prompted him to abridge and hoist the pithy and now famous 32 flag signal 'England expects that every man will do his duty'. Warships at anchor usually fly their national flag and the ensign while those under way hoist only the ensign. When going into action a ship hoists an extra battle ensign. In naval parlance, ships do not fly flags but 'wear' them and when ships are decorated with flags on ceremonial occasions, they are 'dressed'.

Soldiering in India has traditionally been a matter of honour. To uphold honour meant to live by the *Naam-Namak-Nishan* of one's regiment: its Name, Fidelity (by virtue of the salt eaten) and the Flag. The world over when a soldier dies on duty, his coffin is draped in the national flag symbolizing the nation's debt and responsibility for the soldier's death in its service and as a mark of national honour. The flag is usually handed over to the family.

Flying a 'flag of distress' to indicate an emergency meant flying the flag upside down or at half-mast. Captured enemy flags are similarly displayed upside down. Flags flying at half-mast (actually three fourth up the mast) today signify grief and respect for the dead. 'Dipping' the flag denotes a mark of respect. Ships at sea salute each other by 'dipping', that is, lowering the flag slowly and then rapidly hoisting it.

National colours are only dipped for the head of state, while regimental colours are also dipped for the supreme commander, which in our context, is the President of India in both cases. The only exception, and a singular privilege, is the entitlement of field marshals to have regimental colours dipped in their honour. Field Marshal Sam Manekshaw, popularly known as 'Sam Bahadur', was first accorded this singular honour at the Army Day Parade on 15 January 1973.

# CROSSING THE KHARDUNG LA

## From *The Ice World of Himalaya,* Fanny Bullock and William Hunter Workman, 1900

Having secured this valuable addition to our menial staff, our other preparations were soon completed, and at noon, on 4th July, we left Leh to cross the Kardong Pass. We were able to procure only a few riding *yaks,* which animal is preferred in Ladakh and other neighbouring mountain regions to the pony, as being more secure-footed, and having more endurance. Most of our equipment was carried on ponies.

The route rises continuously from Leh to the pass, situated about ten hours march to the North, and the last half is rough, boulder-covered and steep, which conditions, combined with the altitude, make the ascent a fatiguing one. We followed the custom of breaking the journey by encamping for the night at a spot four hours above Leh, at an altitude of 14,000 feet, from which the passage over the pass to the village of Kardong was made the next day.

At this point, we, for the first time, mounted *yaks.* In the course of the summer we had considerable experience with them. The *yak* is about as large as a medium-sized ox and resembles a buffalo, perhaps, more than any other bovine in shape. It is covered with long, glistening, black hair, which hangs from the shoulders, flanks, thighs, and tail in a shaggy profusion that obscures all outlines. Its horns often curve forward so as to form an almost horizontal circle like those of certain beetles. Indeed, as the rider sits upon its broad back, and looks down on the massive shoulders and curving horns, he may easily imagine himself seated astride a huge horned beetle. Its vocal utterance is a short, low-pitched grunt, which, though seemingly threatening, betokens no ill-nature, for its disposition is mild. Its gait is easy, and it is very sure-footed. Moving with slow and measured tread and lowered head, the *yak* carefully selects a place for every step and seldom puts its foot on an insecure stone or foothold. Often in passing boggy and treacherous places, our *yaks*, after examining the footprints of animals and men who had preceded them and sunk in, would walk around the bad places, choosing in every case a firm foothold.

On steep mountainsides, we have seen *yaks* go in safety over places without a semblance of anything that could be called a path, which one would not suppose a large four-footed animal could pass, and where experienced mountaineers would tread with caution. On the present occasion, the *yaks* performed their part well. It was interesting to note that although they are said in their natural state to range from 15,000 to 17,000 feet, above 15,000 feet they seemed to suffer quite as much from exertion and altitude as the human attendants, who were on foot, indeed, more so than some of them. At 17,000 feet and above, where the path was both steep and bad, only twelve to twenty steps forward could be taken without a rest, when the rapidity and force of their respiration were very marked.

We reached the top of the Kardong, 17,574 feet, towards noon, and stopped to look around. We had ascended from the South side between two mountain spurs, presenting nothing remarkable, and had encountered no snow. On the top, and for some distance down on the North side, lay a large snow-field. The view compared favourably with that from most passes. To the South, beyond Leh, some fine rock mountains were seen, while to the North three handsome snow peaks loomed up in the distance with large snow-fields from which rose impressive snow-covered walls. These were evidently mountains in the Korakoram Range and appeared to be at least 25,000 feet high. Snow peaks rise on each side of the pass, seemingly 1000 to 1500 feet above it, which looked as if they could be scaled, and from which, in clear weather, an extended view ought to be obtained.

The descent was steep and rough, over snow and rock debris for some 2000 feet, then easier till Kardong Village was reached at 13,500 feet. On the way two small lakes were passed, one of them, just below the snow-field, being remarkable, in that the water, as seen from above, appeared to be of several colours. Edelweiss was found on the North side of the pass at an elevation of 16,000 feet, about the highest altitude at which we have found it growing. The plant was small, the stem being from one to two inches high, and the flower, about the size of an ordinary Swiss or Tyrolean edelweiss, being of a dull green colour with a centre of somewhat lighter shade. Also at 17,000 feet, in a wilderness of snow and rocks, far above vegetation of any kind, where nothing that could serve as food for bird or animal could be detected, plump, well-nourished, slate-coloured pigeons, with white stripes across the wings, were flying about, evidently perfectly at home.

From Kardong Village the dusty path descends sharply, along the face of high cliffs of clay and glacial deposit of pyramidal and various fantastic shapes, to the bottom of the narrow valley, which it follows for a short distance, through a vigorous growth of tamarisk, to its opening into the broad valley of the Shayok. We crossed the Shayok, flowing with swift current and billows two feet or more high, in a flatboat, at a point just above its junction with the Nubra River. The bed of the Shayok Valley is here about 10,000 feet above sea level and its width about four miles. Another hour's march brought us to Tsati at the opening of the Nubra Valley.

# FORGING THE KHARDUNG LA

*Great things are done when men and mountains meet;*
*This is not done by jostling in the street.*
—William Blake

GAZETEER OF KASHMIR AND LADAK COMPILED UNDER THE DIRECTION OF QUARTER MASTER GENERAL IN INDIA IN THE INTELLIGENCE BRANCH 1890

KHARDONG PASS, ALSO CALLED LEH PASS AND LAOCHE LA

Latitude 34 deg 20 min Longitude 77 deg 42 min Elevation 17900 ft

On the range of mountains lying between the Indus and Shyok valleys. Is crossed from a camping ground 7 miles north of Leh on the summer route to Yarkand, and is very difficult for ponies. Yaks are used in carrying goods across. Dr. Thomson crossed it from the Leh side on the 20th July. The pass is usually open from 15 July to 15 December.

"The morning was intensely frosty. The path lay close to the stream, ascending somewhat rapidly. The last part of the ascent was extremely steep, among immense, angular, granite boulders, with here and there a little snow in the crevices. From the summit the view to the south was very extensive, embracing a great extent of snowy mountains with numerous lofty peaks, as well as a part of the Indus valley, and the town of Leh. To the north it was much more limited, as hills close at hand completely excluded all distant view, except directly in front where one snowy peak could be seen a long way off, evidently beyond the Shyok. On the north side of the pass snow commenced at the very top, and continued for at least 1,200 feet of perpendicular height. The descent for this distance was extremely steep, over a snow bed, which appeared to cover an incipient glacier. About 1,200 feet below the top, I came to a small oval – shaped lake, completely frozen over. Beyond this the descent became more gentle and was partially free of snow". (*Thomson – Trotter*)

Ladakh – the 'Land of Many Passes' – lies at the crossroads of the ancient trade routes from the Indian subcontinent to the great East-West trade highway or the 'Silk Route'. The traditional trade caravan routes traversed the passes of Zojila, Namik La and Fotu La from Kashmir, and Baralacha La, Lachulung La and Tanglang La from Punjab across the Great Himalayan and Zanskar Ranges into the Indus River Valley, converging at Leh. From here movement along the Indus was possible to Tibet and Baltistan. Northwards from Leh, trade caravans carrying pashmina shawls, spices, opium and saffron crossed the Ladakh Range through the Khardung La (Pass Of Lower Castle) or Chang La, traversed the forbidding Karakoram Range through the Karakoram Pass and thence to the Central Asian towns of Yarkand and Kashgar on the Silk Route. The caravans brought back tea, precious stones, hashish, tobacco and silk. Leh was the largest barter centre on these routes.

The route from Leh across the Ladakh Range traversed the Khardung La or Chang La to descend into the Nubra Valley. The caravans thereafter followed the frozen Shyok River in winters – the steep gorges and raging torrents of glacier melt precluding move along the river in summers. In summers, they moved along the Nubra River and across the Saser La to reach the origin of the Shyok and cross the Karakoram Pass.

A motor able track had been constructed across the Zojila to Kargil in 1948. Construction of a road link between Kargil and Leh commenced in 1959 and a convoy of seven jeeps traversed the distance on 03 August 1961.

The ancient caravan route from Leh to the Nubra Valley, across the Khardung La, carved out over the centuries, followed the naturally convenient alignment for man and beast. The first attempt, albeit unsuccessful, to construct a road along this caravan route was in 1963 by the Jammu and Kashmir Public Works Department. However, it could only be converted into a four-wheel-drive gravel-track allowing limited movement of light vehicles during the summer months.

Consequent to the 1971 War and the Army deployment towards Turtuk along the Nubra Valley, the need for a motorable road from Leh across the Khardung La became imperative. Conversion of the track into a motorable road was taken up by the Indian Army in 1972, and work commenced on 27 August 1972 by the 201 Engineer Regiment, Madras Sappers. Amongst other expedients and innovations adopted, jeeps were dropped by helicopters along the route and coal tar drums were lifted by helicopters to the work sites. In the absence of any heavy machinery, the road was cut through the granite rocks by sheer physical effort. The Regiment lost 18 men in forging the Khardung La. The road-alignment entailed a crossing at 18,380 feet, 866 feet higher than the traditional pass at 17,574 feet, and was opened to motor traffic on 27 August 1973.

A glaciated patch of hard, frozen ice, 500 meters ahead of the Pass, was spanned by a 110-foot Bailey Bridge launched by the Border Roads Organization. It became the highest bridge in the world. It was also unique in that its ends rested on hard ice. After being repeatedly swept away by avalanches, and being relaunched, this patch was finally overcome by constructing a wire-crated stone-masonry causeway in 1994.

The Pass experiences snow accumulation of approximately ten feet in winters. The temperature averages a maximum of 20 degrees Celsius in summers and a minimum of minus 40 degrees Celsius in winters. Wind speeds up to 100 km per hour are common. The road is also prone to avalanches and landslides, yet it counts as the highest motorable road in the world. Marsimik La in Eastern Ladakh at 18,632 feet, though higher than Khardung La, is not 'motorable' as it allows very limited move by four-wheel-drive vehicles over a rough track. As a comparison, the highest point in Europe – Mt Blanc – is 4808 meters (15,962 feet). The road is kept open round the year being an important link with Siachen. No visit to Ladakh today is complete without going up to the Khardung La. In a land of superlatives, Khardung La is one of them. You cannot drive nearer to God.

*While far below men crawl in clay and clod,*
*Sublimely I shall stand alone with God.*
—Mary Sinton Leitch, *The Summit*

# WHEN WAR DRUMS BEAT

An 1812 music score sheet titled *The Drummers Call Barred With Music* explains that:

> The General is to be beat when the whole are to march, and is the signal to strike tents and prepare for the march.
> The Assembly is the signal to repair to the Colours
> The March, for the whole to move.

When war drums beat the purpose remains to 'march to the sound of guns' but the scene changes over the years. Subedar Sita Ram, a 'Native' in the service of the Bengal Army of the East India Company, recounts the march into Afghanistan in the First Afghan War 1839 in his fascinating autobiography, *From Sepoy To Subedar*, which was translated in 1873 and made compulsory reading for British Officers in India:

> In the year 1837 it was common gossip throughout India that the *Sirkar* was going to assist Shah Suja-ul-Malik, the Amir of Kabul, to regain his throne. The sepoys dreaded crossing the Indus as it was forbidden by our religion and many obtained their discharge or deserted. Nevertheless troops began to move and a force was assembled at Ferozepur. An army in the pay of Shah Shuja was also gathered. I was offered a *havildar's* appointment with higher pay in this Legion and I joined.
>
> We marched by the side of large rivers and arrived at Rohri on the

> Indus which we crossed after a good deal of trouble. The Baluchis now began to harass us by night and carried away our camels. Then we came to the Bolan Pass where many were killed by the tribesmen. Torrential rains added to our misery and it took nearly eight days to traverse the pass. Every yard of the way was marked by an abandoned camel, a foundered horse, or a camp follower dying of exhaustion. Tents, camel trunks, wine chests, cooking pots, bundles of blankets, and overturned carts marked the progress of the Army of the Indus.
>
> We next arrived at Quetta and eventually Kandhar came into sight which we entered on 26 April 1839 and Shah Suja was installed on the throne. After some months stay we moved to Ghazni which was captured on 23 July 1839. A garrison was left at Ghazni and our army marched on to Kabul. If the officers had taken counsel from some of their wives the calamities that afterwards befell the English army would never have occurred.

The biographer of the notorious William Hodson, his namesake Rev GH Hodson, writes in *Hodson of Hodsons Horse* what his subject observed on the march to Mudki for the First Anglo Sikh War 1845:

> There was something wholly distinctive about soldiering in India and the ancient splendour of the pre-Mutiny army. I wonder more every day at the ease and magnitude of the arrangements, and the varied and interesting picture continually before our eyes. Soon after 4 am the bugle sounds the reveille and the whole mass is astir at once. The smoke of the evening fires has by this time blown away and everything stands out clear and defined in the bright moonlight. The sepoys bring the straw from their tents and make fires to warm their faces on all sides and the groups of swarthy redcoats stooping over the blaze with a white background of canvas and the dark clear sky behind all produces a most picturesque effect as one turns out into the cold. The multitude of camels, horses and elephants, in all imaginable groups and positions - the groans and cries of the former as they stoop and kneel for their burdens, the neighing of the hundreds of horses mingling with the shouts of the innumerable servants and their masters' calls, the bleating of the sheep and goats, and, louder than all, the shrill screams of the women, almost bedevil

> one's senses as one treads one's way through the canvas streets and squares to the place where the regiment assembles outside the camp.
>
> The stern, determined-looking British footmen, side by side with their tall and swarthy brethren from the Ganges and Jumna – the Hindu, the Mussulman, and the white man, all obeying the same word, and acknowledging the same common tie; next to these a large brigade of guns, with a mixture of all colours and creeds; then more regiments of foot, the whole closed up by the regiments of native cavalry; the quiet looking and English dressed troopers strangely contrasting with the wild Irregulars in all the fanciful uniforms.

Military historian Richard Holmes, in his insightful narrative of the pre-Independence British and Indian Army, *Sahib,* describes the plodding siege trains towards Multan in 1848 during the Second Anglo-Sikh War and into Afghanistan in 1879:

> Such a curious sight! First came the escort and the twenty-four pounders each drawn by twenty magnificent bullocks with an elephant behind each one. This put down its head and gave the gun a shove whenever they got to a steep place. In the rear came the smaller guns and mortars, then the stores, and finally the ammunition camels carrying thousands of rounds of ammunition on their backs.
>
> The armament of the battery consisted of a couple of muzzle loading 40-pounders, each of which was drawn ordinarily by two elephants with a spare elephant kept handy to hook in on occasion, and of a couple of 6.3-inch howitzers, each of which was drawn by a team of sixteen bullocks - or *'bhails'* in native parlance. A couple of sixteen-*bhail* teams were also kept in reserve, that were intended to be attached to the 40-pounders in case of the battery going into action against the enemy; for elephants are intelligent animals, and entertain a strong objection to the ping of a bullet. Besides the guns and howitzers, the battery has its limbered ammunition wagons, drawn by *bhails* ... Even when this imposing caravan was properly closed up in column of route on a level road, it of necessity extended several hundred yards from head to tail.

Major, later General, Sir George MacMunn, marching for the Tirah Campaign 1897 on the North West Frontier, recorded the scene:

> The roads in every direction were full with gathering troops, Highland regiments, Gurkhas, Sikh corps ... long lines of Indian cavalry, their lances standing high above the acrid dust that they stirred. By the sides of the roads strings of laden camels padded on besides the troops, the jinkety-jink of the mountain guns, the skirling of the pipes ... all contributed to the wild excitement and romance of the scene.

The assassination of Archduke Franz Feridnand of Austria on 28 June 1914 in the faraway Balkans soon set the war drums beating in India. India's immense contribution to the Great War and her vital part in the critical initial days on the Western Front was never fully acknowledged. Nevertheless, Lieutenant Colonel WB Merewether's detailed account, *The Indian Corps in France During The First World War,* recalls the Indian Army's arrival in France:

> On 08 August 1914, the 3rd Lahore and 7th Meerut Indian Divisions mobilised and began embarking from Karachi and Bombay on 24 August. *SS Taiyebeh,* followed by *Mongara* and *Castilia* berthed at Marseilles on 26 September where everything was given over to war. The scene on the quays was a sea of regimental colours, bizarre and incongruous; machine gun mules and horses, Indian troops in khaki mixed with French seamen and colonial troops, British troops and labourers. Nobody understood anyone else's language. Leaning over the ship's bulwark young British officers called out to learn whether they were coming too late. In six months nearly all were dead.
>
> When the 129th Baluchis, among the first Indian regiments to arrive in France, disembarked on 30 September 1914 and marched through the streets, they were met with raucous cheers from the French. Massia Bibikoff, a Russian artist wrote: 'It was a delirious scene. People who were drinking in the cafes of the Canebiere, men, women, officers, stood up on their chairs and shouted *'Vive Angleterre! Vivent les Hindous! Vivent les Allies!"* (Long live

> England! Long live the Hindus! Long live the Allies!)
>
> The Army of India was little understood by the general public and many thought that Indian Brigades and Divisions were composed of Sikhs and Gurkhas alone. A newspaper writing of the arrival of the Corps at Marseilles solemnly announced that 'this Corps has been raised and equipped entirely at the expense of three great Indian Princes, who are now occupying the finest hotels in Marseilles. Their names are Prince Sikya (a corruption of Sikh), Prince Gorok (Gurkha) and Prince Baluin (Baluchis).
>
> At the race-course camp by the sea were twenty or thirty French men, women and children leaning on the rails and watching Indian soldiers cooking their evening meal in their khaki uniform ... they exchanged words, French and Hindustani, a French child offered one of them a sweet, the Indian gave *chaipatty* in return, cigarettes were offered by a passer-by, a Mohammedan pulled out from his haversack a bamboo flute and played a ditty; all laughed heartily.
>
> On 30 September the Lahore Division entrained for Orleans after being hurriedly re-equipped with .303 Lee Enfield rifles. Enormous crowds gathered at the stations where the trains stopped; fruits, biscuits, coffee and flowers were lavished on the men as the flag waving crowds shouted *Les Hindus.*

I was attending a course of instruction at Pune which had commenced in August 1971. Talk and certainty of war lay thick in the air. Pune Cantonment was emptying out as units and formations were mobilised and moved to their operational areas. By the time the course terminated in end October, Pune Cantonment was a deserted place. My fellow course mates would regularly receive instructions to report to new locations on termination of the course. I had left my regiment in J&K, and it would likely have been deployed in its operational area by the time I rejoined it, but there was no change to the railhead at Pathankot.

As the train approached Pathankot, military special trains were unloading troops, guns, tanks and stores at nearby railway stations. On detraining, I found a JCO from the regiment waiting to receive me. As expected, he informed me that the regiment was deployed and we could go the 'rear' to collect my kit before moving off to join the regiment. Having done that, we set out and on crossing the Ravi at Madhopur we joined an unending stream of military transport of all types on the then two lane road towards Jammu. Full mobilisation of the army had commenced by now and 1 Corps – the 'Strike' Corps – was on the move. There was no civilian traffic on the road.

Troop-carrying lorries with helmeted infantrymen holding rifles between their knees, columns of heavy guns with the lead vehicle flying a chequered black-and-white flag indicating priority for move and deployment, large transport-trailers carrying tanks, wheeled armoured personnel carriers (APCs), ammunition lorries flying red flags, anti-aircraft guns with radars, bridging equipment and bulldozers on trailers, rover vehicles flying distinguishing pennants on radio antenna and command post vehicles. In the body of all vehicles were soldiers doing what soldiers of all armies do under such conditions – dozing off. All movement very efficiently controlled and directed by the military police.

The mass of vehicles belching exhaust smoke created a haze. Heavy vehicles in low gear pulling up the incline of causeways emitting thick diesel fumes added to it and reduced visibility to a few hundred yards. The cumulative sound of engines created a roar like swarms of bees overhead. At road level, it was wheels and wheels as far as the eye could see.

Above the moving panoply of the wherewithal for war, Hunter fighter aircraft in pairs flew Combat Air Patrols (CAPs) to thwart any enemy surprise pre-emptive attack.

All this made for a memorable and uplifting scene.

As we neared Samba, the road on either side was dotted with signposts with coded letters and figures indicating where each unit or formation headquarters was to turn off. By late afternoon, and a little ahead of Samba, we turned south and after a few km, we were in our regiment location. The regiment was deployed; guns dug down and camouflaged with the ammunition ready. I was greeted with the cheerful exuberance of the men and a hot mug of sweet tea. I was back to where I belonged: Gun Position Officer of a 130mm Medium Artillery Battery.

Next morning a Pak Mirage III reconnaissance aircraft darted in, and flying over our position, turned to sweep the highway. The ack-ack guns deployed with us opened up. All talk of war was now a certainty. More action was to follow.

Twenty years later, on the third day of my assuming command of a regiment, we were mobilised and concentrated at Bareilly airfield to be airlifted to Sri Lanka for *Operation Pawan.* As Kipling said "but that's another story ...".

# THE GOD OF WAR

> A man with artillery on his side might dice with the Devil and rise from the table the victor.
> —Richard Holmes

When the Uzbeks ousted Babur from Samarkand, he set out southwards to seek his fortune. Taking Turkish guns and gunners from Kabul, he met Sultan Ibrahim Lodhi at Panipat on 21 April 1526. Babur's guns wrought havoc in enemy ranks, with war elephants running wild in panic. Babur's victory laid the foundation of the Mughal Empire. Akbar, the third in succession, called artillery as the *Locks and Keys of Empire. Ultima Ratio Regum* – The Final Argument of Kings – was inscribed on his cannons by Louis XIV of France. Stalin called it the *God of War.*

By World War I, industrial and scientific developments had resulted in breech-loading, hydraulic recoil absorbing, quick-firing guns. The French *Soixante-Quinze* or the '75' developed in 1897 with a hydraulic recoil and fixed ammunition could pump 20 rounds in a minute. Their capacity to fire and expend ammunition was so great that normal methods of production simply could not cope with the requirement. By the spring of 1915, shells were being rationed by the British on the Western Front. The 'Shell Crisis' brought down the British government and the new government appointed a Minister of Munitions. Total reconfiguration of industries followed. Nothing signified industrialization of war more than the gun and the shell. Massed artillery delivering unimagined quantities of shells was now a reality. Heavier guns with heavier shells delivering thousands of tons of munitions over days became the norm. Like huge drums emitting a continuous roar, a rolling thunder pervaded the battlefields. Those who have experienced being under heavy shelling describe the helplessness and buffeting like that by scores of trains screaming and hurtling towards them.

In 1906, Britain launched the battleship *HMS Dreadnought*. Its steel hull, steam-turbine, speed and massive guns outclassed all other fighting ships of that time. Bigger ships like the German *Bismarck* and American *Maryland* followed. Mounting up to nine guns of 16-inch calibre, with armour-piercing shells as big as a medium-stature man and weighing 2700 lbs, they fired up to a range of 24 miles. The 70,000 ton Japanese *Yamato*, mounting 69 feet long 18.1-inch guns, firing 3200-lbs shells with a range in excess of 26 miles, was the largest ever. Such ships became the terror of the seas. This was to last well into the century. But that is another story.

When the unexpected resistance by the Belgians in August 1914 at the fortress of Liege, on the bank of the River Meuse, along with twelve other forts in a 60-mile radius, threatened to throw the German plans out of gear, they brought up the monsters developed in secrecy by Krupps of Germany and Skoda of Austria in the years preceding the war. Heavy siege guns had until then been restricted by the ability of horses to pull them. Steam locomotives and the internal-combustion engine unshackled their size. The German rail-mounted 16.5-inch gun had a crew of 200, weighed 98 tons, and fired an 1800-pound shell to 9 miles. It was named *Big Bertha* after the wife of the head of the Krupp works. The Austrian 12-inch mortar was broken up in three parts for movement and towed on iron pads around its steel wheels. A steel platform was laid to bring it into action, and the mortar assembled and bolted onto it. It lobbed a projectile to 7 miles. The crews wore padded covers over their mouths, eyes and ears and lay flat on the ground, 300 yards away, to fire them electrically through a wire. The bombardment of the forts began on 12 August, and by 16 August all had been reduced to rubble.

The fortress complex of Verdun boasted of 60 individual forts and outposts. It held great symbolic and historic significance for the French and had been successfully held at the outbreak of the war. Then on 21 February 1916, the German attack commenced with some

1600 artillery pieces, the largest artillery concentration till date, with 20,00,000 rounds to be fired in the first six days, and another 20,00,000 shells in the next twelve. On 25 February, the prime fortification of Fort Douaumont fell.

The Battle of the Somme was preceded by a seven-day bombardment of the German line by 1437 guns delivering 17,38,000 shells over a 14-mile front. The plan envisaged a five-day bombardment preceding the attack over V, W, X, Y and Z days commencing V Day 24 July 1916. Bad weather forced a two-day postponement of the attack, with inadequate ammunition for another two days of bombardment. When the attack went in on 01 July, the effect of the bombardment had petered out. The allies suffered 57,470 casualties, including 19,240 killed, on the first day.

Increasing reliance on artillery to seek a breakthrough in the stalemate of the trenches saw over 3000 guns firing 4.5 million shells over ten days on an 11-mile front before the battle of Passchendaele on 18 July 1917. Rain and mud, compounded by the destruction of the drainage by the shelling, simply bogged down any progress.

The German spring offensive of 1918 was launched on 21 March with 3500 field and 2500 heavy guns. Employing the innovative 'fire-waltz', they delivered a mix of high explosives, smoke, tear-gas, and poison-gas shells on the front lines and accurate bombardment of allied guns in depth. This was followed by a massive creeping barrage behind which the stormtroopers broke through the defences. The British line collapsed with the Germans advancing 40 miles over a 50-mile front, to within 60 miles of Paris, when Haig issued the famous last-stand order 'With our backs to the wall...' on 11 April. Three heavy Krupp railway guns were now brought up. These 'Paris Guns' were 15-inch guns with an 8-inch tube inserted inside, making them 112 feet long and weighing 138 tons. They had a barrel life of 65 rounds, with each round wearing away the barrel, causing each shell to be slightly larger than the last-fired shell. The 65 shells were, therefore, to be fired in a set sequence. Only 20 could be fired in a day. On 23 March 1918, the three guns opened fire on Paris from over 70 miles away creating panic. 183 shells were fired. At the end of the war, the Germans destroyed the heavy monsters, to prevent them from falling into Allied hands.

The final British offensive around Amiens and St Quentin saw an eight-hour bombardment with 126 shells landing every minute over every 500 yards of German defences. By the end of the war, the Royal Artillery had half-a-million officers and men, more than what the entire British Army had at the commencement of the war.

The static attrition of the Great War had brought the massed artillery to its heyday. By World War II, manoeuvre had been largely restored on the battlefield, nevertheless, where static defences had to be broken, massed and heavy artillery prevailed. The Germans once again produced the *Schwerer Gustav* and its sister the *Dora* for tackling the French fortifications of the Maginot Line and the Russian defences of Sevastopol. These rail-mounted 31.5-inch behemoths produced by Krupp weighed 1344 tons, with a barrel length of 33 yards, and a shell weighing seven tons fired up to a range of 29 miles. Both were destroyed before the surrender. The Germans also fielded the 28-cm rail mounted K5 *Leopold* which bombarded the beaches at Anzio, Italy, and nicknamed the *Anzio Anne* by the Allies. The British developed the 250-ton 18-inch rail-mounted *Boche Buster*, and the Americans the 914-mm *Little David*, but these were never used in action.

At 9.40 pm on 23 October 1942, the British artillery at El Alamein opened a five-and-half-hour barrage over a 40-mile front with 908 field and medium guns, each firing over 600 rounds, totalling 5,29,000 before it ended. In the plain open desert, the rolling thunder could be heard in Alexandria, 40 miles away. The mass of World War I had arrived in this war. At the Battle of Kursk, 1943, nearly 50,000 Soviet guns and mortars delivered 42 million rounds in July-August. The Allied assault on the Gustav Line in Italy in 1944 was backed by 2000 guns firing 1,74,000 rounds.

Perhaps nothing delivered more mass-energy in the shortest time than the Soviet-pioneered multi-barrel truck-mounted rocket-launchers, firing salvos and saturating the target with high explosive. The BM 13 *Katyusha* fielded in 1941, mounting 48 tubes with each firing at a few seconds interval, could deliver the equivalent of 18 field guns. The whining sound of the rockets in flight earned it the nickname *Stalin's Organ*.

By April 1945, the River Oder, 60 miles east of Berlin, had

become the front-line between Nazi Germany and the Soviet Union. Two and a half million Red Army troops, 6000 tanks and over 40,000 artillery pieces were deployed for the final assault on Berlin. The Seelow Heights, 35 miles from Berlin, was the last organised German defensive position before Berlin. On 16 April 1945, the Soviet attack commenced with over 9000 guns and rocket launchers firing over an 18.5-mile front, making it one gun or launcher every three yards. Approximately 5,00,000 shells were fired in the first 30 minutes. The heat and the blast of the firing generated a hurricane-like wind. For the next three weeks, till the capture of Berlin on 02 May 1945, Soviet artillery fired over two million shells and rockets into the city. When the firing ceased the silence was deafening.

When the Communist Chinese entered the Korean War, overwhelming the UN forces with their sheer numbers, the Americans responded with what came to be termed as the 'Meat Grinder' – massed artillery supplemented by air power. American artillery in Korea fired five times more ammunition than the average fired by the Allies in all of World War II.

On major battlefields last century, more than any other weapon, artillery shells did the butchers work: 58 percent British casualties on the Western Front in World War I, 75 percent in the Western Desert and 51 percent Russian casualties on the Eastern Front in World War II and 60 percent American in Korea.

By the end of the last century, technology brought about pin-point accuracy in target acquisition and designation, precision-delivered munitions and terminally guided projectiles, all resulting in 'mass' being transformed into 'effect' by a few guns. The days of the massed big guns were over. It had been a century of The God of War.

*The angel of Death spread his wings on the blast*
*And breathed in the face of foe as he passed ...*
—Lord Byron, *The Destruction of Sennacherib*

# BATTLE OF HALDIGHATI AND CHETAK

Nearly four thousand years ago, the horse was tamed, domesticated and brought on the battlefield for chariots. Two thousand years later the horse mounted warrior appeared on the scene giving rise to the concept of cavalry. The stirrup introduced in 800 AD gave stability and firmness in the saddle to the rider which enabled him to dominate the battlefield till the machine gun, barbed wire and finally the tank sounded the horseman's death knell. Tank mounted warriors were now the prima donnas.

Maharan Pratap and his mount Chetak epitomise the romance and chivalry of the medieval mounted warrior. The insignia of the Indian Army 10 Corps depicts a horseman with a spear poised to strike. The Corps goes by the moniker 'Chetak Corps'. On assuming command of the Corps, I enquired if a painting of the Battle of Haldighati featuring Rana Pratap and Chetak could be obtained or commissioned for display in the headquarters. My query led my staff to the Custodian of the House of Mewar who very graciously offered to present the painting to the Corps. It arrived a few days later – a composite painting that depicted all the major events of the battle.

The Battle of Haldighati was precipitated by the Mughals seeking suzerainty over the kingdoms of Northern India. Babur's victory at the field of Panipat on 21 April 1526 laid the foundation of the Mughal Empire. It was followed by the Battle of Khanwa on 17 March 1527 against the forces of Rana Sangha of Mewar. The efforts to subdue the Rajputs continued. Following the siege of Chittorgarh, Maharana

Udai Singh, Maharana Pratap's father, left the fort before it was captured and moved to the city of Udaipur, which he had founded in 1559. Akbar sent six diplomatic missions to Pratap seeking to negotiate an alliance similar to the one he had concluded with the other Rajput chiefs. However, Pratap refused to accept Akbar's suzerainty, prompting Akbar to initiate hostilities.

On 18 June 1576 (or possibly 21 June as per some other calendar calculations), the armies of Pratap and Akbar met at Haldighati near the town of Gogunda where Pratap's army had taken up a position at the entrance of a defile. Akbar's army, under Maan Singh I of Amber who was now a Mughal General and Commander-in-Chief, was led by Syed Hashim in the field. Pratap's army had the Tanwars of Gwalior and the Rathores of Merta as also a contingent of Afghan warriors led by Hakim Khan Sur and a small contingent of Bhil Adivasi archers. His army is estimated to have had 3000 horse-borne soldiers, 2000 infantry soldiers, 100 elephants, 100 spearmen and 400-500 Bhils. The Mughals numbered about 40,000.

Commemorated as the most important event in Rajput history, the Battle of Haldighati was an indecisive battle. For an event that spawned a legend in the annals of Rajasthan, the battle of Haldighati was a short affair; it lasted for only four hours.

The Rajputs initiated a full frontal attack taking the Mughals by surprise. However, the numerical superiority of the Mughals and the efficiency of their artillery soon began to tell. Seeing that the battle was favouring their opponents, Pratap's generals prevailed upon him to flee the field to fight another day. Sardar Maan Singh Jhala took the royal silver insignia from the wounded Maharana Pratap's back and placed it on his back, thus confusing the enemy, and taking the entire attack of the Mughal hordes upon himself. He was eventually killed. It was his sacrifice that let Maharana Pratap live and continue fighting the Mughals, eventually liberating all of Mewar except for Chittorgarh.

Maharana Pratap's horse Chetak, wearing an elephant mask to deceive the war-elephants who had swords tied to their tusks, was seriously wounded too. Nevertheless, he took the wounded Maharana away from the battlefield across a river-bed about two miles distant, before he collapsed and died.

The other lesser known heroes of Haldighati were the Bhil

Adivasis of the Aravallis, whose intense showers of arrows inflicted considerable casualties on the enemy. In recognition of their extraordinary contribution, a Bhil stands alongside a Rajput on either side of the Royal Coat of Arms of Mewar.

The Battle of Haldighati has commanded a lasting presence in Rajasthani folklore, and the persona of Pratap is celebrated in many folk songs, the most popular being *O Neele Ghode Raa Aswaar* (O Rider of the Blue Horse).

The legend of Pratap and Chetak lives on and recalls the glory of the cavalryman. The Chetak Corps and its insignia embody the spirit of the horseman and the dominance of the tank mounted warrior of today.

> *Four things greater than all things are,*
> *Women and Horses and Power and War.*
> —Rudyard Kipling, *The Ballad Of The King's Jest*

# THE SAM BROWNE BELT

The Indian Army did away with the Sam Browne Belt in the 1980s. When the end came, it was like the buglers sounding the last post. Sam Browne had been a vital part of the ceremonial rig; closest to the heart, quite literally.

The Sam Browne, colloquially called the Cross Belt, was distinctly different from the cross belt which was a functional piece of equipment of a bygone era. The cross belt had pouches or gibernes in which the Infantry kept ammunition, the Grenadiers kept fuses and some regiments even pushed in the bugle-horn. It saw extensive use in World War I and was thereafter replaced by canvas web equipment with pouches and backpack. The Sam Browne Belt, on the other hand, was a sheer ceremony – all Kiwi/Cherry Blossom and Brasso, spit and polish. Its very name conjured up visions of fine men astride magnificent horses, gleaming leather and polished brass, burnished sword, colourful pennants and guidons generating incredible pride, pomp and show.

Just as the Crown sometimes stood for the Empire, and the Ashoka Lions stand for the State, the Sam Browne denoted authority, like Under Officers being privileged to wear it at the Indian Military Academy. Non Commissioned Officers, on promotion as Junior Commissioned Officers, eagerly wore the Sam Browne with pride. In a similar imitation, a canvas belt worn with one brace and shoulder strap across the chest conveyed authority of the regimental police or the military policeman. It also represented formal proceedings. At the conclusion of a court-martial, all the members would don the Sam

Browne and full medals to pronounce the verdict. A Young Officer, on first joining his unit, was likely to be interviewed by his Commanding Officer with both wearing the Sam Browne.

The Sam Browne belt was named after Lieutenant General Sir Samuel James Browne, VC, a British Army Officer, who died in 1901. Consequent to the Anglo-Sikh Wars, the East India Company raised 'Irregular' cavalry and infantry units for managing the frontier with Afghanistan. These formed the Punjab Irregular Force – the PIFFERS. In 1849, Lieutenant Browne commenced raising the 2nd Punjab Irregular Cavalry at Lahore. His regiment saw action at Delhi, Agra and Kanpur in 1857. On 31 August 1858, the then Major Samuel Browne, was severely wounded and lost his left arm, and won the Victoria Cross (VC) for his gallantry. With the loss of an arm, Samuel Browne found it difficult to support his sword from the belt and therefore added the shoulder strap. A leather pistol holder also formed part of the original belt. It gained formal acceptance in the 1860s and remains one of the few accoutrements still in service worldwide with little or no change over 150 years. The original belt is now on display in the India Room at the Royal Military Academy, Sandhurst.

Samuel Browne became the Commandant of the Corps of Guides. Twenty years later, as Lieutenant General Sir Samuel Browne, he commanded the Peshawar Valley Field Force assembled at Jamrud for intervention in Afghanistan in the autumn of 1878 on the eve of the Second Afghan War. In 1861, the 2nd Punjab Irregular Cavalry, on regularisation, became the 2nd Punjab Cavalry. Redesignated in 1903 as the 22nd Cavalry (Frontier Force), a year later it became the 22nd Sam Browne Cavalry (Frontier Force). The 22nd and 25th Cavalry then amalgamated in 1922 and became the 12th Cavalry (Frontier Force) (Sam Browne Cavalry). It dropped out of the Order of Battle in 1937 when it gave birth to the Cavalry Training Centre at Ferozepur during the reorganization of the Army. In 1947 it went to Pakistan becoming the Armoured Corps Centre. Pakistan reactivated it as the 12th Cavalry (Frontier Force) in 1955.

An interesting tradition of 3rd Cavalry, associated with the Sam Browne, was the wearing of the cross strap buckle at the back instead of the front. It came about when the commanding officer turned up on parade inadvertently wearing it in reverse and all officers did the same rather than embarrass him.

What led to the sad demise of the Sam Browne? Use of the Sam Browne had proliferated to include all and sundry such as security guards and doormen. The web belt had hastily retreated in face of the new leather belt having a rectangular, nickel-plated buckle surmounted by the regimental crest, capable of acquiring a shine as swiftly as the shoe. Then came a phase of misplaced enthusiasm to standardise, Indianise and do away with all accoutrements peculiar to each arm and regiment, resulting in much tinkering with badges of rank, shoulder titles and the like. The straight sword associated with a straight-backed Army was replaced by the curved Indian *Talwar*, but due to its imbalance and unwieldiness in performing ceremonial drills, discarded just as quickly. The new dark green 'Service Dress' was designed to be worn without a belt. All factors combined dictated the fading away of the Sam Browne from the Indian Army.

The eclipse of the Sam Browne belt marked the passing away of an era, remembered by old soldiers, who do not die but just fade away.

# A SLICE OF THE SILK ROUTE

On being posted at Leh, I commenced familiarization of our forward deployments in Kargil, Siachen and Eastern Ladakh. We took off from Leh in a Cheetah helicopter, and having climbed to 20,000 feet, we flew across the Khardung La and along the Shyok River to Daulet Beg Oldi (DBO) and then up to the Karakoram Pass. I realized I was traversing a part of the ancient and fabled Silk Route. Ladakh, being an important way station along this route, was known as 'Little Tibet'.

*Seidenstraae* – or 'Silk Route', a name given by the German geographer Ferdinand von Richthofen – is the world's oldest trading route linking the East and the West. The formidable barriers of Hindu Kush, Karakoram and Kun Lun could not prevent the Indian subcontinent from being linked with this trading highway. Hazarding these high mountains, Indian merchants also acted as a conduit for the exchange of art and culture. Indian traders carrying considerable amounts of gold and silver preferred the Leh-Karakoram Pass-Yarkand-Kashgar route as it was much safer than the route through Afghanistan. The main 4000-mile Silk Route connected China with Syria and thence to Europe. From Peking to Venice it traversed the Taklimakan Desert and the Pamir Knot; Taklimakan meaning 'If you go there you will never return'. Around the 8th century, the route was at the height of its activity and stretched approximately 8000 miles. Chinese silk, finding favour with the royalty of Central Asia and Europe, was the first impetus for the establishment of the silk route. The fundamental driver – silk – ceased to be the primary trading commodity around 1400 AD. The route itself fell into decay and disuse with the discovery of a sea route from Europe to India and the Far East, around the Cape of Good Hope, by Vasco de Gamma. Religious conflicts of the 13th century – the Crusades – also contributed to the decline.

In its heyday, it was the pathway for the trading of exotic commodities and, above all, for the free flow and exchange of ideas and inventions. What passed through the route was transformed progressively through local influence, be it food, language or even religion. Gunpowder, rocket science, porcelain, and paper invented in China were received and exploited by the West. Astrological findings added to the prevailing knowledge. The major route lay between 30 and 40 degrees latitude, thus allowing the same astronomical observations and inferences to be used along its entire length. 'Cotton Rock', the fireproof fibre extracted from rocks on the edge of the Taklimakan, was the precursor of asbestos. The route was not free from medieval brigands. Muslim bandits performed religious rituals after consuming Hashish before setting out to kill and loot. The practice gave rise to the term Assassin – derived from hashish. Muslim Turks controlled most of the route in the 10th century and it was the natural highway for the Mongol armies in the 13th century.

Very few, if any, travelled the entire length of the route. Products and requirements of a region were bartered with the next one and goods travelled as far as they were required. While the main artery ran from the east coast of China to the Mediterranean, through Kashgar, Yarkand, Khotan, Samarkand, Baghdad and Damascus, subsidiary routes joined up to spread the network. Spices, pashmina, opium and precious stones moved from the Indian subcontinent through Afghanistan and Kashmir-Ladakh to join the route at Khotan, Bukhara and Kashgar. Silk, tea, hashish and jade came in return. Areas along the trade routes became famous for their products: Khotan for jade, Bukhara for carpets, Badakhshan for lapis-lazuli and rubies, Tibet for musk and pashmina wool, Kashmir for its saffron, fine shawls and calligraphed books. Kashmiri shawls were much prized in the Imperial Russian Court. Yangisar remains famous for its knives even today.

Buddhism, perhaps the most widespread and unique export, travelled from India through Ladakh to Tibet, China and beyond. It took various forms and hues along the way. Leh was an important barter junction, lying as it did at the confluence of routes from Kashmir, present-day Himachal Pradesh, Tibet, Gilgit and Baltistan. The route from Kashmir through Leh and beyond the Karakoram Pass to Yarkand was negotiable only during the winters when the Shyok River was frozen and movement over it was possible. Deep gorges through which the glacier melt torrents raged in the summers precluded any movement. Extreme altitudes across the Karokaram and the numbing cold – up to minus 40 degrees Celsius – made it an extremely hazardous undertaking. But perhaps the gains to be made were worth the risks.

Not many in the Occident believed all the stories of the trade link till Marco Polo returned to Venice with exotic merchandise. At his death, when asked to confess his false narratives, he replied, 'I did not tell half of what I saw'. Marco Polo described Kashgar as the biggest Asian Bazaar.

The name Daulet Beg Oldi (DBO), practically the last staging site of the subcontinent before the Karakoram Pass, itself sums up the riches and hazards of trading on the route – where *Daulat* (rich) *Beg* (great) *Oldi* (died).

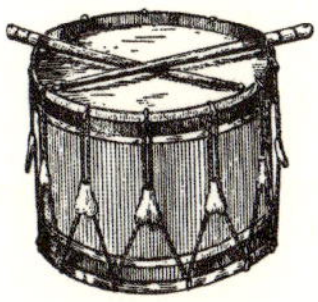

# ASAL UTTAR

## The Battle that defined the 1965 Indo-Pak War

Post India's humiliation in 1962, when Pakistan made incursions into Kutch in April-May 1965, India agreed to a delineation of the Kutch border by a three-member international tribunal. This emboldened Pakistan to attempt to take Kashmir by force. The Pakistan Army, boosted by its qualitative and quantitative superiority in artillery and armour, and believing the post-1962 expanded Indian Army to be ill-trained and ill-equipped to stand against them, considered it a very opportune time to settle its political problems with India by military action.

Rapidly increasing Pakistani infiltration activities in J&K indicated that a crisis would develop and culminate into hostilities. The threat to Punjab stemmed from the configuration of the canal and river systems, which suggested a Pak offensive along the grain of the country in the Khem Karan-Khalra sector between the Ravi and Satluj Rivers, where there were no natural obstacles, and aimed towards the vital bridge at Beas. Accordingly, the defences in this sector were strengthened by an additional brigade, and 2 (Independent) Armoured Brigade was located at Tarn Taran to be available at short notice.

The security of Punjab was to be ensured by a surprise pre-emptive offensive up to the Ichogil Canal with a view to lean on this obstacle and deny bridges across it to Pak. 11 Corps' *Operation Riddle* envisaged a move from peace-stations directly into action, securing of territory across the International Border up to the east bank of the Ichogil Canal and the capture of vital bridges over the canal intact.

Balance was to be retained to meet any threat in the Khem Karan-Khalra areas. 4 Mountain Division, equipped and trained for the mountains, was nevertheless tasked with an offensive in the plains of Punjab.

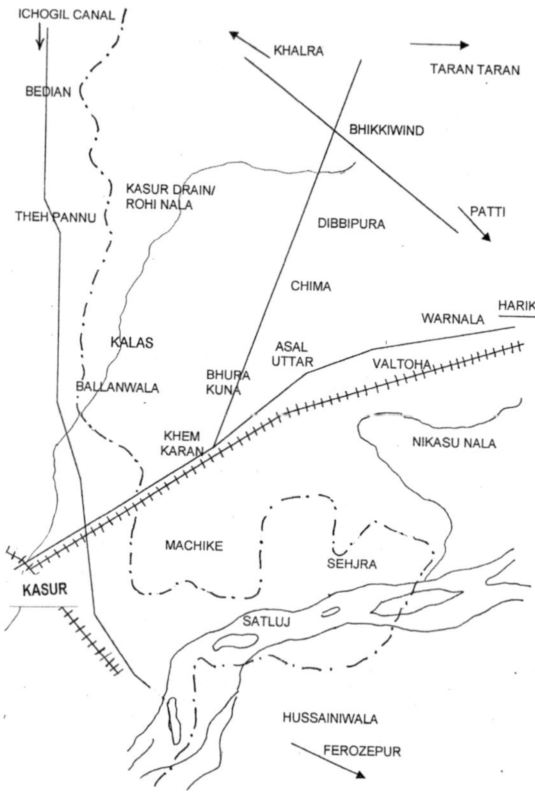


The offensive plans, therefore, were as follows:

15 Infantry Division was to advance along the GT Road axis up to the Ichogil Canal.

7 Infantry Division was to progress operations along the axis Bhikkiwind-Khalra-Barki up to the Ichogil Canal.

4 Mountain Division was to capture areas east of Ichogil Canal, destroy the bridge over the canal on the Khem Karan-Kasur road and occupy a defended sector to meet any enemy offensive.

29 Infantry Brigade Group was to destroy the Pak bridgehead in the area Dera Baba Nanak while 67 Infantry Brigade Group was to hold Hussainiwala and contain Pak in the area of Sulaimanke. These actions were intended to secure the northern and southern flanks of the Corps.

2 (Independent) Armoured Brigade and 96 Infantry Brigade from 15 Infantry Division were earmarked as Corps reserve and located at Taran Taran.

The major Pak offensive by their 1 Armoured Division and the newly raised 11 Infantry Division was also planned along axis Kasur-Khem Karan. These formations were accordingly concentrated in the area of Kasur. The objective was the Beas Bridge and the Pakistanis saw this as the 'Fourth Battle of Panipat' which would once again change the history and geography of India.

The Indian offensive commenced on 06 September 1965. While the 15 Infantry Division offensive met partial success, 7 Infantry Division was able to progress operations generally as planned and captured Barki after a grim hard-fought battle. 4 Mountain Division operations, which were to culminate in the battle of Asal Uttar, commenced at 0500h on 06 September 1965. In its initial phase, 62 Mountain Brigade secured the area up to Rohi Nala, while 7 Mountain Brigade secured the area north of the line Rohi Nala-Ichogil Canal East Bank-Theh Pannu. The Shehjra Bulge was also captured. However, Ballanwala could not be captured, nor the bridge over the Ichogil Canal destroyed. Pak forces were already poised for their own offensive and the enemy reaction was, therefore, quick and violent. By the afternoon of 07 September, the enemy had built up intense pressure on the isolated defended localities of 18 Raj Rif ahead of Khem Karan, 4 Grenadiers at Theh Pannu and 1/9 GR less two companies spread in area Kals-Khem Karan-Machike. Some of the newly raised units lost cohesion and practically disintegrated with their remnants later merged into other units.

At this stage, it was decided to readjust the dispositions of 4 Mountain Division by withdrawing and establishing a defended sector astride the axis Khem Karan-Bhikkiwind in the area Asal Uttar. The Rohi Nala in the north, and the Nikasu Nala along with the Khem Karan Distributary in the south, combined to form a horseshoe with little scope of bypassing the defended sector. *Time* magazine, in its issue of 23 September 1965, commented that 'The Indian strategy resembled that of Hannibal when he caught the Romans in a bag-like trap and decimated them at Canne'. This readjustment gave the Division a clean break and forced the enemy to redeploy his artillery, thus giving 4 Mountain Division time to prepare the defences. 9 Horse and a company of 1/9 GR deployed south-west of Khem Karan also helped delay the enemy who was also delayed in crossing the Rohi Nala. While all troops were ordered to pull back to Asal Uttar, two companies of 9 Jak Rifles held out for the whole of 07 September 1965 on the Rohi Nala, and 40 Medium Regiment refused to redeploy rearwards as it did not want to abandon the large quantities of ammunition dumped in the gun positions, and continued to engage enemy concentrations around Kasur. 'For Kasur the war began on 07 September 1965 when an Indian column advanced to within two miles. For seven hours an artillery barrage rolled across the town bringing ruin and death': *Time* magazine, 23 September 1965.

18 Raj Rif, 1/9 GR, 4 Grenadiers and the remaining troops from 9 Jak Rif and 7 Grenadiers immediately set about preparing the defences. By the morning of 08 September the available troops with 4 Mountain Division were deployed as under :

> 18 Raj Rif in the area south of Asal Uttar covering the axis Khem Karan-Patti.
> 1/9 GR less two companies in the area south-west of Asal Uttar covering the axis Khem Karan-Bhikkiwind.
> 4 Grenadiers in the area south of Chima in depth to 1/9 GR and covering the axis Khem Karan-Bhikkiwind.
> 9 Jak Rif north of Asal Uttar and in-depth to18 Raj Rif.
> The gun areas were north-west of Valtoha and north of Chima.
> Remnants from 7 Grenadiers and 13 Dogra were employed to reinforce these battalion-defended areas.
> An advance party of 17 Sikh of approximately a company strength was rushed from Ambala and deployed with 4 Grenadiers.
> 9 Deccan Horse was deployed within the defended areas for anti-tank protection and the defence of gun areas.
> Gap to the south of Valtoha was plugged by flooding the area after breaching the Khem Karan distributary.

The Rohi Nala was also breached to flood the area.

Meanwhile 8 Cavalry less a squadron from 2 (Independent) Armoured Brigade had been moved out to the area Amritsar-Wagah on 06 September 1965, thus leaving only 3 Cavalry and a squadron of 8 Cavalry with the Armoured Brigade.

The Pakistani offensive *Operation Talwar* was to be spearheaded by their elite 1 Armoured Division. Pak 4 Armoured Brigade Operations Order and maps captured later by 3 Cavalry, revealed their plan as under:

> 4 Armoured Brigade to advance along the road Valtoha-Patti, capture Harike by 1430h 08 September and secure Raya-Beas on the road Amritsar-Jallandhar by last light 09 September 1965.
> 3 Armoured Brigade to advance along the road Khem Karan-Bhikkiwind and secure Jandiala Guru, thus cutting the GT Road by last light 09 September 1965.
> 5 Armoured Brigade was to protect the left flank of the advance along the road Khem Karan-Bhikkiwind and interpose between 7 Infantry Division and 4 Mountain Division.

The stage was now set for the Battle of Asal Uttar.

The enemy offensive on 07 September was delayed due to problems in bridging the Rohi Nala. Khem Karan was captured by the enemy on 08 September and at 1000h the enemy carried out a reconnaissance in strength with two squadrons of Chaffees and one squadron of Pattons in an attempt to break into the gun areas. The guns were pulled out of gun-pits and brought into the open to engage enemy tanks by direct fire from 3.7-in Howitzers. Simultaneously, 9 Horse also engaged the enemy tanks. The enemy withdrew with 14 tanks destroyed or damaged. Interestingly, the puny 3.7-in Howitzer, introduced into service in 1919, was designed for carriage by mules and employment in rugged inaccessible mountain terrain. It not only proved its worth in support of operations in the plains of Punjab but was also used with great effect against enemy tanks in a direct-firing role at Asal Uttar.

The initial probing was followed by an attack at about 1130h on 1/9 GR and 4 Grenadiers defended areas by a regiment of Pattons, one squadron of Chaffees and a motorized battalion in APCs. A portion of the defended area of 1/9 GR was overrun. The combat group then attempted to swing around the northern flank towards the rear but was intercepted by a squadron of 3 Cavalry lying in wait near Bhikkiwind. An attack on 4 Grenadiers was also repulsed with five enemy tanks knocked out.

> Remember we are fighting to defend our homes and hearth, the enemy shall not get through.
> —A tank squadron commander to his troops.

With the enemy intentions becoming clearer and a major armour thrust being imminent, 2 (Independent) Armoured Brigade was placed under command 4 Mountain Division and moved on night 8/9 September to the area of Bhikkiwind. Up to the middle of 1965, the regiments of 2 (Independent) Armoured Brigade were equipped with World War II vintage Sherman tanks. Their 75/76 mm guns were largely ineffective against the Patton's armour. The Brigade was provided with a Centurion regiment (3 Cavalry) and an AMX regiment (8 Cavalry) prior to the outbreak of hostilities. This proved to be an extremely fortuitous decision. The regiment equipped with Shermans (9 Horse), though theoretically no match against the Pattons, proved invaluable in providing anti-tank defence to the defended areas at Asal Uttar. During the night, extensive mine-fields were also laid. In fact, 51 Engineer Regiment of 4 Mountain Division laid a record one lac mines in just two days from 07 September to 09 September 1965.

By the morning of 09 September, the dispositions of 4 Mountain Division were as under:

> Defended sector in the area Asal Uttar comprising three battalions and two companies with 9 Horse less a squadron in an anti-tank role.
> Squadron 9 Horse in the rear of the defended sector for protection of gun areas.
> 3 Cavalry less two troops in the area of Dibbipura-Chima.
> Squadron 8 Cavalry east of Valtoha covering the left flank up to the Satluj River. 8 Cavalry less a squadron reverted back to 2 (Indep-

endent) Armoured Brigade on the evening of 09 September and was deployed in depth in the area of Warnala.

HQ 2 (Independent) Armoured Brigade in Dibbipura.

On the afternoon of 09 September, the enemy made an abortive attempt to bypass the defended sector from the southern flank. However, the tanks were bogged down in the flooded area and destroyed at leisure. Simultaneously, another attempt to clear 4 Grenadiers and advance towards Bhikkiwind was frustrated. At 2100h, yet another attempt was made to overrun the 18 Raj Rif positions with enemy tanks using infrared night-vision equipment. This too was beaten back by the infantry with own artillery fire compensating for the lack of night-fighting capability of Indian tanks.

With defences barely holding out and the increasing weight of enemy assaults, the situation was indeed critical. Any breakthrough would enable the enemy to head towards the Beas River cutting out a major portion of Punjab and all forces west of the river. An unsettled controversy suggests that the Western Command was ordered or suggested to withdraw to the Beas River which was refused. Be that as it may, the defences at Asal Uttar were held.

The climax of the battle was reached on 10 September. At 0700h the enemy made yet another determined attempt with two armoured regiments and a motorized battalion to outflank the defences from the north and break into the gun areas at Chima, while simultaneously assaulting the 4 Grenadiers defended area. A squadron of 3 Cavalry lying in wait amidst maize and sugarcane fields engaged the enemy with a single executive word of command *Maro* as the line of Pattons presented their broadside. The initial outflanking manoeuvre having failed, the enemy attempted a wider hook to get to the gun areas. This too was broken up by 3 Cavalry. Meanwhile, the assault on 4 Grenadiers was beaten back with CQMH Abdul Hamid knocking out three Patton tanks and disabling another with his jeep-mounted recoilless gun before he was hit by a tank shell and killed. His gallant action won him the PVC posthumously. Around midday, an enemy radio transmission was intercepted:

"From Imam to Imam Baaz: In the name of Islam and Pakistan,

push forward. Get through the b__s."
"Just can't sir, Indian tanks all around."
"All right. You stay put. I am coming forward."

Following this intercept, at about 1430h, the Reconnaissance Group of GOC Pak 1 Armoured Division, the 'Imam', was engaged by own artillery fire at Mile 38 on the road Khem Karan-Bhikkiwind. The GOC, Major General Nasir Ahmed Khan, was seriously wounded and the Commander Artillery, Brigadier AR Shammi, killed. The radio intercept now revealed '*Hamara Subse Bada Imam Mar Gaye*.' With that, the momentum of the enemy offensive petered out. General Mohammed Musa of the Pak Army writes in his book *My Version – Indo-Pak War 1965*:

> The offensive was called off because ... Practically, the entire divisional command set up had become paralyzed due to the confusion that prevailed ... .

The decisive victory at Asal Uttar resulted in the decimation of Pakistan's 1 Armoured Division and became a graveyard for the much vaunted Patton tanks. The enemy lost 97 tanks, including 72 Pattons, destroyed or abandoned, which included the virtual decimation of Pak 4 Cavalry, whose Commanding Officer along with 12 Officers, 58 Other Ranks and 11 running tanks surrendered on 11 September 1965. *The Tribune* reported on 15 September 1965: 'The battlefield presented the picture of a graveyard of tanks'. Superior gunnery of the Indian tank crews had prevailed.

Pak 1 Armoured Division less 5 Armoured Brigade was moved to Pasrur on 11 September 1965 to counter the Indian 1 Corps offensive. This signalled the end of their offensive. 4 Mountain Division made an unsuccessful attempt to capture Khem Karan on 11 September 1965 with 4 Sikh, moved from 7 Infantry Division, suffering considerable casualties. The Division was reinforced by 29 Infantry Brigade and 41 Mountain Brigade on 17 September 1965. Another attack on Khem Karan on 21-22 September 1965 was also unsuccessful. The ensuing cease-fire thereafter terminated hostilities.

The peaceful green countryside around Asal Uttar gives no hint of the bloody battles fought in September 1965. The sugar cane and maize fields now grow paddy. A number of small memorials to the dead lie scattered around Asal Uttar. Havaldar Abdul Hamid's grave and memorial near Chima on the Bhikkiwind Road reminds one of his valiant action and supreme sacrifice. In memory of those killed in action during the epic battle, the Gram Panchayats of Asal Uttar and the neighbouring villages hold a *Shaheedi Mela* on 09 September each year. It is evocative of the couplet – '*Shaheedon ki chitaon par jutege har baras mele, watan par marne walon ka yahe baki nishan hoga*'.

INDIAN ARMY ORBAT: PUNJAB SECTOR

| | |
|---|---|
| 11 Corps | Lt Gen JS Dhillon |
| 4 Mountain Division | Maj Gen Gurbaksh Singh |
| 4 Mountain Artillery Brigade | Brig JS Sandhu |
| 91 Mountain Regiment (3.7-in How) | |
| 92 Mountain Regiment (105-mm Pack How) | |
| 84 Light Regiment (120-mm Tampella Mor) | |
| 40 Medium Regiment (5.5-in How) from Corps Artillery | |
| 7 Mountain Brigade | Brig DS Sidhu |
| 4 Grenadiers | |
| 7 Grenadiers | |
| 1/9 GR | |
| 2 Mahar – after 10.09.1965 | |
| 62 Mountain Brigade | Brig HC Gahlaut |
| 18 Raj Rif | |
| 13 Dogra | |
| 9 Jak Rif | |
| 9 Horse (Sherman MK IV 76-mm Gun) | |
| 51 Engineer Regiment | |
| 29 Battalion Punjab Armed Police | |
| 7 Infantry Division | Maj Gen HK Sibal |
| 7 Artillery Brigade | Brig CV Advaney |
| 48 Infantry Brigade | Brig KJ Shahaney, up to 14.09.1965<br>Brig Piara Singh, VrC, MC, 15.09.1965 onwards |
| 65 Infantry Brigade | Brig Lerb Ferris |
| 15 Infantry Division | Maj Gen Niranjan |

| | |
|---|---|
| | Prasad up to 08.09.1965<br>Maj Gen Mohinder Singh, 09.09.1965 onwards |
| 15 Artillery Brigade | Brig MR Vardharajan |
| 38 Infantry Brigade | Brig FW Pathak up to 12.09.1965<br>Brig UK Gupta 13.09.1965 onwards |
| 54 Infantry Brigade | Brig MS Rikh up to 06.09.1965<br>Brig DS Kalha up to 12.09.1965<br>Brig Niranjan Singh, MC 13.09.1965 onwards |
| 96 Infantry Brigade | Brig V N Malhotra |
| 2 (Independent) Armoured Brigade | Brig T K Theogaraj |
| 3 Cavalry (Centurions) | |
| 8 Cavalry (AMX 13) | |
| 1 Dogra (Motorised) | |
| 1 Field Regiment (SP) (25 Pr Sexton) | |
| 29 Infantry Brigade Group (Under Command 4 Mountain Division after 17.09.1965) | Brig Pritam Singh |
| 67 Infantry Brigade Group | Brig Bant Singh |
| 50 (Independent) Parachute Brigade | Brig A M Nambiar |
| 21 (Independent) Artillery Brigade | Lt Col Sucha Singh |
| 474 Engineer Brigade | Col R M Rao |
| 41 Mountain Brigade (Under Command 4 Mountain Division after 17.09.1965) | Brig M R Rajwade<br>1 TAC |

PAK ARMY ORBAT: LAHORE-KASUR-SULAIMANKE SECTOR

1 Corps

| | |
|---|---|
| 1 Armoured Division | Maj. Gen. Naseer Ahmad Khan |
| 12 Cavalry (Divisional Recce Regiment) | |
| Division Artillery | Brig AR Shammi |
| 3 Field Regiment (SP) | |
| 15 Field Regiment (SP) | |
| 16 Field Regiment (SP) | |
| 21 Medium Regiment | |
| 19 Light Anti-Aircraft Regiment (SP) | |
| 3 Armoured Brigade | Brig Moen |

| | |
|---|---|
| 19 Lancers | |
| 7 Frontier Force (Armoured Infantry) | |
| 4 Armoured Brigade | Brig Lumb |
| 4 Cavalry | |
| 5 Horse | |
| 10 Frontier Force (Armoured Infantry) | |
| 5 Armoured Brigade | Brig Bashir |
| 6 Lancers | |
| 24 Cavalry | |
| 1 Frontier Force (Armoured Infantry) | |
| 1 Engineer Battalion | |
| 11 Infantry Division | Maj. Gen. Abdul Hamid Khan |
| 15 Lancers (I Corps Recce Regiment) | |
| 32 Tank Delivery Unit | |
| Division Artillery | Col Shirin Dil Khan Niazi |
| 26 Field Regiment | |
| 38 Field Regiment | |
| 12 Medium Regiment | |
| 9 Medium Regiment | |
| 35 Heavy Regiment | |
| Troop 88 Mortar Battery | |
| 37 Corps Locating Regiment | |
| 21 Infantry Brigade | Brig Sahib Dad |
| 5 Frontier Force | |
| 13 Baluch | |
| 52 Infantry Brigade | Brig SRH Rizvi |
| 2 Frontier Force | |
| 7 Punjab | |
| 12 Baluch | |
| 106 Infantry Brigade | Brig Nawazish Ali |
| 1 East Bengal Rifles | |
| 7 Baluch | |
| 3 Engineer Battalion | |

BATTLE OF ASAL UTTAR: HONOURS AND AWARDS

Battle Honour 'Asal Uttar'

- 9 Horse
- 3 Cavalry
- 4 Grenadiers
- 18 Raj Rif (Saurashtra) now 11 Mech Inf
- 1 Dogra now 7 Mech Inf
- 2 Mahar
- 9 Jak Rif

Honour Title 'Asal Uttar'

40 Medium Regiment now 40 Medium Regiment (SP)
91 Mountain Regiment now 91 Field Regiment

Theatre Honour 'Punjab'

8 Light Cavalry

Param Vir Chakra

CQMH Abdul Hamid 4 Grenadiers (Posthumous)

Maha Vir Chakra

Maj Gen Gurbaksh Singh 4 Mountain Division
Brig TK Theogaraj 2 (Independent) Armoured Brigade
Lt Col Salim Caleb 3 Cav
Lt Col Raghubir Singh 18 Raj Rif (Saurashtra)
Lt Col AS Vaidya 9 Horse

Vir Chakra

Ris Achhar Singh 9 Horse
Nb/Sub Ambhore Shiwash 2 Mahar
L/Nk Bhanwar Singh 18 Raj Rif (Saurashtra)
Capt Prabhu Singh 18 Raj Rif (Saurashtra)
Hav Raghunath Singh 1 Dogra
Maj Ram Swarup Sharma 18 Raj Rif (Saurashtra)
Lt Teja Singh 9 Jak Rif
Maj SC Vadera 3 Cav
Nk Jagdish Singh 18 Raj Rif (Saurashtra) (Posthumous)
Dfdr Tarlok Singh 9 Horse
Capt Reet MP Singh 8 Cav

Sena Medal

Maj Ram Nath 40 Med Regt
Lt Col PR Jesus 91 Mtn Regt
Maj JM Vohra 9 Horse
Maj Ajit Singh 91 Mtn Regt
Capt Kartar Singh 4 Grenadiers
Capt PR Janu 4 Grenadiers
2/Lt Dharambir Singh 1 Fd Regt (SP)
2/Lt SS Sirohi 9 Horse
Ris Risal Singh 9 Horse
Ris Nihal Singh 3 Cav
Sub Bakshi Singh 4 Grenadiers
Sub Mool Chand 4 Grenadiers
Sub Daryao Singh 4 Grenadiers
Sub Umrao Singh 4 Grenadiers
Nb/Ris Jagdeo Singh 3 Cav
Nb/Ris Bakhshish Singh 3 Cav
Dfr Balu Singh 9 Horse
Hav Janak Singh 4 Grenadiers (Posthumous)
Hav ORA Chandu Ram 36 Fd Hosp
L/Dfr Sahib Singh 3 Cav (Posthumous)

Nk Shri Ram 4 Grenadiers
Sowar Sant Singh 9 Horse
Sowar Daya Chand 3 Cav
Sowar Nek Singh 3 Cav
Sowar Udai Singh 3 Cav
Gdr Akhtar Ali 4 Grenadiers
Gnr (OWA) Alagar Arjuna 84 Lt Regt (Posthumous)
AA NP Pandey 44 Med Bn (Posthumous)
Nk Hanuman Singh 18 Raj Rif
Rfn Pitam Singh 18 Raj Rif (Saurashtra)
Rfn Shaitan Singh 18 Raj Rif
Nb/Ris Nasib Singh 3 Cav

Vishist Seva Medal

Lt Col F Bhatty 4 Grenadiers
L/Nk Hawa Singh 4 Grenadiers

# GUNNER JANG SINGH

Pre-commission training at the Indian Military Academy, Dehradun lays particular emphasis on physical fitness. A young officer on joining his unit is expected to lead his men in any physical endeavour. Two mile 'Battle Physical Efficiency Test' (BPET) runs with full equipment and weapon are routine weekly features in units. On joining my unit in 1970, BPET runs were de rigueur and I was expected to lead the men. The one individual who would not let me outrun him was Gunner Jang Singh.

Gunner Jang Singh was a typical Indian soldier of those days. Barely educated, physically tough, stoic and unyielding under physical pressure, loyal, willing executant of the letter and spirit of an order and most importantly a true comrade-in-arms. No one could handle the heavy artillery ammunition better than him. We saw action together in 1971. Having served the colours, he faded away, and I continued to serve.

More than a decade later, the emotional turmoil following *Operation Blue Star* saw men in some Sikh units deserting. In the military action that followed, most were apprehended and some, unfortunately, killed. One of our units was also affected. As the Brigade Major, I was charged with compiling the record of all such individuals. There would be a steady flow of their relatives to enquire about such persons and they were all directed to me. On meeting me, they were appraised about the person whom they had come to enquire about. Thereafter they were offered refreshments and a meal and helped make their way home.

One morning a rustic, tough-looking man with a flowing grey beard stood in front of me. I had him seated. Something about him seemed familiar. The moment he spoke I recalled he was Gunner Jang Singh. I asked him if he recognised me. Perhaps worries about his son weighed far more heavily on his mind to enable him to recollect. When I gave him my name he jumped from his chair, stood ramrod straight and saluted me. I got up, and we hugged each other. On checking the records, it emerged that his son too had deserted and was now in military custody. A big sense of relief came over his face. Apparently, he wanted to say something but refrained from doing so. We then chatted about the good old times and revived old pleasant memories; the BPET runs, events and episodes of the 1971 War, whereabouts of others, the present location of the Regiment and so on. As he prepared to leave, I insisted he stay on for the night and leave the next day as it was past midday and he had a long way to go.

He spent the night in the barracks and was ready to leave the next morning when he came over to wish me goodbye. The lingering impression of him wanting to say something the previous day prompted me to ask if there was anything I could do for him. Yes, he said, his son had not been true to his salt. He had violated the honourable code of a soldier, notwithstanding the charged environment and provocation. Without asking me the likely disciplinary action against him, he requested me to award him whatever punishment was due and to make sure that he was not retained in the Army. With that he shook hands, saluted and departed.

# THE MILITARY STAFF AND THE COLLEGE

*Good morning; good morning! The General said*
*When we met him last week on our way to the line.*
*Now the soldiers he smiled at are most of 'em dead,*
*And we're cursing his Staff for incompetent swine.*
*'He's a cheer old card' grunted Harry to Jack*
*As they slogged up to Arras with rifle and pack.*
*But he did for them both with his plan of attack.*
—Siegfried Sassoon, *The General*

'What about the Staff? I had heard and stored away in my memory several definitions of it: The staff is a bloody nuisance, inefficient where it isn't actually crooked. The staff exists in order to deprive the 2/4th Gurkhas of their rights. This was, naturally, Willy's opinion (Commanding Officer 2/4 Gurkha Rifles). The function of the staff is to so foul up operations, by giving contradictory orders and misreading their maps, that wars will be prolonged to a point where every staff officer has become a general – a fairly common view.' This extract from John Masters *Road Past Mandalay* echoes a common perspective of diehard regimental officers. But then, like any complex organization, the army needs professionals to feed, equip, move, coordinate and administer it in peace and war. And concomitantly, staff colleges to train such professionals.

Although 'military staffs' can be traced back to the earliest recorded warfare when a warrior-chief asked for advice from one of his colleagues, it was in the late eighteenth-century that the increasing and complicated requirements of logistics necessitated specialized staff. The key staff figure thus became the Quartermaster General. The second half of the eighteenth-century also saw extensive road building and the introduction of greater firepower with longer range. This afforded greater scope for manoeuvre, thus resulting in the break-up of a single massed army under the general's eye into a group of smaller armies. This logically necessitated a specialist group of men to assist the commanding general to coordinate all activities, resulting in the General Staff. However, the duties of the General Staff were discharged by the Quartermaster General till about the middle of the nineteenth century, when the two were bifurcated, and separate staff heads appointed. Thus, we read of Wellington's Quartermaster General ordering the movement and deployment of troops on the night of the Duchess of Richmond's ball for the battle at Waterloo the next day. Logistics was, and remains, a critical staff function for the successful outcome of any military undertaking.

Formal education in staff schools and colleges was initiated by Frederick the Great of Prussia (1712-86), who established the *Academie des Nobles* in 1765, which became the forerunner of the *Kriegasakademie*, established in 1810 at Berlin.

> The world does not rest as securely on the shoulders of Atlas as Prussia relies on her army.
> —Frederick the Great

A military academy to train French officer cadets was established at Saint-Cyr in 1802 and the same year the US Military Academy was also established at West Point. The French Staff School was founded in 1811.

The British staff college has its origins in the Royal Military College established in 1799 at High Wycombe to train 'Gentlemen Cadets' as officers. In 1802, it became the Senior Department of the new Royal Military College at Great Marlow. It moved to and joined the Royal Military College, Sandhurst in 1820. The Senior Division at Sandhurst was moved to Cambridge Town (later Camberley) and designated as the Staff College in 1858, was then separated from it in 1870, and finally merged into the Joint Services Staff College in 1997.

The symbol '*psc*' (passed staff college) first appeared in the British Army List in 1864. In 1904, the instructors who were hitherto titled 'Professor' were re-designated as 'Directing Staff'. With the inclusion of two naval officers in the Staff Course of 1906, the Staff College acquired its Joint Service character. Field Marshal Robertson – Chief of the Imperial General Staff (1915-18) during World War I – was the first officer from the ranks to enter the Staff College Camberley in 1897 and later became Commandant from1910-13.

The Prussians under Moltke refined their staff in the second half of the nineteenth century. The Prussian Chief of General Staff was an institution independent of the war minister, responsible only to the king. He was also the de facto commander-in-chief of the Prussian forces in war. It was also permanent thus ensuring continuity. Moltke held the position for thirty-one years, and the position was held by only seven men for the period from 1821 to 1914. Their exclusiveness was visibly manifest in the red stripe along the length of their uniform trousers. The 'Great General Staff' was organised into sections with specific responsibilities covering practically all facets of war-making, especially the Railway Section, which supervised civil construction, troop movement, mobilisation plans and even the railway traffic management in war. The Franco-Prussian War of 1870-71 indicated their staff efficiency when they mobilized and moved into barracks 11,83,000 men in 18 days and transported 4,62,000 men to the French frontier during the same period culminating in their resounding victory over the French at Sedan and entering Paris on 26 January 1871. So confident was Moltke of the efficiency of the German General Staff that on mobilization day 1870 he was found reclining on a couch reading a thriller. At the outbreak of World War I, when the Russian offensive into East Prussia threatened to overwhelm the Germans, brilliant staff work in moving troops from the West and simultaneously redeploying troops in the East resulted in the great victory at Tannenberg. The German Staff College was also instrumental in introducing the modern 'war game'.

When Lord Raglan ordered the Light Brigade to attack the withdrawing Russians at Balaclava pulling away cannons captured from Turkish emplacements, the order wrongly conveyed by Captain Nolan, the 'Staff Officer', was to charge the Russian gun emplacements ringing the valley. Of the 673 cavalry, the loss amounted to 247 men and 497 horses. The disastrous consequences of incompetent staff work in the Crimean War of 1854-56, including the glorified disaster of *The Charge of the Light Brigade* where 'Not though the soldier knew, someone had blundered', abject mishandling of supplies and near neglect of casualties and medical aid prompted the establishment of the British Staff College for proper staff training. Interestingly, one of the pre-requisites for entry into the Staff College was a 'distinct and legible handwriting' – a requirement stipulated by the Prime Minister, Mr Palmerston, who likened the handwriting of army officers to that of kitchen maids! Also, the emphasis of instruction was on mathematics as it was expected to sharpen the staff officer's mind. Artillery and Engineer officers were not required to undergo the Staff Course as their pre-commission training at the Royal Military Academy, Woolwich, was considered good enough to qualify them for staff appointments! In any case, aspiring for and entering the Staff College was considered bad form amongst regimental officers till the beginning of last century. It was considered to be a 'mugs game' – a mug being someone who did not pursue equestrian sports, did not shoot, drank water instead of wine, went to bed early and slogged at algebra, trigonometry and fortifications and learnt German and French.

Staff appointments were dictated more by an officer's social standing and background than by being qualified at the Staff College. The Duke of Cambridge advising a staff officer in 1857 said, 'If your General keeps a girl, it is your duty to squire her to all public places and to make a humble third of a party at whist or quadrille; but be sure never to win'. While all European armies had created General Staffs decades ago, the British were reluctant to do so. The Secretary for War declared in 1890 that a general staff 'would be absolutely mischievous and dangerous to the state'. It was finally created in 1906 and charged with organisation, training and operations while the Adjutant General was responsible for manpower and discipline, the Quarter Master General for supplies and transport and the Master General of Ordnance for equipment and arms.

The abolition of the system of purchase of commissions and promotions in 1871 and the introduction of competitive exams was also adopted for entry into the staff college. 'Crammers', which coached and prepared candidates for entry into the Royal Military College, Sandhurst, soon found officers looking for entry into the staff college. Nearly fifty percent of those entering these institutions had been through such crammers.

The German system of stiff competitive examination for entry into all the staff colleges became universal in due course. General Kurt Hammerstein-Equord, Chief of the General Staff of the *Reichswehr* in 1930, had this to say: 'I divide my officers into four classes; the clever, the lazy, the industrious and the stupid. Those who are clever and industrious are fitted for the highest staff appointments. Use can be made of those who are stupid and lazy. The man who is clever and lazy however is for the very highest command; he has the temperament and nerve to deal with all situations. But whoever is stupid and industrious is a menace and must be removed immediately'. Staff training, especially German, was rigorous and exacting:

> For several years the bell of my flat would ring on Christmas Eve. A courier would bring his Christmas present, a great military situation designed by him for the set task of working out an operational plan. He would have been very surprised if the solution had not been in his hands on the evening of Christmas Day.
> —Von Kuhl, aide of Field Marshal Alfred von Schlieffen (Gerhard Ritter, *The Schlieffan Plan*)

Upto 1903, when the General Staff was created, the Indian Army staff was organised under the Adjutant General, Quarter Master General and Military Secretary. The Master General of Ordnance was also added. The structure remains unaltered till today.

A staff college for India was suggested as early as 1875, but amongst other objections, the lack of a suitable climate for serious study except in the hills, prevented it being established. Nevertheless, in 1905, due to the efforts of Lord Kitchener, the C-in-C, a Staff College was opened at Deolali. In 1907, it was moved to its permanent location at Quetta. The Deolali buildings today house the Military Hospital. The first foreign officer to attend a staff course at Quetta was an Australian. In 1933, the future General (later Field Marshal) KM Cariappa become the first Indian to enter the Staff College.

Following the partition of the subcontinent, the Indian Staff College was opened at Wellington in October 1947 and housed in the old Hastings Holiday Home Barracks for British other ranks. The main administrative building, 'Ashoka', was completed in 1957 and bears a resemblance to the Quetta Staff College building with a similar porch and wings.

The Staff College at Wellington had only the Army Wing to start with. The Air Wing was added in 1949, and with the addition of the Naval Wing in 1950, it became an inter-service establishment. Brigadier (later Lieutenant General) SD Verma was the first commandant, followed by Major General WDA Lentaigne of Chindits fame.

The owl surmounted by a crown was adopted as the British Staff College crest in 1868, the owl symbolizing the wisdom of Minerva. It was successively adopted by the Staff College, Quetta, and the Indian Staff College, Wellington, though it raises questions at times as the owl is considered singularly foolish in Indian folklore. On India becoming a Republic, the crown was removed from the crest and the motto *Tam Marte Quam Minerva* substituted with the Sanskrit *Yuddham Pragnya*.

# THE BOYS AT BADGAM

## Kashmir, October 1947

## Recollections of Major General Rajendra Prakash, VSM

In October 1947 we (my parents, my two younger brothers and I) lived in Badgam, a small village south-west of Srinagar in the Kashmir Valley, fairly close to the only airfield there. My father (late) Sardar Om Prakash was the revenue officer-in-charge of what is now the Badgam District. We lived in a solitary cottage, poised on the very edge of *Karewa,* a vast upraised geological formation, typical of the Valley, stretching away towards Gulmarg-Baramulla to the north-west. My father's office and the Government Treasury were housed in a U-shaped building, on lower ground in the vicinity of our cottage, while the small village of Badgam lay a few hundred yards further down.

I used to cycle down to Sri Amar Singh Degree College, on the outskirts of Srinagar, where I had obtained a provisional admission, because results of my FSc examination had not be declared by Panjab University, due to the disruption caused by the partition of the country, including Punjab, on 15 August 1947. I was subsequently granted an FSc diploma in 1948, having rendered three months 'service' in a refugee camp in Pathankot, as per rules then prevalent.

Around 25th or 26th October, while returning from my college, I saw a couple of tall, hefty men in *salwars* lurking in a village half-way to Badgam. These men did not look like Kashmiris, and on return, I mentioned it to my father. We were all blissfully unaware of what was happening in the country, except for word-of-mouth rumours, as there was no TV or Internet in those days. To hear All India Radio, you needed bulky and expensive batteries (wet or dry) to run the radio, while newspapers – *The Tribune* and *Civil & Military Gazette* in English, and *Milap* and *Pratap* in Urdu – came all the way from Lahore, which was in Pakistan by then. There was general unease all around heightened by vague rumours about an invasion by tribals and massacres in Muzaffarabad and our hometown of Mirpur, but nothing specific was known at that time.

On the night of 26 or 27 October, we saw a wide circle of fires blazing in the far distance on the *Karewa* towards Tangmarg-Baramulla. These were rumoured to be the Sikh villages being burnt by the tribal invaders. Around midnight the next day, we were woken up by a mounted cavalry patrol of J&K Bodyguards, who were out on a reconnaissance, but they were as much in the dark as us about what was happening around. Not knowing the situation in the larger context, we blissfully carried on hoping for the best, though full of vague apprehensions.

The next night, probably 28/29 October, two or three rifle shots were fired at our cottage, perhaps by a local mischief-maker, hitting the tin roof and making a lot of noise. We also saw some panicky Sikh villagers passing through in our vicinity during the night. My father then decided that under the circumstances, my mother and us siblings (17, 11 and 3 years old) should leave Badgam and go to the airfield where Indian troops were rumoured to have landed on 27 October. After spending an uneasy and watchful night, my father asked for our Peshawari tonga to be made ready at dawn, but the horse was found to be missing from the stables. My father, with his loyal Jamedar Chaprassi, then raged around the village and eventually found our horse hidden away in a dilapidated hut at the outskirts. Hitching up the horse to the tonga, the family took off for the airfield with some hand-carried essentials only.

We reached the airfield in the early morning, passing Bakshi Gulam Mohammad (then a vigorous National Conference leader) en route, where he seemed to be energetically trying to restore some order amongst milling and panicky crowds. My father exchanged courtesies with Bakshi Sahib and we drove on to the airfield, which was just a few ramshackle huts then. There were about four or five Dakotas on the ground with more taking off and landing. Many busy-looking soldiers with maroon berets [1 Kumaon (Para) possibly] and many distressed looking civilians, mostly women and children, were milling around the airfield.

A para-trooper major was organizing the civilians into Dakota-loads and he asked me why I was not staying back to fight the tribals. I told him that I had to escort my mother and young siblings to India and my father was staying on. My mother and two brothers were sent to a Dakota (Dalmia-Jain Airways, I remember) which took off immediately and landed them at Ambala. I was herded into another Dakota (my first air experience) and landed at Safdarjung Airfield in New Delhi, not knowing what to do next. Fortunately, after an anxious hour, my mother and two brothers were flown-in from Ambala and the family was reunited.

My father went back from the airfield to Badgam and resumed his duties though the administration was in complete disarray by then. On 03 November, a fighting patrol of 4 Kumaon reached Badgam and the company commander, Major Som Nath Sharma, came to meet my father in his office. While they were talking some disturbance was heard and Major Sharma quickly rejoined his command. What ensued was the Battle of Badgam where the gallant officer and his Kumaonis held up 700 tribal marauders who intended to capture the airfield, the only access into the Valley that day, and thus secure the Valley for Pakistan. In the ensuing battle, 4 Kumaon killed over 200 attackers and Major Sharma was awarded the first Param Vir Chakra posthumously for his bravery.

After observing the battle from his office for some time, my father perforce had to leave Badgam along with his faithful chaprasi. The rest of the staff and the populace had deserted the village by then. Before leaving, he collected the contents of the Government Treasury and some important official papers, and then made his way to Srinagar cross-country, across a marsh, with great difficulty. On reaching Srinagar, he deposited the contents of Badgam Treasury in the Srinagar Treasury. Subsequently, he served as Deputy Commissioner of Ladakh when the first encounter with the Chinese took place at Konka La on 20 October 1959 resulting in capture of Deputy Commandant Karam Singh and his CRPF patrol. My father retired as the Principal of J&K Revenue Training School in 1961 and passed away in 1978. A deep personal regret remains with me that while serving in the Army from 1949 to 1983, I never found the time to sit with my father and amongst other things, record in detail his 'live' recollections of the Battle of Badgam.

All our goods and chattels in our Badgam cottage were burnt and destroyed on 03 November, but the only thing my father managed to retrieve intact was a suitcase belonging to a Muslim friend, a World War II paratrooper from 3 Rajput (Para), who was spending his leave with us in the Valley but had to rejoin duty when Partition took place. This piece of retrieved luggage was restored to the owner in January 1948 at Kasur (Pakistan) where I travelled courtesy 2/8 Gurkha Rifles, then at Ferozepur.

Having foregathered at Safdarjang Airport on 29 October, we managed to locate an uncle in nearby Lodi Colony, then went on to shelter with my aunt in Lucknow, and finally to Gurdaspur to stay with my maternal grandparents. I joined the Army in 1949, as did my younger brothers (Late) Brigadier Brijendra Prakash, SM, VSM, Signals and Intelligence Corps and Admiral Arun Prakash, PVSM, AVSM, VrC, VSM, Indian Navy.

I am still mystified as to why the *Lashkars* waited till 03 November to reach Badgam when they could easily have walked up to the airfield on 26 or even 27 October when the Indian troops had just started landing. Probably due to the bigger attractions of Baramulla, including St Joseph's, my old college, where the poor nuns were besieged!

# FEROZEPUR VIGNETTE

Stretching northwards from the Rann of Kutch, the great expanse of the Thar Desert once encompassed the present-day areas of Bathinda, Moga, Ferozepur and Kasur. The Satluj sliced through this desolate country, its banks spawning villages and hamlets, which rose and went into oblivion as the river swung and changed its course, swollen with the flood waters of the rains in the North. Sandstorms that raged for days still form a part of living memory. Storms that would cast a dark envelope blocking out the sun and bringing darkness at noon. Then came one of the greatest canal irrigation systems of the world, which first contained, and then tamed the desert with the waters of the Satluj, Ravi and Indus rivers. The green countryside around Ferozepur is still dotted with mounds of earth – the remnants of dunes which once dominated the landscape. Just as the Satluj is linked with the transformation of the country around Ferozepur, so is the history of Ferozepur inexorably interwoven with this river.

Any experienced surveyor would agree that the ideal alignment of a road in the mountains would invariably correspond to that of the ancient footpath carved out by the passage of man, as this would have a convenient gradient, least crossings of rivers and streams and not be prone to slips and slides. So also in the plains, the old caravan routes sought the fords over rivers, water sources en route and, of course, the shortest distance. It was, therefore, inevitable that the present-day location of Ferozepur should have merited attention, lying as it did on the edge of the desert on the route to Delhi from the Khyber and Lahore, as well as from the Bolan and Multan, and commanding the fords over the Sutlej just below the confluence of the Sutlej and Beas rivers. Having crossed the Sutlej, one would be on his way to the heartland of India, with the rivers of Punjab behind him and no major river ahead.

The earliest known invaders and occupants of the territories in and around Ferozepur and up to the Satluj were the Punwar Rajputs from Rajasthan who established their capital at Janer, located between Harike and Moga. They were followed by the Bhattis who held sway over areas extending from Bikaner to Hissar and Kasur and set up their capital at Bhatiana, the land of the Bhattis, which is today called Bathinda. The Bhattis are credited with the founding of Ferozepur by one of their chiefs – Feroze Khan – in the mid-sixteenth century. However, more reliable and authentic sources indicate that Ferozepur was founded by Firoz Shah Tughlag, the Emperor of Delhi (AD 1351-88).

Following the invasion of Mahmud of Ghazni in 1001 AD, the Afghans made repeated forays to loot and plunder. Then came the terrible visitation of Taimur in 1398 which signalled the end of organised governance in Northern India, till Babur laid the foundation of the Mughal rule at Panipat in 1526. The declining Mughal influence once again attracted the Afghans who entered Lahore under Ahmed Shah Abdali in 1748. The unsettled and chaotic conditions nurtured and encouraged the Sikhs to carve out principalities for themselves between 1750 and 1761. These came to be called 'Misls'. To the north-west of Ferozepur was the Bhangi misl which held Lahore, Amritsar and Sialkot. Between the Ravi and Chenab Rivers was the area held by the Sukercharkiyas.

Ranjit Singh became the chief of the Sukercharkiya Misl at the age of twelve. He soon set about consolidating and taking under his fold all the adjoining territories. The growing Sikh empire under Ranjit Singh, with its military capability and the resultant British apprehensions, brought about the Treaty of Amritsar signed on 25 April 1809 between the British and the Sikhs, consequent to which the Sikh state was mutually restricted to the Satluj as its eastern limit. Other Sikh states east of the Sutlej became feudatories of the British. Important crossings over the Satluj, including Ferozepur, thereafter assumed political and military importance and were developed as outposts of the British-Indian territories. While Ferozepur was only 40 miles from the capital city of Lahore with one river crossing, the British garrison town of Ludhiana was 130 miles with two rivers interposed in between. However, the occupation and development of Ferozepur as a cantonment was not immediate for fear of it being taken as an offensive act and thus initiating hostilities. Ferozepur was initially occupied by the British in 1835 and built up as a forward supply depot. It was made a military cantonment in 1838. The appointment board in the Garrison Engineer's (GE) office indicates the first GE being appointed in that year. The building is also the first to be constructed in Ferozepur in 1840. As per an 1838 census, the population of Ferozepur town was 2732. This had increased to 16,890, including military personnel, by 1841. A century later, subsequent to the partition in 1947, Ferozepur once again emerged as an important forward cantonment for the same basic reasons.

The British force assembled for intervention in Afghanistan in 1838 was denied passage through Sikh territory and beyond to the Khyber. It was, therefore, mustered at Ferozepur to move astride the Sutlej along with boats and barges, link up with the other part of the force from Sind at Rohri-Indus, and thereafter march through the Bolan in Baluchistan into Afghanistan. The 10,000 fighting men assembled at Ferozepur were accompanied by 38,000 camp followers, 30,000 camels and a large number of pack animals. A classic picture of an Indian Army on the move. On 27 November 1838, Lord Auckland, the Governor-General and Sir Henry Fane, the Commander-in-Chief, met Ranjit Singh at Ferozepur where a farewell review of the 'Army of the Indus' was held. A magnificent durbar was set up by Ranjit Singh near the bank of the Satluj and the Sikh Army put through its paces with impressive manoeuvres and rapid volleys of gunfire. The 'Army of the Indus' thereafter set out on the ill-fated Afghan venture. Some withdrawing troops were back in Ferozepur in December 1839. Within a few years, the Sikh Army would be at war with the British on the battlefields around Ferozepur.

Ranjit Singh died on 27 June 1839. Intrigues and conspiracies compounded by rival and ineffectual claims to power resulted in chaos and anarchy. The Army – the Khalsa – the one united power left, acquired a praetorian character and decided the fate of king and country. Narrow self-serving interests urged the army to challenge the

British. If it was shattered, the court would be rid of its masters, if triumphant, the court would claim credit. The British, on the other hand, wanted all along to destroy the last power on the subcontinent and consolidate their hold up to the Khyber. The die was cast when on 11/12 December 1845 the Sikh Army crossed the Sutlej and entrenched themselves near Ferozepur, garrisoned at that time by four artillery batteries of six guns each, eight infantry battalions and two cavalry regiments; a total strength of 10,472 men and 24 guns. The First Anglo-Sikh War (1845-46) which followed became known as the 'Sutlej Campaign' and was fought on the battlefields of Mudki, Ferozshah, and Sabraon near Ferozepur, besides Aliwal near Ludhiana.

The first encounter of the Satluj Campaign took place between the British force, advancing from Ambala, and the Sikhs, at Mudki, 16 miles from Ferozepur, on 18 December 1845. The engagement started at four o'clock of that winter afternoon and went on well into the night earning the nickname 'Midnight Moodkhee'. Three days later, the battlefield shifted to Ferozshah. Ferozshah, 12 miles from Ferozepur, was the scene of the most terrible battle of British-Indian history. It was won by the Sikh soldiery and lost by their leader's treachery ... but that is another story. The inconclusive action on 21 December 1845 was clinched the next day by General Littler's force from Ferozepur affecting a junction with the main British force under Sir Hugh Gough on the afternoon of 22 December 1845 at Misriwala village near Ferozshah, much like Field Marshal Blucher coming to the rescue of the British at Waterloo thirty years earlier. The 748 British dead at Ferozshah, including 54 officers, were buried beside the St Andrew's Church on the Jhoke Road at Ferozepur. The church retains its original bell and pipe organ, as also the pulpit carved out of a single stone, even though it was rebuilt after 1857 as a memorial to the dead of the Sutlej Campaign. A marble slab near the entrance is inscribed:

THIS CHURCH WAS ERECTED
TO THE GLORY OF GOD
IN MEMORY OF
THOSE WHO FELL FIGHTING FOR
THEIR COUNTRY IN THIS DISTRICT
DURING THE SUTLEJ CAMPAIGN
1845-46

In the open burial ground, now a playground for the local children, and recently converted into a mini-stadium, stood a marble cross on a red stand-stone platform with a marble plaque at the base which read:

IN MEMORY OF
THOSE WHO FELL IN THE
SUTLEJ CAMPAIGN
1845-46

In a misplaced sense of 'beautification', the cross was uprooted from where it had stood for a century and a half, and relocated on a cross road on the Mall, beside the existing memorials. Major General Sir Robert Sale, the commander at the siege of Jalalabad 1842, and Major General John McCaskill, killed at Mudki, lie buried in Ferozepur Cemetery.

On 10 February 1846, the Battle of Sabroan was fought on the east bank of the Satluj, about 30 miles from Ferozepur. The Sikh leaders had been in treasonable contact with the British and that night the Satluj rose seven feet, due to rains in the north, further damaging the sabotaged bridge of boats and precluding reinforcement or withdrawal. Treachery and nature decided the outcome. Fifty-six boats built on the Indus were brought up to Ferozepur in September 1845 and were used to construct a bridge of boats at Khoonda Ghat, adjacent to Ferozepur, to enable the British Army to cross the Sutlej after the Battle of Sabraon. The army consisted of over 24,000 men, 40 heavy guns, 1,00,000 camp followers and 68,000 baggage animals.

While Governor-General Sir Henry Hardinge had subordinated himself to Commander-in-Chief Sir Gough during the First Anglo-Sikh War, his successor, Lord Dalhousie, positioned himself at Ferozepur during the Second Anglo-Sikh War at the end of which Maharaja Duleep Singh, the last Sikh ruler, was escorted out of Lahore on 21 December 1849 and arrived at Ferozepur on 26 December 1849. Departing for Mudki the next day, he was exiled at Fatehgarh.

The British erected brick obelisks commemorating the battles at Mudki, Ferozshah and Sabraon which still stand today. In commemoration of the deeds of the Punjabi soldiers, the Anglo-Sikh

War Memorial came up at Ferozshah in 1976 on the Ferozepur-Ludhiana Road near the twin canals. It has, besides other things, ballads by the poet Shah Mohammad inscribed on copper plates.

The Golden Arrow House, the official residence of the General Officer Commanding 7 Infantry Division, was built in 1879 and was occupied by the Commander Ferozepur Brigade. Some barracks built in the eighteen-sixties and named 'Mudki Lines', 'Sabroan Lines' and 'Aliwal Lines', besides 'Gough Lines', still stand today, though no longer very habitable. The 'Ferozeshah Hospital' for British troops built in 1890 today houses the Military Hospital. The Indian Troops Hospital built in 1928-30 is now the Divisional Headquarters.

The first fort constructed at Ferozepur during the reign of Ferozshah of Delhi (1351-88) had been reduced to a mound by the end of the 19th century. The present fort and arsenal were constructed from 1840 onwards when an ordnance magazine was built. In 1858, the arsenal and gunpowder magazine was built. The fort was finally completed in its present form in 1886. The 65-acre brick-and-mud structure has an inner quadrangle surrounded by a hexagon-shaped wall and a star-shaped ditch surrounding the outer wall. It also houses some of the oldest military buildings in Ferozepur. Recent digging of foundations for new buildings threw up a number of cannons of early 19th-century vintage.

In the years following the events of 1857, the 'Ferozepur Brigade' forming part of the 'Lahore Division' garrisoned Ferozepur. The presidency armies were abolished in 1895, and organisationally, Ferozepur formed part of the Punjab Command, which included the North-West Frontier, and now became an important garrison for Frontier duties. On mobilisation in 1914, the Ferozepur Brigade, forming part of the 3rd Lahore Division, landed in France as part of the Indian Corps with 129th Baluchis, 57th (Wilde's) Rifles (FF), 89th Punjabis and 9th Bhopal Infantry. Khudadad Khan of the 129th Baluchis was awarded the first VC of the Indian Army in October 1914. Mir Dast of 57th (Wilde's) Rifles and Chatta Singh of 9th Bhopal Infantry too were awarded the VC.

Between the two World Wars Ferozepur also housed the Royal Indian Army Service Corps Records, an Armoured Corps Training School and the 14 Punjab Regimental Centre. Like all other colonial cantonments, Ferozepur had its *Lal Kurti* (Red Coat) or BI (British Infantry) Bazar – the Sadar Bazar being out of bounds for British troops. Post Independence, 5 Infantry Division was stationed at Ferozepur until it was flown out to the Eastern Sector in the turmoil of 1962. Ferozepur became the home of the 7 Infantry Division on its raising in 1963.

The second half of the nineteenth-century witnessed the spread of the railway network and development of an extensive irrigation system in Punjab. The nearby Hussainiwala Headworks, along with the road and rail bridges over the Satluj, which carried the trunk routes from Delhi to Lahore and beyond, added their own importance to Ferozepur. The first railway bridge across the Sutlej – The *Kaiser-i-Hind* – came up at Hussainiwala in 1885-87 linking Lahore with Ferozepur. The romance of the Punjab Mail originating from Bombay and running upto Peshawar through Ferozepur, though much diminished from its heyday, still lingers, with the train now terminating at Ferozepur. It was the fastest train of those days. Khushwant Singh's village of Mano Majra and its environs in his celebrated novel *Train to Pakistan,* though fictitious, is set on the banks of the Satluj, where the rail bridge spans the river, and would, in reality, correspond to Hussainiwala and the surrounding countryside near Ferozepur. The spot where Bhagat Singh, Rajguru and Sukhdev were cremated on the banks of the Satluj at Hussainiwala after their execution in the Lahore Jail on 23 March 1931, a National Martyrs Memorial has now been developed. The Harike Headworks were completed on 12 April 1952.

On 12 September 1897, in a deed of collective heroism perhaps unsurpassed in the annals of war, 21 soldiers of the XXXVI Sikh Regiment (present-day 4 Sikh) died to a man in defence of Fort Saraghari in Waziristan on the North-West Frontier against an attack by thousands of Pathans. To raise a suitable memorial to the dead, who were all awarded the then-highest award of the IOM, the *Pioneer* newspaper of Allahabad raised voluntary subscriptions, and a memorial gurudwara was constructed at Ferozepur at a cost of Rs 27,118. It was declared open in 1904 by the then Lieutenant Governor of Punjab. All twenty-one men belonged to villages around Ferozepur. The Saraghari Gurudwara is a fine piece of symmetrical architecture.

The bloody action fought by the troops of 7 Infantry Division to capture Barki on the Ichogil Canal on 10 September 1965 is commemorated by the Barki Memorial, constructed in 1969, adjacent to the compound of the Saraghari Memorial. Coincidentally, one of the units which fought at Barki was 4 Sikh of Saraghari fame. The roundabout near the memorial was also named 'Barki Square' by the citizens of Ferozepur.

On a prominent crossing on the Mall are two sandstone obelisks and a column erected as memorials to the dead of the Great War 1914 -19. The column is of the VI King Edward's Own Cavalry (present-day 18 Cavalry, Indian Army); the other two are of the 19, 22 & 24 Punjabis and 20 Duke of Cambridge's Own Infantry (Brownlow's Punjabis). These went on to form part of the 14 Punjab Regiment in 1922 and went to Pakistan in 1947. The last named memorial is similar to the Cenotaph outside Whitehall in London.

Ferozepur was always an important artillery station. Positioning artillery on the then 'frontier' was essential to save on the time and effort required to move the artillery train and siege artillery from other important military stations like Delhi, Meerut and Ambala. A large number of memorial tablets in memory of 'Gunners' in the churches and the cemetery at Ferozepur bear testimony to their service here. One cannot fail to notice numerous antique guns mounted at various places around Ferozepur Cantonment. The ones at Barki Square were cast in 1798 and were used as the 'Mid-Day Gun' until World War 1, being fired at noon to announce the time. Many of these guns were cast in the foundries of Lahore and Amritsar and are a part of those captured and 'spiked' during the Satluj Campaign of 1845-46. Recent digging for construction in the fort unearthed some old cannons.

From 10 January 1960 to 05 July 1961, the construction of married accommodation and a sports stadium by troops of 5 Infantry Division was undertaken under the controversial Project Jyoti. 137 Officers, 228 JCOs and 1890 OR quarters were constructed. The present-day NP (Near Permanent) type houses for officers, JCOs and ORs and the Jyoti Stadium is a legacy of this project.

Ferozepur's extreme climate recorded a maximum of 47 Degrees Celsius on 31 May 1954 and a minimum of Minus 3 Degrees Celsius on 29 January 1964. In an otherwise rain-starved area, a maximum of

301 mm of rain fell on 17 September 1950. Frequent flooding of the town by the Satluj was tamed by the Harike Barrage and dams upstream.

Perhaps the most poignant reminders and authentic chroniclers of the station's military history are the headstones in the local cemetery. In their own silent way, they recount the tenures of regiments, both British and Indian, which include Her Majesty's 10th Foot in 1849, 2nd Battalion The Royal Sussex Regiment in 1895 and 32 Field Regiment in 1984. Though time and weather have taken their toll, some of these are exquisite pieces of craftsmanship. One erected by the comrades of Private JM Donald of the lst Dorset Regiment laid to rest in 1906 reads:

HIS TOUR OF DUTY HERE IS DONE
NO MOTHER WATCHED BESIDES HER SON
NO FRIENDS OF CHILDHOOD THERE COULD LEND
SWEET SOLACE TO THEIR AILING FRIEND

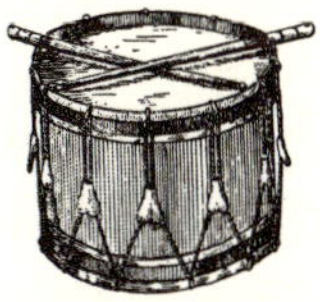

# THE MILITARY BAND

> No one can say for certain where the soul of the battalion lives, but the expression of that soul is most often found in the band. A wise and sympathetic bandmaster can lift a battalion out of depression, cheer it up in sickness, and steady and recall it to itself in times of almost unendurable stress.
> —Rudyard Kipling, 1915

Military music has evolved from its primeval purposes of invoking fear in the enemy, relaying orders, urging soldiers into battle, controlling troops on the battlefield, keeping them in marching step and enhancing military prestige. It finds a usage and reference in the Mahabharata and the texts of the ancient Greeks and Romans. These purposes were served by bugles, trumpets, natural horns and the drum. Signalling in the field and regulating a soldier's activities during the day from Reveille to Lights Out was done by drum beats, sounding of trumpets or bugles, or even by a single piper. Trumpets and kettledrums have traditionally announced the arrival of royalty or important persons. Onboard ships, the drummer would sound change of the watch, and when required, 'beat to action'. This is referred to as field music. Following the development of other wind instruments and their harmonisation with the primary instruments, the military band as we know it came about. Thus, the military band consists of percussion, woodwind and brass instruments, and does not have string instruments for obvious reasons. It is, therefore, sometimes referred to as a brass band.

Medieval Europe relied upon the horn and trumpet till the

Crusades when European armies encountered the drums and cymbals used by the Islamic armies. It proved particularly unnerving for western cavalry as their horses had not heard and were not accustomed to such sounds. By the 13th Century, the drums had been adopted by the Crusaders as well, thus fusing the European trumpets and horns with the Asiatic drum and cymbal.

Turkish military power had brought most of Eastern Europe under its sway until they were checked at the gates of Vienna in 1683. Expectedly, they also pioneered military bands and had military musicians around 1650, which gave impetus to similar European bands. The Ottomans are credited with the oldest marching band in the world. These were and are known as *Mehtaran* from the Persian *Mehtar* (musician) and are also referred to as *Mehtar Takimi* (a group of musicians). Traditionally, their clothing was extremely elaborate and colourful which found expression in later European bands too. Ottoman military bands set the trend for their European equivalents, and Turkish instruments were freely amalgamated into European military bands.

The Bagpipe has enthralled listeners for centuries. Its wild and exciting skirling has spurred men into battle as far back as the days when the Bible first made mention of it in the Old Testament. The Romans brought the instrument to Britain who introduced it to India. The Scots made it a national tradition. The Rifle regiments and most Infantry regiments are today associated with the 'Pipes and Drums'.

Harmonic military music developed in Europe in the eighteenth century in Germany and England. It assumed the rhythmic and martial character in the nineteenth century. In 1763, Frederick the Great of Prussia first defined the composition of the military band. It comprised trumpets and other wind instruments with percussion instruments like the drum and cymbals. Formalised bands producing a systemic score set the trend for each of the arms and their regiments to adopt their own marching tunes and raise their own bands. The British Army regiments initially maintained bands by hiring civilians paid for by the colonel commanding the regiment. The Grenadier Guards of Britain is credited with raising the first band of enlisted men in 1749. These regular enlisted men also acted as stretcher bearers on active service. The drummers were invariably young boys who were not old enough for regular soldiering. The rise of military powers also saw the enhancement of military music. The British brought this practice to India.

Much like the officers' messes where the china and cutlery were paid for and maintained by the officers, the regimental band instruments were similarly subscribed for by the officers till the Second World War. There is a story of one Major General Sir Dudley, General Officer Commanding at Ambala in the 1860s, who ordered a regiment to send their band to his residence for a ball. The bandsmen duly reported as ordered but without their musical instruments as he had not requested the officers who had provided the instruments!

'If the trumpet give an uncertain sound, who shall prepare himself to battle?' ask the Corinthians in The Bible. In the din and confusion of the battlefield, musical instruments were the primary means of conveying orders to advance, attack or retreat. Military music provided greater service to the infantry than the cavalry as the beating of hooves drowned out the sound of instruments. The cavalry, therefore, laid great stress on the trumpet which could be heard above the sound of the horse's hooves, whereas the infantry relied on the drum to set the beat and rhythm for marching and relaying orders with drum rolls. The bugle was particularly useful in conveying standard commands over long distances above the din of battle. A copper bugle carried the sound farther than a brass bugle. Regulation bugle calls were composed by Austrian composer Franz Joseph Haydn. On troopships the calls took on different meanings: 'Retire' meant turn out to clean the deck, 'Commence Firing' meant to man the pumps while 'Charge' was permission to smoke. The Marathas and Rajputs used the *Tutari* or *Ranbukara* – a long curved trumpet – on the battlefield. The *Nagara* war drums used in Punjab and Rajasthan were brought to India in the middle ages by the Arabs and Persians. The loud and thundering beat of the huge drums produced by two sticks usually meant that the army was marching into the battle.

'Military Music' instinctively evokes the 'pomp and circumstance of glorious war'. Images of 'flags flying, bayonets fixed and drums beating' instantly come to mind. The rhythmic marching music attracted composers and found expression in the creations of Mozart,

Beethoven and Johann Strauss, often inspired by classical Ottoman music. Special scores have been composed for landmark events. Elgar's *Imperial March,* composed for the Diamond Jubilee of Queen Victoria in 1897, and *Pomp and Circumstance* in 1901, on which was imposed *Land of Hope and Glory,* became an expression of Britain's imperial pride and glory. Similarly, *Crown Imperial* was created for the coronation of King George VI in 1937. Tchaikovsky composed exceptional Russian scores. The ever-popular *Radetzky March* was composed in honour of General Radetzky of Austria for his successful Italian Campaign in 1848.

The tradition of adopting a Regimental March is linked to the troop's folk songs sung on the march and are often the same folk songs set to music. Most popular pipe scores are traditional Scottish folk numbers. The French Foreign Legion had the popular *Le Boudin* composed by a German bandmaster. Troops on the march, both British and Indian, often sang unprintable songs to break the tedium, and among them was *Zakhmi Dil* (Wounded Heart), a popular Pathan love song. It was adopted by the 40th Pathans as their regimental march. In a land where pederasty has always been a way of life, it was not surprising that the song goes as: 'There is a boy across the river with a bottom like a peach, but alas, I cannot swim'. Then there were those recalling home like *It's a long, long way to Tipperary,* popular during the First World War, and *Lili Marleen* during the Second, or the Garhwali *Bedi Pako Bara Masa* – Passion Fruit Ripens all Twelve Months. On the 150th anniversary of the raising of the Sikh Regiment, the popular Scotch whisky brand 100 Pipers brought out a commemorative pack with labels showing Sikh pipers; *100 Pipers* having been the regimental march of the Sikh Regiment. Today, Indian Army regimental marches set the troop's popular folk songs to their traditional music as far as possible. Stirring verses from the scriptures are also set to military music and adapted as regimental marches.

While most British cavalry regiments had a mounted band, with the drum horse being the pride, the 31 Lancers, later reorganized as the 13 Lancers, were the only Regiment of the Indian Army to maintain a mounted band from 1846 onwards till the Regiment was mechanized in 1938. By the end of World War II and Independence, the regular Indian Cavalry regiments had been mechanized. The only surviving horse cavalry units were those of the State Forces. These were amalgamated and perpetuated into 61 Cavalry which survives as the only horsed cavalry regiment in service in the world. The mounted band of Gwalior Lancers formed part of 61 Cavalry till 1975 when it was finally disbanded. The Bikaner Camel Corps too had a mounted band. This tradition is now perpetuated by the Border Security Force camel-mounted band.

In 1897, following a tribal revolt on the North-West Frontier, a punitive expedition was launched. The Malakand Field Force assembled for the expedition included the young Second Lieutenant Winston Churchill and the action that followed saw the famous stand at Saragarhi on the Samana Ridge by 36 Sikh on 12 September 1897. What was unique was the award of the Victoria Cross to Piper Findlater of the Gordon Highlanders. The attack on the Dargai Heights having failed twice, it was launched for the third time by the Highlanders and Gurkhas on 20 October 1897. Piper Findlater, while playing his battalion into the attack, was wounded in both legs. Lying down near a rock he continued to play *Cock O The North* urging his battalion into the attack. His action inspired the men to carry the heights.

Pipers had traditionally played soldiers into attack, however, very heavy casualties during World War I put an end to this practice. Nevertheless, going against regulations and wearing the kilt his father had worn in World War I, Piper Bill Milin accompanied the first wave landing on Sword Beach at Normandy on D Day, 06 June 1944. He began playing the troops into battle even when he was still in the water. Once on the beach his commander, Lord Lovat, ordered "Give us *Highland Laddie* man!" and he played on under enemy fire walking up and down the beach. Miraculously, he survived. Captured German snipers later confirmed they avoided shooting him thinking him to be mad! Fifty years later he was to play the lament at his commander's funeral. His action is depicted in the 1962 Hollywood classic *The Longest Day*. Yet again pipers played the men into battle during the Falkland War in 1982.

On 02 November 1965, the Sikh Light Infantry, as part of a brigade, was tasked to capture OP Hill near Poonch which had been occupied and heavily fortified by the enemy after the ceasefire. Earlier attempts had failed. As the attack progressed and uncertainty prevailed, the Sikh Light Infantry had pushed on and captured their objective. Their bugle sounded in the pitch-dark night, conveyed the pre-arranged success signal to others, preventing any friendly fire on the captured objective and generating all round elation.

Military music can be extremely stirring and uplifting for weary souls. In the relentless retreat from Mons in August 1914, about 300 exhausted British troops had abandoned their weapons and equipment and simply lay down in the town square of St Quentin, prepared to surrender to the advancing Germans. A cavalry major, seeing them, said to himself, 'If only I had a band'. Seeing an abandoned toy shop nearby and picking up a tin whistle and drum from there, he along with his trumpeter struck up *The British Grenadier*, a popular regimental march and *Tipperary*. One by one the men got up, cheered, organised themselves and were back as a fighting unit. The French Foreign Legion believed 'music to be the perfect drug for the soldier. It chased away reason which would render sacrifice difficult or impossible. It abolished fear'.

In the heyday of the British Empire, perhaps no Army matched the Indian Army in colour and pageantry with the military bands being the centrepiece. That tradition endures. Besides individual regimental marches, *Sare Jehan Se Acha* set to Iqbal's poem and *Kadam Kadam Bharae Ja*, the marching tune of the Indian National Army composed by Captain Ram Singh, have come to be the marching tunes of the Indian Army. And then, of course, there is *Auld Lang Syne* by the Scot, Robert Burn, played to Scot folk melody – 'Should old acquaintance be forgot, and never brought to mind? ...' – which is invariably played at passing out parades at military academies and at farewells.

Ceremonies of state and national days, celebrations of victories, military pageants and the soulful sobriety of funerals are invariably set to the beat and rhythm of military music. No one can fail to be stirred by the sound of trumpets, the beat of the drum, the crash of cymbals or the poignancy of the lone piper playing the lament. Among the well-known military music performances is the Beating the Retreat at Vijay Chowk, New Delhi since 1961, and the Edinburgh Military Tattoo.

Amongst the most sombre and touching field music is the bugles sounding the *Last Post* – its American equivalent being the *Taps*. It has its origins in being sounded at the end of the inspection of sentry posts and signified that the camp had been secured. The *First Post* marked the commencement of the inspection. *Last Post* also signalled the end of the day's battle. Throughout the army the *Last Post* was sounded at 10 pm, except in Lord Cardigan's regiment, where it was sounded at 9.50 pm, the time at which he died. Today the *Last Post* is sounded at remembrance ceremonies or funerals. It signifies the end of the soldier's duty and the infinite night of rest. Followed by a two minutes silence, *The Rouse*, historically played to awaken soldiers at the beginning of the day before *Reveille*, is then played to resume normal activities by those present. Edward Honey, an Australian newspaper correspondent and former soldier, recalling times spent in silence remembering dead colleagues, put forward the idea of observing a two-minute silence. It was projected to King George V and adopted on Armistice Day 1919.

Rudyard Kipling encapsulated the spirit and purpose of the military band in his poem *Route Marchin'*:

*We're marchin' on relief over Injia's coral strand,*
*Eight 'undred fightin' Englishmen, the Colonel, and the Band;*
*Ho! get away, you bullock – man, you've 'eard the bugle blowed,*
*There's a regiment a – comin' down the Grand Trunk Road.*

# THE FIELD MARSHAL AND THE BATON

General GG Bewoor, when designated as the Chief of the Army Staff, was asked by a reporter as to how he felt on reaching the top of the ladder. 'Every soldier carries a field marshal's baton in his knapsack' said he. He was quoting Napoleon, who in these words had summed up the ultimate ambition of every soldier: to be a Field Marshal!

The word 'Marshal', in German Marschall, in French Marechal, in Scottish Marichal, is derived from the German Marsh (Horse) and Scalc (Caretaker). A similar word of Latin origin is 'Constable' – originally Comes Stabuli – meaning a person in charge of the stables. These two personages, the Marshal and the Constable, were always closely linked, as any large domestic establishment would have a 'head groom' and 'groom' or so to say a Marshal and a Constable. The founding of various continental monarchies in the age when cavalry dominated the battlefields, and when no educated and trained class of administrators existed, ensured that those who looked after horses and managed stables developed into high military officials. The Chambers Dictionary defines a Marshal as 'an officer in a royal household, originally the king's farrier, later having care of military arrangements'. The two, therefore, originally performing domestic duties, came to be high officials in royal households and ultimately of the army and the state.

While the French monarchy instituted the 'Marshal de France' in the eighteenth century, Napoleon abolished the title and designated eighteen of his most talented generals as Marshals of the Empire. After 1815, the title reverted to the old 'Marshal de France'. The last

Marshals of France were six generals so promoted in the First World War, Joseph Joffre being the first. There are none today. The Austrian Army, credited as the oldest standing army on the continent, was the first to adopt the title of Field Marshal, instead of the historic and simple Marshal, as a title of the highest grade of General Officer. Johann Strauss composed the *Radetzky March* in 1849 in honour of the Austrian Field Marshal Radetzky. It remains popular even today and is generally included in the performance of most Philharmonic Orchestras. The Germans created the first Field Marshal in 1658, the Imperial Russians under Peter the Great in 1716, and Italy and Poland during World War I. Count Hermann Wrangel and his son Count Karl Gustav Wrangel were the first two Swedish Field Marshals. The present-day 84-mm Rocket Launcher is named after the latter.

Following the Russian revolution and the communists coming to power, the Soviets created the title of Marshal of the Soviet Union. The American Army, in contrast, has never had any Marshals or Field Marshals. Their highest-ranking officer being a General, followed by Lieutenant General, Major General and Brigadier General. Till the First World War, Washington and Grant had been the only Generals, and Pershing became a General during the war. Grant, in fact, had been the first Lieutenant General of the US Army so promoted during the Civil War. During the Second World War, the Americans created the 'General of the Army', usually called a 'Five-Star General', to ensure parity with the British and other allied armies. General MacArthur was appointed Field Marshal by the Philippines in 1936 and became the first American to be so appointed by another country.

As the Indian Army has drawn so heavily upon British precedent and military heritage, the evolution of British Field Marshals is so much more relevant in our context.

While the standing army was established in Great Britain in 1660, the rank and title of Field Marshal was created in 1736. Over a hundred Field Marshals were appointed up to the Second World War, and many of them were from the British royalty. The British generally followed the practice of conferring the rank on veterans who were too old for active service, and it was rare to find a British Army in the field commanded by a Field Marshal before 1914. General George

Pollock, who led the British troops in Afghanistan in 1839, was elevated to a Field Marshal in 1870, and the Earl of Lucan, who commanded the cavalry at Balaclava in the Crimea in 1855, was promoted in 1887. The sole distinction of a foreign general being conferred this rank by the British was Marshal Ferdinand Foch of France in 1919. During Queen Victoria's reign, an 'establishment' of eight Field Marshals on pay came about, of which six were to be from the British Army and two from the Indian Army. This induced the practice of filling up the establishment with those whose services in other armies would have hardly merited such promotion. After 1914, the situation changed and Field Marshals were the ones commanding armies in the field, while the others like Allenby were appointed later for services rendered during the Great War. Similarly, Slim was elevated after World War II.

According to British regulations, the appointment of a Field Marshal is 'at the will of the sovereign'. In our context, it is at the 'pleasure of the President'. A newly created Field Marshal is received by the sovereign or the head of state and is personally handed over the baton – The Field Marshal's Baton! The announcement for General Sam Manekshaw being appointed Field Marshal for his service during the 1971 War was made on 31 December 1972, and a special investiture was held at the Rashtrapati Bhavan on 03 January 1973. The badges of rank, similar to that of a British Field Marshal, which include crossed batons surrounded by a wreath and surmounted by miniature Ashoka lions, were fabricated overnight at the Army Workshop in Delhi Cantt. The baton was a slightly different matter. The Ministry of Defence finally approved it, but not without their obduracy compounded by ignorance. The design was adapted from a Polish Field Marshal's baton, and it is covered by red velvet studded with gold buttons and topped by golden Ashok Lions. It had then cost seven thousand rupees.

The British Baton, on the other hand, is an extremely fine piece of jewellery. It is 22 inches in length, and one inch in diameter, covered with red velvet, with eighteen gold lions studded equally over its entire length. The top is mounted by a gold St George and the Dragon, and the bottom has a gold ring with the name of the recipient. The Duke of Wellington was perhaps the greatest collector of field marshals batons. In addition to the service baton, he was presented an extraordinarily elaborate and special baton by the Prince Reagent, besides batons from Austria, Russia, Prussia, Portugal and the Netherlands.

Drawing on the British precedent of honouring old and distinguished soldiers, General Carriappa was promoted Field Marshal on 15 January 1986, very appropriately on Army Day, which itself is commemorated for the date on which Carriappa became the first Indian C-in-C of the Indian Army on 15 January 1949. Unlike other General Officers, there is no age limit for Field Marshals, and they remain on the active list for life. The Indian Army List of 1988-89, therefore, has two Field Marshals: Manekshaw, Sam Hormusji Framji Jamshedji and Carriappa, Kodandera Madappa. Air Chief Marshal Arjan Singh, who led the Indian Air Force in the 1965 Indo-Pak War and retired in 1969, was elevated as Marshal of the Air Force on 26 January 2002.

A Field Marshal, if on parade, has the unique privilege of having the colours lowered in salute with the 'General Salute', as also while marching past. This honour is otherwise accorded only to the sovereign or head of state with the 'National' or 'Rashtriya Salute'. Field Marshal Manekshaw was so honoured during the Army Day Parade on 15 January 1973 when he relinquished the office of Chief Of Army Staff.

On matters of pay, the British precedent was to place the Field Marshal on half-pay, when not employed, and for the Parliament to vote him a special grant. Field Marshals Haig and Allenby were each voted a grant of Pound Sterling 1,00,000 for their war services. MacArthur was voted $5,00,000 by the Philippine Government for his war services. Our Field Marshals were sanctioned Rs 400 per month in addition to their pension. However, Field Marshal Manekshaw was restored full pay and arrears shortly before his death.

When life's bugles sound truce, a Field Marshal is entitled to a military funeral which otherwise is accorded to those who die in service.

# ZULU THREE FIVE NINE

By a mix of fortuitous and frustrating circumstances, I found myself waiting at a helipad at Ferozepur. I was accompanying the General Officer Commanding the Division on reconnaissance and was thus hitching a ride on the helicopter. It was a clear, bright and sunny March day; just the perfect day for flying. The helicopter arrived and landed. All helicopters in the Indian Air Force, and now the Army Aviation, are numbered prominently on the tail boom with the letter prefix `Z'. Their registration number, so to say. This one was Z 359, or in service parlance 'Zulu Three Five Nine', a Chetak. I was transported twenty years back in time to the days when I had flown Z 359. It was called an Alouette III then.

I had earned my pilots 'Wings' and joined an Air Observation Post Squadron at Bagdogra in 1974. Keen to fly and be fully operational, I had appeared before the Aircrew Examining Board and been rated 'C White': fully operational, though in the lowest acceptable category to carry passengers and fly cross-country. I eagerly looked forward to my first long-distance cross-country flight or a 'ferry'.

Soon the impending orders for a Flight of five helicopters to move to Patiala came through. While all else would move by train, the helicopters would be flown or 'ferried' subject to being airworthy. Being the junior-most and the least experienced pilot, I could be part of the ferry, along with my co-pilot, if all five aircraft were airworthy. Very disappointingly, four were, while the fifth one had been grounded for quite some time. It was Z 359. If it was not made airworthy before the Flight departed, it would be ferried later by an experienced pilot.

Now began our endeavours to get Z 359 to fly. We met the engineering officer, coaxed the ground crew, tapped sources to obtain some spares and had the aircraft ready for an air test a day before the ferry was to commence. We arranged to do the air test ourselves, but when we took her up, we found the fuel consumption a little high. Unable to attain maximum speed at full power, she vibrated excessively, indicating that the rotors were out of alignment. After some effort by the ground crew, we took her up again, and it was a little better. To certify the aircraft fit or otherwise would decide if we went on the ferry or not. Keenness and youthful exuberance decided it. We cheated a bit though not grossly violating safety parameters. I declared her fit. The ferry was on! My flying log book records:

24 April 1975: Bagdogra - Purnea - Patna - Varanasi - Allahabad:
5 hours 30 minutes.
25 April 1975: Allahabad - Kanpur - Agra:
3 hours 30 minutes.
26 April 1975: Agra - Palam - Patiala:
3 hours 5 minutes.

Z 359 vibrated all the way and barely kept up with the others, but we had ferried her with the Flight.

In the twenty years since the ferry, Z 359 would have gone through base overhaul a number of times, and I had been through the vicissitudes of life and service. Here we were together again.

The General Officer arrived, and we took off. Zulu Three Five Nine flew sure and smooth, but I was just a passenger.

# GUNNERS AT THE INFANTRY DAY

The Gazetteer of Kashmir and Ladakh of 1890 records –

> The territories of the Kashmir State comprise two provinces, Jamu and Kashmir, each of which is administered by a Chief Officer, or Governor, styled *Hakim-i-Ala*. The districts of Baltistan or Skardu and Ladak are included in the province of Jamu; and the district of Gilgit, including Astor, in Kashmir. The territory of Punch is administered by Raja Moti Singh, who holds it under a grant from the Maharaja. When the treaties of 1846 were made, Gulab Singh held, as Raja of Jamu, the hill chief ship around Jamu and a more or less complete state of subjection, and Ladak and Baltistan by right of conquest, and Gilgit had become an appendage of the Sikh governorship of Kashmir. The general and practical result therefore of the treaty of Amritsar was to confirm Gulab Singh in what he already possessed, and to transfer to him the province of Kashmir with it's newly acquired authority over Gilgit.

At 0500 hours 27 October 1947, six requisitioned civil Dakota transport aircraft took off from Safdarjung (then Willingdon) Airport, New Delhi. Simultaneously, three Dakotas of the Royal Indian Air Force (RIAF) were getting airborne from Palam Airport. By 1000 hours, they had landed the first elements of the Indian Army at Srinagar. Four decades later, 27 October came to be commemorated as Infantry Day. 1st Battalion The Sikh Regiment is acknowledged as the first troops to be so air-landed and credited as the saviours of Srinagar and, consequently, Kashmir. Much less acknowledged, and nearly forgotten, are the Gunners who formed part of the landing and the critical days thereafter.

The events leading up to 27 October 1947 began with Lord Louis Mountbatten being appointed Viceroy by Prime Minister Atlee to "take Britain out of India before June 1948". Lord Mountbatten, a man in a hurry, arrived in Delhi on 22 March 1947 and set 15 August 1947 as the date to end British rule. The leaders of the emerging Dominions of India and Pakistan, as also the 565 Princely States, were expected to resolve the merger of these states with either of the Dominions by then, when British paramountcy would lapse.

Having failed to convince the Maharaja of Jammu and Kashmir to accede to Pakistan, and notwithstanding the standstill agreement, Pakistan launched a tribal invasion on 22 October 1947. The plan envisaged a force of six *Lashkars* of about 1000 men each, stiffened with regular Pakistani troops, to advance along Muzaffarabad-Domel-Uri-Baramula-Srinagar axis, capture Srinagar and the airfield and, thereafter, capture Banihal to isolate the Valley. Other *Lashkars* were to ingress into the other parts of the state. On 24 October, the Raiders captured Mahura and the powerhouse, plunging the valley into darkness. Brigadier Rajendra Singh, Chief of Staff of the State Forces, personally assumed command of the State Forces troops at Uri and held the Raiders for four crucial days. The steel bridge over Uri Nallah was destroyed to delay them. He was posthumously awarded the first Maha Vir Chakra.

After a period of dithering and uncertainty of acceding to the Indian Union, the Maharaja of Jammu and Kashmir signed the instrument of accession on 26 October 1947 when the enemy was literally at the gate. The same evening at about 2200 hours, Army Headquarters was asked to airlift troops to Srinagar early on 27 October. No Britisher was to be involved in active operations. The only unit readily available and commanded by an Indian officer was 1 Sikh which had moved from Clement Town, Dehradun, on 27 August for internal security duties and was strung out around Gurgaon and Rewari. The Commanding Officer, Lieutenant Colonel Dewan Ranjit Rai, had assumed command on 21 October. The Battalion also had a Sikh company of the 3/15 Punjab Regiment (MMG) under command, however, the Battalion could barely muster two weak companies immediately. Another company was organised from three officers and 104 Sikh troops of 13 Field Regiment, Royal Indian Artillery (RIA) under Captain RL Chauhan, then stationed at the Red Fort Delhi, again on internal security duties, and some Sikh personnel from 2 Field Regiment RIA (the prefix Royal was dropped by all the services on 26 January 1950). Thus 1 Sikh less two companies and the Composite Company RIA was ordered to be airlifted on 27 October. The remainder Battalion was to be mustered and flown in subsequently. The troops for the initial airlift were concentrated at the airports by 0400 hours and the remainder later in the morning. The Operations Order was handed over to the Commanding Officer by Captain (later Lieutenant General) SK Sinha at the airfield.

No 12 Squadron of the RIAF, the only transport squadron, could also muster only three aircraft. These were augmented by the available civilian Dakota aircraft. Each RIAF and civilian Dakota was to carry 17 and 15 personnel respectively along with 500 lbs of stores.

Tactical Headquarters 1 Sikh and a platoon were assigned the three RIAF aircraft from Palam. The six civilian aircraft from Safdarjung were to lift the C Company of 1 Sikh. The second wave of eight aircraft was to lift the Composite Company RIA at 1100 hours and the third wave of eleven aircraft to lift the D Company of 1 Sikh at 1300 hours. One officer and two NCOs from the Royal Indian Engineers were also to form part of the initial airlift while the remainder of the Battalion would be airlifted the next day.

Thus the stage was set for the historic airlift though it was not totally unexpected nor without any warning. Requests for help emanating from the Maharaja of Jammu and Kashmir since 22 October had initiated some contingency planning on 25 October. Army Headquarters was warned on 26 October to prepare for intervention in Kashmir. An Oxford aircraft from Ambala carried out reconnaissance of the Srinagar Airfield on 26 October and confirmed the absence of any invaders. Nevertheless, the airlift on 27 October was fraught with uncertainties and hazards reflected in the directions to the Commanding Officer to circle the airfield and land if it did not appear to be held by the raiders.

> In all my extensive experience as Allied Commander in South-East

Asia and Pacific during the Second World War, I have never seen an airlift of this magnitude with such slender resources and at such short notice.
—Lord Louis Mountbatten, last Viceroy & Governor-General of India

The first wave took off well before dawn. The leading aircraft (VP 905) was very appropriately piloted by the Commanding Officer No 12 Squadron RIAF, Wing Commander KL Bhatia, with Lieutenant Colonel Dewan Ranjit Rai, Commanding Officer 1 Sikh, on board. It was a clear, bright and sunny day. After nearly three and a half hours, the first lumbering piston engine aircraft landed at Srinagar airfield at 0830 hours, and by 1000 hours the first wave had disembarked. The second and third wave consisting of eight and eleven Dakotas took off at 1100 hours and 1300 hours, and by the end of the day, the 28 sorties had landed 1 Sikh less two companies and the Composite Company RIA at Srinagar comprising a total of 300 men. While C Company and the Composite Company RIA were dispatched immediately on arrival to reinforce the State Forces troops at Baramula covering the main Uri -Baramula-Srinagar axis, D Company was tasked to deny the bridge over the Jhelum at Sopore and secure the airfield and the town. C Company and the Composite Company RIA took up a defensive position at Mile 32 east of Baramula.

Lieutenant Colonel Rai, along with A and D Company, set out towards the C Company position on 28 October. He was killed in action that evening and awarded the MVC posthumously. Under pressure from the overwhelming strength of the invaders, the Battalion, along with the Composite Company RIA, withdrew and took up a defensive position at Mile 16 near Pattan, holding it and keeping the raiders at bay. This enabled the build up of troops at Srinagar on 28 and 29 October. Two Spitfire fighter aircraft operating from Ambala carried out strafing of the enemy on 28 October helping the defenders to hold their ground. These aircraft thereafter landed at and operated from Srinagar.

On 29 October, Tactical Headquarters 161 Indian Infantry Brigade was established at Srinagar airfield. 56 men of 1 Sikh and 218 men of 1 Kumaon (Para) were also flown in. The defence of Srinagar airfield was now taken over by 1 Kumaon (Para), while the remaining troops of 1 Sikh under Major Harwant Singh, MC, who had assumed command of the Battalion, moved forward to Pattan where the situation was critical. Repeated enemy attacks on the Pattan position were beaten back by 1 Sikh with the company of 3/15 Punjab Regiment (MMG) and the Composite Company RIA.

On 30 October, two 3.7-inch howitzers of the Patiala State Forces under Lieutenant Jabar Jang Singh were flown in. It so happened that the Indian Army had loaned these guns to the Patiala State Forces for the duration of World War II. The written instructions to the troop commander were to hand over the guns at Srinagar and return. He and his men were not to be involved with the ongoing operations. The guns were without dial sights. As the guns were being unloaded, a group of raiders was observed preparing to move towards the airfield from the direction of Badgam. The guns were immediately brought into action and fired by sighting along the barrels and the raiders dispersed. Thereafter the two guns were moved to Pattan with an escort from 1 Kumaon (Para) and handed over to the gunners of the Composite Company RIA. Two more guns arrived the next day and were also moved up. These were then manned by detachments formed from the gunners of the Composite Company RIA. Notwithstanding the non-availability of dial sights, the guns were immediately deployed in direct firing role and continued to do so till the sights arrived. The four 3.7-inch Howitzers remained with 1 Sikh at Pattan till 04 November and redeployed with the Battalion when it withdrew to Mile 4.

Subsequently, these four howitzers continued to be manned by detachments formed from the personnel of the Composite Company of 13 Field Regiment RIA and were referred to as 13 Field Battery in all dispatches. To avoid confusion, it was designated as 17 Mountain Battery.

33 men of 1 Sikh were flown in on 30 October and 184 men on 01 November. D Company of 4 Kumaon under Major Somnath Sharma was flown in on 31 October. On receiving information on 03 November about the concentration of raiders near Badgam, about five km from the airfield, A and D Companies of 4 Kumaon and a company of 1 Kumaon (Para) were sent out to reconnoitre. While returning, D Company was surprised by the raiders. However, the company held its

ground with the active support of 17 Mountain Battery and strikes by the fighters operating from Srinagar. In the fighting that ensued, Major Somnath Sharma was killed and won the Param Vir Chakra posthumously.

On 03 November, Major SP Kapila, MC, flew in as artillery advisor. His first task was to arrange ammunition for the howitzers, some of which arrived the same day. 32 Field Battery of 11 Field Regiment under Major Udham Singh arrived by road at Srinagar on 06 November, in time to support the attack of 161 Infantry Brigade on 07 November, to throw back the invaders from around Srinagar. What followed became known as the Battle of Shalateng where the enemy suffered heavy casualties from the combined firepower and bayonets of the infantry, two Daimler armoured cars of 7 Cavalry under Lieutenant David, artillery and strafing from the air. By the evening of 07 November, Pattan was recaptured, and Baramulla captured the next day. 32 Field Battery and 17 Mountain Battery deployed near Baramula the same day. Uri was captured on 13 November. The threat to the Valley stood eliminated.

Composite Company RIA and the Sikh company of 3/15 Punjab Regiment remained under the command of 1 Sikh for subsequent operations that followed. The Patiala Mountain Battery flew in with six gunners per gun in November, and its main body, with the animals marching from Patiala, reached Srinagar in April 1948 under Major Kuldip Singh, MC. Composite Company RIA of 13 Field Regiment returned to Ambala on 16 May 1948.

Captain RL Chauhan was awarded the Vir Chakra and Jemadar Pritam Singh Mentioned in Despatches on 14 April 1948. The ad hoc battery of 3.7-inch Howitzers – 17 Mountain Battery – ceased to exist on 28 April 1948 when the guns were handed back to the Patiala Mountain Battery, which was operationally inducted on the request of the Maharaja of J&K. Wing Commander KL Bhatia landed a section of 4 (Hazara) Mountain Battery at Poonch, which was besieged, on 13 December 1947. He was awarded the VrC for his services in the J&K operations.

Aircraft returning from Srinagar were invariably overloaded for evacuating civilians. The Revenue Officer of Badgam District dispatched his family of four on 29 October from Srinagar airfield. While the mother and two younger boys landed at Ambala, the elder boy, the future mountain gunner, Major General Rajendra Prakash, VSM, landed at Safdarjung, Delhi.

By 30 October 1948, 30 Field Battery of 11 Field Regiment, 51 (Para) Field Battery of 17 (Para) Field Regiment and the J&K Mountain Battery were grouped for the capture of Zojila by 77 Para Brigade. They were temporarily designated as 17 Composite Regiment under Lieutenant Colonel Gyan Singh, Commanding Officer 11 Field Regiment. As Kipling said 'but that's another story ...'.

# COURAGE AND CHARACTER

> Courage is rightly esteemed the first of human qualities ... because it is the quality which guarantees all others
> —Sir Winston Churchill

World War I saw battlefield casualties unprecedented in human history. The average life expectancy in the trenches of the Western Front was a few weeks. Lord Moran served as a Medical Officer with the First Battalion of the Royal Fusiliers from 1914 to 1917 in the trenches. Based on his experiences, and the diaries he maintained during that period, he set out to find 'how courage is born and how it is sustained in a modern army of free people'. This culminated in his classic book *The Anatomy of Courage*. He analysed fear, how fear causes courage to be expended, and the care and management of fear.

Lord Moran says 'Courage is a moral quality. It is a cold choice between two alternatives, the fixed resolve not to quit which must be made many times by the power of will'. Courage is an expendable commodity. Courage is willpower where-of no man has an unlimited stock and when in war it is used up, he is finished. A man's courage is like his bank balance from which he is always spending. The call on his balance may be a routine daily expenditure or maybe a sudden draft which threatens to lead to bankruptcy. Discipline keeps this expenditure under control and is a vital element in the management of fear.

During World War I, 3080 British soldiers were awarded the death sentence for cowardice. 346 sentences were carried out, being 'shot at dawn', out of which 266 were for deserting their posts under fire. It was in the intervening years between the two World Wars that the concept of 'shell shock' and 'battle fatigue' began to be accepted as one of the reasons for 'cowardice' in battle. Death sentence for cowardice was abolished in the British Army in 1930.

Lord Moran had come to these conclusions having observed fear first-hand in the trenches. He categorised men into four classes – those who do not know fear (these are very few), those who feel and know fear but do not show it (a majority of the leaders), those who feel fear and show it but do their job (a fair majority) and those who feel fear, show it and shirk (again a very few). He goes on to suggest the management of fear by dealing with these four classes. With the all-pervading certainty of death in the trenches, he courageously wrote that 'As the odds shortened and it became plain that death was to be the common lot I thought less of its coming until at last I saw no cruelty in its approach...'. As personal physician to Sir Winston Churchill from 1940 to 1965, Lord Moran is also the author of the book *Winston Churchill–The Struggle for Survival 1940-1965*, which again is a study of an individual under immense stress. He maintains that a man of character in peace is a man of courage in war.

And what of character? In a profession where the currency is men's lives, character must rank very high. Perhaps the most incisive analysis of character appears in Von Clausewitz's *On War*. He writes:

> If we consider how men differ in their emotional reactions, we first find a group with a small capacity for being roused, usually known as 'stolid' on 'phlegmatic'. Second, there are men who are extremely active, but whose feelings never rise above a certain level, men whom we know to be 'sensitive but calm'. Third, there are men whose passions are easily inflamed, in whom excitement flares up suddenly but soon burns out, like gunpowder. And finally, we come to those who do not react to minor matters, who will be moved only gradually, not suddenly, but whose emotions attain great strength and durability. These are the men whose passions are strong, deep and concealed.
>
> Stolid men are hard to throw off balance, but total lack of vigour cannot really be interpreted as a strength of character. It cannot be denied, however, that the imperturbability of such men gives them a narrow usefulness in war. They are seldom strongly motivated, lack

initiative and consequently are not particularly active, on the other hand, they seldom make a serious mistake.

The salient point about the second group is that trifles can suddenly stir them to act whereas great issues are likely to overwhelm them. This kind of man will gladly help an individual in need, but the misfortune of an entire people will only sadden him; they will not stimulate him to action. In war, such men show no lack of energy or balance, but they are unlikely to achieve anything significant unless they possess a very powerful intellect to provide the needed stimulus. But it is rare to find this type of temperament combined with a strong and independent mind.

Inflammable emotions, feelings that are easily roused, are in general of life and therefore of little value in war. Their impulses are strong but brief. If the energy of such men is joined to courage and ambition, they will prove most useful at a modest level of command, simply because the action controlled by junior officers is of short duration. Often a single brave decision, a burst of emotional force, will be enough. A daring assault is the work of a few minutes, while a hard-fought battle may last a day, and a campaign an entire year. Their volatile emotions make it doubly hard for such men to preserve their balance, they often lose their heads, and nothing is worse on active service. All the same, it would be untrue to say that highly excitable minds could never be strong – that is, could never keep their balance ever under the greatest strain. Why should they not have a sense of their own dignity since as a rule, they are among the finer natures? In fact, they usually have such a sense, but there is no time for it to take effect. Once the crisis is past, they tend to be ashamed of their behaviour. If training, self-awareness, and experience sooner or later teach them how to be on guard against themselves, then in times of great excitement an internal counterweight will assert itself so that they too can draw on the great strength of character.

Lastly, we come to men who are difficult to move but have strong feelings – men who are to the previous type like heat to a shower of sparks. These are men who are best able to summon the titanic strength it takes to clear away enormous burdens that obstruct activity in war. Their emotions move as great masses do – slowly but irresistibly. These men are not swept away by their emotions as often as the third group, but experience shows that they too can lose their balance and be overcome by blind passion. This can happen whenever they lack the noble pride of self-control, or whenever it is inadequate. We find this condition mostly among great men in primitive societies where passion tends to rule for lack of intellectual discipline. Yet even among educated people and civilized societies, men are often swept away by passion.

To repeat: strength of character does not consist solely of having powerful feelings, but in maintaining one's balance in spite of them. Even with the violence of emotion, judgement and principle must function like a ship's compass, which records the slightest variations however rough the sea.

*We say a man has a strength of character, or simply has character, if he sticks to his convictions, whether these derive from his own opinions or someone else's, whether they represent principles, attitudes, sudden insights or any other mental force.* Such firmness cannot show itself, of course, if a man keeps changing his mind. This need not be the consequence of external influence; the cause may be the workings of his own intelligence, but this would suggest a peculiarly insecure mind.

Obviously, a man whose opinions are constantly changing, even though this is in response to his own reflections, would not be called a man of character. The term is applied to men whose views are stable and constant. This may be because they are well thought-out, clear, and scarcely open to revision, or in the case of indolent men, because such people are not in the habit of mental effort and, therefore, have no reason for altering their views; and finally, because a firm decision, based on fundamental principle derived from reflection, is relatively immune to changes of opinion. Often there is a gap between principles and actual events that cannot always be bridged by a succession of logical deductions. Then a measure of self-confidence is needed, and a degree of scepticism is also salutary. Frequently, nothing short of an imperative principle will suffice, which is not part of the immediate thought process, but dominates it. That principle is: in all doubtful cases to stick to one's first opinion and to refuse to change unless forced to do so by a clear conviction. A strong faith in the overriding truth of tested principles is needed; the vividness of transient impressions must not make us forgot that such truth as they contain is of a lesser stamp. By giving precedence, in case of doubt, to one's earlier convictions, by holding to them stubbornly, one's actions acquire that quality of steadiness and consistency which is termed strength of character.

Strength of character can degenerate into obstinacy. The line between them is hard to draw in a specific case, but surely it is easy to distinguish them in theory. Obstinacy is not an intellectual defect; it comes from a reluctance to admit that one is wrong. To impute this to the mind would be illogical, for the mind is the seat of judgement. Obstinacy is a fault of temperament. Stubbornness and intolerance of contradiction result from a special kind of egotism, which elevates above everything else the pleasure of its autonomous intellect, to which others must bow. It might also be called vanity if it were not something superior; vanity is content with the appearance alone; obstinacy demands the material reality. The argument, therefore, is that strength of character turns to obstinacy as soon as a man resists another point of view not from superior insight or attachment to some higher principle, but because he objects instinctively. Admittedly, this definition may not be of much practical use; but it will nevertheless help avoid the interpretation that obstinacy is simply a more intense form of strong character. There is a basic difference between the two. They are closely related, but one is so far from being a higher degree of the other, that one can find extremely obstinate men who are too dense to have much strength of character.

Character isn't made during a crisis, but that's when it comes out.

# FEROZEPORE BRIGADE AREA 1935

Rummaging through a pile of old documents intended to be destroyed in the Station Headquarters at Ferozepur in 1995, I chanced upon a folder with frail yellowing pages tagged inside. It was titled 'Ferozepur Brigade Area Orders 1935'. The contents, though of routine administrative nature, were a window into the world as it existed at Ferozepur over six decades ago. But first a word about the 'Ferozepur Brigade Area'.

The Presidency Armies of Bengal, Bombay and Madras were amalgamated on 01 April 1895 creating a unified Indian Army, and organised into Military Districts under four Commands: Punjab Command (including the North-West Frontier and Punjab Frontier Force), Bengal Command, Madras Command (including Burma) and the Bombay Command (including Sind, Quetta and Aden). The 1908 reorganisation structured it into the Northern and Southern Commands made up of nine divisions and five cavalry brigades. Then the post-war reorganisation in 1919 formed four Commands with headquarters at Muree (Northern), Quetta (Western), Nainital (Eastern) and Madras (Southern). With the abolition of Western Command in 1938, the remaining survived up to the Second World War.

In the 1930s Lahore District [3 (Lahore) Division] formed part of the Northern Command and Ferozepur Area fell under the Lahore District. The latter comprised Ferozepur and Multan under a brigade headquarters at Ferozepur and was called the 'Ferozepur Brigade Area'. Therefore, the 'Ferozepur Brigade Area Orders'.

The Orders revealed that the allotment for fuel for warming and drying purposes totalling Rs 1603 As 4 and Ps 1 was allotted to Ferozepur Garrison comprising 3 Field Battery Royal Artillery, 20/21 Medium Battery Royal Artillery, 2nd Battalion The Border Regiment, 1st Battalion The 2nd Punjab Regiment (later 1 Punjab and now 1 Para), 10th Battalion The 14th Punjab Regiment (Regimental Centre 14 Punjab Regiment transferred to the Pakistan Army and merged into Punjab Regiment Centre, Mardan), 2 Royal Lancers [Gardener's Horse] (2 Lancers today) and 13 Duke of Connaught's Own Lancers (transferred to the Pakistan Army and now 13 Lancers), besides the British and Indian Military Hospitals and services units. Rs 799 As 4 and Ps 2 was allotted to the Multan Garrison for 1st Battalion The Leicestershire Regiment and 5th Battalion The 13th Frontier Force Rifles (transferred to the Pakistan Army and today 10 Frontier Force) again with the British and Indian Military Hospitals.

Contrary to the general perception, the state of discipline of British troops does not appear to be good – there were six District Court Martials convened for offences relating to theft and striking superior officers.

Breakout of Equine Influenza was frequent and widespread as some station or the other in Northern Command was placed in quarantine with no movement of animals in or out. Anti-rabic vaccine was available from the newly opened Pasteur Institute, Kasauli for Rs 5 per doze. The government had not approved provision of bleaching powder and copper sulphate for disinfecting swimming baths and the Orders advised that these were to be procured through subscription!

The Orders stated that visitors to Afghanistan were to be allowed by the Torkham-Kabul Road, while an amendment to the Manual of Ceremonials permitted carriage of King's Colours on all Ceremonial Parades. A government horse or pony was prohibited to be played at polo, hunting or pig sticking without the permission of the officer commanding the unit. An insurance fee of Rs 7 As 8 per month had to be paid into the government treasury. The horse or pony was to be considered as 'played at polo' from the time it first went into a 'chukkur', whether first or last. And 3 Cavalry relieved 2 Royal Lancers (Gardener's Horse) in November 1935.

Promulgated every month, the Orders were initialled by the adjutant. This folder belonged to 10th Battalion The 14 Punjab Regiment as anything concerning the battalion was marked and highlighted with a thick red or blue coloured pencil. The adjutant was someone with the initials 'MAK'. As I flipped further, I came across a list of officers granted leave in the month of July, and amongst them was Captain Mohammad Ayub Khan – MAK. His initials did not appear in the Orders during the months of his leave. Thirty years later, the President of Pakistan – MAK – would lead his country into a war with India.

# THE MILITARY UNIFORM

> The better you dress a soldier, the more highly will he be thought of by the women, and consequently by himself.
> —Field Marshal Lord Wolseley

Military uniforms first appeared in the armies of Europe towards the end of the 17th century. Though the cost of supplying the elaborate standardised uniform was prohibitive, economies of scale made them affordable. The creation of standing armies required them to be uniformly disciplined and, therefore, uniformly dressed. Since discipline on the battlefield was a fundamental requirement for victory, it gave rise to a mass of drill books and rules that commanders were expected to enforce. Correspondingly rules, regulations and specifications for uniforms followed. The most comprehensive *Regulations for Clothing of the Army*, running into 200 pages, was published by the British War Office in 1914. *Dress Regulations for Officers* were published in 1911.

As European empires expanded into new territories, the culture, military traditions and local conditions led to the incorporation of local items of dress into the European military uniform to produce colourful and functional hybrids like the *Spahis* of the French light cavalry, recruited from their North African colonies, wearing distinctive long white cloaks called *Burnos*. This was nowhere more true than in India where, for instance, the cummerbund was the regimental *pagri* wrapped around the waist.

Imposing European military dress conventions on locally recruited soldiers was equally prevalent. A controversial item was the high, stiff leather collar or the 'stock' intended originally to protect the neck and later supposed to improve military bearing and appearance by keeping the chin high and posture erect. In an attempt to make the sepoys look more 'English', its introduction for the sepoys of the Madras Army in 1806 was one of the major causes of the Vellore Mutiny as the leather was repugnant to both the Hindus and Muslims.

All uniforms and accoutrements start as a functional requirement. Up to the era of close combat on the battlefield, they were also designed to make the wearer look broader and taller to awe the opponent. This could also become absurdly impractical like the magnificent brass helmets with a long horse hair plume worn by the Bengal Horse Artillery. Such embellishments were modified in due course to suit changing requirements or retained as part of regimental traditions. Ethnic pride too dictates adopting regional wear like the Scottish kilt. While the government specified the basic overall colour and material of the uniforms, details of lining, facing and other embellishments were left to the commander in charge of his regiment. This gave rise to regimental distinctions. The facings: cuff, turn-back cuff of a coat and lapels were invariably those of the regiments distinguishing colours. This even led to the naming of regiments like the 'Buffs' or *Kali Chindi* – Black Patch of the Indian Army. The presentation of some items of a uniform, like the paratroopers red beret, also symbollised acceptance and entry into a military group. In 1703, the Duke of Marlborough introduced the system of approved patterns being 'sealed' to ensure uniform pattern and quality. This is still followed in the Indian Army with the specified 'Authority Holding Sealed Approved Pattern'. By the end of the 18th century, the British Army had adopted buttons and shoulder belts bearing the number of the regiment. Inscribing names of famous battles and adopting regimental distinguishing signs culminated into regimental badges. This created a sense of belonging and *esprit de corps*. These badges could also have some very un-military origins like the British Special Air Service Regiment adopting their badge modelled on a fresco in Shepherds Hotel, Cairo or the Indian 17 Division insignia of a black cat taken from a toy catalogue during World War II. Till this time, rank had been easy to determine by the style and quality of an officers uniform. With standardization of uniforms, metallic shoulder knots developed into epaulets for officers, and in 1802, stripes on the sleeves were introduced to distinguish non-commissioned officers. Officers and Non Commissioned Officers (NCOs) nominated for a specific duty, like right markers on parade, usually wore and still wear a sash – officers over the left shoulder and NCOs over the right.

Functionality and practical battlefield expedients were in due course formalised and are now found as accoutrements on uniforms. To protect the throat, 'gorgets' or metallic clasps were worn around the throat, today they are seen as 'Gorget Patches' or what is loosely called 'Red Tabs' or 'Collar Dogs' on the collars of senior officers. British and Indian cavalry often stitched chains into the shoulders of their uniforms to provide protection against sword cuts. The shoulder chains are now worn by cavalry officers on their ceremonial mess dress, both in the British and Indian Army. The Royal Welch Fusiliers have five 7½ inch long black ribbons stitched behind the collar which is a relic from the times a leather pad was worn to protect the uniform from stains from pigtails.

Around this time nationals of armies of Europe began to be associated with the colour of their uniform. The choice of colour for the British, and subsequently the British-Indian Army, was primarily between red and blue. Both colours were widely available due to their dyeing process involving one stage as against other colours involving mixing in two stages. They became a cheap and favourite pigment for the military uniform. Another version for the adoption of red ascribes it to the large quantities of red broadcloth available which could easily be put to use by the Army. While the Army at large chose red, the Gunners chose blue. The officers in turn wore blue jackets while the men wore red. This was to cost them dearly when the Boers picked off the officers at Boomplaats, South Africa in 1848. At Isandhlwana on 22 January 1879, the Zulu chiefs had specifically instructed the warriors of their *impis* (armies) to go for the red coats. 21 officers and 534 men of the 24th Foot fell to the Zulu *assegais*. There were no survivors from the battalion, however, four officers from other units wearing dark coats escaped. The transition from red coats to khaki – from the Persian *Khak* or dust – came about due to the nature of terrain on the North-West Frontier and the need to merge with the surroundings, red being too conspicuous.

The empire building colonial wars of the 18th and 19th centuries brought into focus armies and their uniforms. The British Redcoat, French Foreign Legion's double-breasted blue greatcoat *Capote*, Russian Cossacks *Papakha* or Astrakhan Hat, the German spiked leather and metal *Pickelhaube* and the French *Kepi* are some examples. During Napoleon's reign, the French had one of the most ostentatious uniforms of that time. Victorian England glamorised the military uniform, and the writings of Kipling, Tennyson, Thomas Hardy and others added to that appeal. European royalty invariably appeared in military uniform for all state functions and still does. At the funeral of King Edward VII on 20 May 1910, nine sovereigns rode behind the cortege, with another forty princes and heirs apparent following, all in resplendent military uniforms. World War I spelt the death of many long-established social orders, political systems and empires, and also the demise of the flashy uniforms prevalent at that time. The elaborate and extravagant uniforms of the 19th century were never to return.

At the beginning of the Great War, 1914, the British-Indian Army had two basic uniforms: Full Dress for ceremonial and state occasions, and Service Dress worn during training and active service. The equipment and accoutrements to be worn with each uniform depended on the task at hand. Officers' uniforms were generally of superior quality and cut and included items like a Mess Dress which was not worn by other ranks. Officers were also able to adopt 'undress' for occasions more formal than actual field service but not requiring the panoply of 'full dress'. Full dress, for all practical purposes, came to an end with the First World War, surviving only for ceremonial use by bodyguards and bands. In 1937, the Service Dress was replaced by the Battledress consisting of a blouse and trousers. The Service Dress, on the other hand, was adopted with variations for ceremonial and regular use. From the beginning of the century till the end of the Second World War, the British and British Indian Army favoured shorts as part of its uniform due to its suitability in the hot tropical climate.

'Kitting Out' – procuring the required uniforms and camp requisites – could be a major expense for a newly commissioned officer and left him in debt. In 1903 it could cost up to £1000. This was partly ameliorated during World War I when a kit allowance was introduced. It still meant about a year's post dated cheques worth a major portion of the pay till the late 1970s. The men paid for getting the issued uniforms altered and fitted, and still do. This too could be expensive, especially the accoutrements of Full Dress. In the 1850s it amounted to nearly Rs 50, about six months pay. Special occasions still demand all ranks procure new and matching uniforms through private means.

While the British Army had headdress adapted from their local dress and ranged from Highland Bonnet to Shako, Bearskin, Glengarry and Tam O'Shanter, the Indian Army by and large wore a *Pagri*, much as all communities wore turbans in some form or the other. The Highland Bonnet and the *Pagri* had the added advantage of providing protection from sword cuts. When most European armies modeled their light cavalry after the 16th Century Hungarian *Huszars* (Hussars), they also adopted its uniform, including the fur cap, named Busby by the British. It had a stuffed cloth bag on top to ward off sabre cuts. The shape and form of the military *Pagri* varied with the region from where the troops were recruited. This finds expression in ceremonial headgear today. British influence and association also caused some Regiments to adopt variations like the Australian slouch hat (Gurkha Hat), Kilmonorock, etc. Mechanization and the requirement of a headgear compatible with fighting vehicles promoted the beret which became universal at the end of the Second World War. While green is the regulation colour of infantry berets and turbans, regimental distinction has promoted varying shades from near parrot green to deep, dark 'rifle green'. The peaked cap of the service dress was adapted for ceremonial use. All such headgear exist in some form and usage today.

Battlefield association also defined headgear. After the Battle of Meanee, 17 February 1843, the 22nd Foot (Cheshire Regiment) presented the cylindrical-shaped Shako to the Madras Sappers in acknowledgement of their action at a critical stage of the battle. Hence, a modified cylindrical cloth *Doopta* is worn by the Madras Sappers ever since. The Pathans, with grudging respect, referred to Sikh troops on the North-West Frontier as *Fakir Ke Fauj* – Mendicants Army or *Kali Pagri Wali Kafir* – Non-believers in Black Turbans; appellations derived from their uniform turbans.

A large number of casualties from head injuries due to shrapnel at the beginning of the First World War prompted introduction of steel helmets. Their useful discomfort replacing the comfortable soft caps. The shape adopted by each country itself became a form of recognition. When British parachute troops were formally organised into the Parachute Regiment in 1940, they adopted maroon as the colour of their berets. This became universal for all commonwealth parachute troops. Popular myth attributes the selection of maroon to the airborne forces commander's wife, the writer Daphane du Maurier, as it was the colour carried by her racehorse. Similarly the black beret adopted by the Royal Tank Regiment (RTR) in 1918 became the headgear for cavalry on mechanisation. General Montgomery was presented a RTR beret with its badge by a tank crew in North Africa during the Second World War. He affixed his general's badge as well and wore it. It became his distinct trademark thereafter.

Battlefield achievements also add to some distinction in the uniform. The Gloucestershire Regiment (then the 26th) beat back a French attack from the front and rear at the Battle of Alexandria, 1801. They symbolically wear a front and back badge on their caps. The Garhwal Rifles were granted the title 'Royal' after the Great War, 1914-18 and entitled to wear a red lanyard on the right shoulder. They insist on proudly wearing it with every uniform; ceremonial, working or combat. Similarly, the 4th Gurkha Rifles cap badge was surmounted by Ashoka Lions after their distinguished performance in the initial stages of the Siachen conflict.

Regular grouping of units with a formation on its 'Order of Battle' was introduced during World War I. The sheer mass of troops made distinguishing troops of one formation from another difficult. Armbands with colour combinations were introduced to indicate the level of the formation: Blue and Red for GHQ, Red and Black for Army Headquarters, Red and White for a Corps and so on with the abbreviated name of the formation on it. These colours are retained today as the background of the formation signs. Each formation thereafter developed its distinguishing signs. These signs were discarded after the war and emerged at the beginning of the Second World War. They were retained thereafter.

All militaries cherish their exclusivity. This finds expression in the pride and meticulous adherence to the colour, cut and accoutrements of the uniform. Uniforms promote bonding and identity of the group, the 'Regimental Spirit'. In India, the discretion with the commanding officers of 'Irregular' units resulted in exotic colours like the peacock-blue turbans of the Bengal Lancers, french-grey of the Madras Lancers and canary-yellow of the Skinners Horse. Nations too identify themselves with their militaries by their uniform. The British eulogized their 'Redcoat' in the *Thin Red Line* after the Battle of Balaclava on 25 October 1854 in the Crimean War. Prior to the outbreak of World War I, the British had adopted Khaki and the Germans Field Grey, but the French Army and public vehemently resisted giving up their blue coats and red trousers worn since 1830. The sentiment attached with *Le Pantalon Rouge* overrode functionality. The Indian Army is associated with and referred to as the Olive Greens. After their humiliation of Vietnam, the American military was reluctant to wear their uniform in public. As General Colin Powell recalled, "The Secretary of Defence came into the Pentagon and said, 'Why aren't people in uniform?' We said, well, we wear it on Wednesday to make sure it still fits. And he said that's the end of that, you are soldiers and you are sailors, you are airmen and you are marines, so you wear them every day. And we did. It was a major step in pride being restored to the Armed Forces".

Another peculiar institution of the British and Indian Army was, and is, the Regimental Tie. It is usually striped and has the regimental colours. The Piffers tie associated with all Frontier Force regiments carries the colours of the *Chakor* or the Himalayan Partridge. The regimental tie marks out such 'tribal' association and mutual recognition, sometimes Freemason style!

Mufti – Arabic for a scholar – was another Indian Army innovation. It meant civilian dress when uniform is not worn, yet a formalised and uniform pattern of civilian dress or 'civvies'. Indian troops moving out of barracks usually wore the loose fitting traditional dress of the region they came from. Each regiment soon laid down its own specifications ensuring regimental distinction and uniformity. British soldiers, on the other hand, could go out only in uniform, especially back in England. Drunken brawls where belts were freely used were common, causing many public places to put up notices saying 'Men In Uniform Not Admitted'. Kipling, on one hand, wrote *Belts* portraying the brawls and, on the other hand, defended the soldier in *Tommy Atkins:*

*I went into a public 'ouse to get a pint o'beer,*
*The publican 'e up an' sez, "We serve no red-coats here."...*
*For it's Tommy this, an' Tommy that, an' "Chuck him out, the brute!"*
*But it's "Saviour of 'is country," when the guns begin to shoot...*

In the late 1930s, Germany developed 'flecked' camouflage to replace the solid olive uniforms that were common around the world during that time. By the 1990s such camouflage patterned uniform designed for the local environment had been adapted by nearly all professional militaries.

Military clothing also had an immense influence on fashion. Khakis, trench coats, berets, cardigans, bomber jackets, wellington boots, double-breasted overcoats, and the T-shirt all owe their origin to military requirements. As new airplanes flew higher in the 1930s, the glare of the sun required protection. A new type of goggle was thus designed resulting in the Ray-Ban Aviators. It remains a popular style today. Inspired by the modernistic Renault tank, Louis Cartier created the Tank Watch in 1917, a prototype of which was presented to General Pershing, leader of the American Expeditionary Force in World War I. It soon acquired a reputation for elegance which persists till date.

Perhaps no army has such a large variation in its uniforms with differentiating waistbands, turbans, facings, headgear colours, shoulder patches, pouch belts and lanyards as the Indian Army. All of which are zealously and proudly preserved as part of its various regimental traditions.

# EASTERN BATTLEFIELD

*Takane No Hana*
—Japanese proverb
Literally: A flower on lofty heights
Metaphorically: Something very tempting but beyond reach

I had heard my father talk of Dimapur, Kohima, Imphal and Rangoon during his service in World War II. Fortuitously, I was to serve and see a slice of that history and area. I landed at Imphal to assume command of a brigade committed to counter-insurgency operations in Manipur. We were mobilised from Manipur for *Operation Vijay* (Kargil) in 1999, and on termination of the operation, we arrived at Dimapur, Nagaland.

British soldiers to a nurse on the Dimapur-Imphal Road before the siege:

> 'What do we find when we get there?'
> 'You'll find a little paradise on earth,' she said.

Dimapur had been a critical logistics base for the battles of Kohima and Imphal and the reconquest of Burma in World War II. The meter gauge railway terminated here. Indian Army and State Forces Sappers had constructed the airfield and railway sidings, critical for supporting the operations, in record time. Entering Nagaland at Dimapur, the Manipur Road climbs 55 miles up to Kohima at 5000 feet, and beyond to Imphal 79 miles away. Small memorials and plaques embedded into the hillside associated with the events and actions of World War II dot the roadside. Short of Kohima, at Jotsoma, stands a memorial at the site of the Headquarters of the 2 British Infantry Division and 161 Indian Infantry Brigade Box. Topping Kohima Ridge and at the bifurcation of the road towards Imphal stands the famous cemetery (at the site of the DC's Bungalow) and the memorial with the inscription 'When you go home, tell them of us and say, for your tomorrow we gave our today'. Attributed to John Maxwell, it is believed to be inspired by the epitaph in honour of the Spartans who fell at Thermopylae, generally translated as 'Go tell the Spartans, thou who passest by, that here, obedient to their laws we lie'. The cemetery has 1420 burials and a memorial to 917 cremations. Moving south along the Imphal Road on the hillside above lies a Lee tank, perhaps knocked out or stranded irretrievably, and now a memorial of sorts. Descending from the Kohima Ridge, a few kilometres to the east, the road leads to Chakabama.

A couple of months later we moved from Dimapur to Chakabama.

Chakabama – meaning crossroads in the local dialect – is where the routes from Kohima, Zunheboto, Pfutsero, Kidima and Jakhama meet. Tracks from here also lead up to the Kohima Ridge. Crossroads in any conflict zone are invariably militarily important, and Chakabama was no exception. It has been a mute witness to a lot of military activity. Kohima and the surrounding areas, including the famous landmarks of the Battle of Kohima, are clearly visible from there. Sitting outside my headquarters and looking westward, I could visualise the battle in relation to the famous features of Kohima Ridge, Garrison Hill, Naga Village, Kuki Piquet, FSD, Jail Hill and Pimple.

The Indian Army has been here since 1956. When the Naga insurgency broke out, 181 Independent Infantry Brigade, which was located at Shillong under Brigadier Sukhdev Singh, VrC, MC, was moved into the then 'Naga Hills' in 1955 and placed under Headquarters Naga Hills and Tuensang Area on its raising in April 1956. The first unit inducted into the Naga Hills was 17 Rajput, followed by 3 Bihar, commanded by Lieutenant Colonel CT Madappa, which arrived at Chakabama in February 1956. On 19 March 1956, Second Lieutenant Muthiah of the battalion was killed in an ambush, becoming the first Army casualty in the Naga Hills. Chakabama remained a battalion base till 1963. With the raising of

Headquarter GOC Nagaland in 1963, later designated as 8 Mountain Division, 81 Infantry Brigade – originally the 1 Patiala Infantry Brigade of the Patiala State Forces – moved into Chakabama under Brigadier Ghasi Ram. The Brigade moved out for the Bangla Desh Operations in September 1971 and returned in January 1972, and was eventually de-inducted along with 8 Mountain Division to Jammu and Kashmir in April 1990. 73 Mountain Brigade of 57 Mountain Division moved in its place in July 1992, but they too moved out to Mokokchung in July 1998. We, 44 Mountain Brigade, arrived in Chakabama in December 1999. When we arrived there, I set about to explore its legacy.

Chakabama had formed part of the Japanese firm base during the siege and Battle of Kohima in 1944. Overshadowed by events in Europe, especially the D-Day landings in Normandy on 06 June 1944 and liberation of Rome a day earlier, the critical strategic significance of the battles of Kohima-Imphal was appreciated much later. A contest run by the British National Army Museum in 2013 voted the battles of Kohima-Imphal 'Britain's Greatest Battles' ahead of Waterloo 1815 and D-Day 1944.

Tokyo announced the invasion of British India on 07 March 1944. The Japanese 31 Division as part of the 15 Army's *U Go* offensive crossed the Chindwin River on 15 March 1944 and pushed through the jungles north of Manipur heading for Kohima to cut off the Kohima-Imphal Road. They herded along 15,000 oxen and goats as 'meat on hoof'. The Japanese 15 and 33 Divisions were to destroy IV Corps (17, 20 and 23 Indian Divisions and 5 Indian Division airlifted later) in the Manipur Plains. 31 Division's advance was delayed by 50 Indian Parachute Brigade at Sangshak, and the newly raised 1 Assam fought the Japanese and imposed valuable delay east of Chakabama at Jessami and Phek. The Japanese pushed on to Chakabama and besieged Kohima on 04 April 1944. The 260 survivors of 1 Assam withdrew into the Kohima defences and were besieged. It was to inspire the regimental ditty *Badluram ka badan zamin ke niche hai aur humko uska ration milta hai* (Badluram lies buried in the ground and we get his rations) sung to the tune of *John Brown's Body lies ...* Kohima was held by 1 Assam, 3 Assam Rifles, 4 Royal West Kent Regiment and 20 Mountain Battery comprising four guns. They were reinforced by a company of 4/7 Rajputs. The defended perimeter measured about 600 by 1000 yards. After 14 days of fighting it had shrunk to about 200 by 200 yards. On 18 April 1944 the garrison was linked up by 1/1 Punjab of the 161 Indian Infantry Brigade of 5 Indian Division flown in from the Arakan. 24 Indian Mountain Regiment deployed at Jotsoma supported the garrison throughout the siege, often firing within 25 yards of the defenders and on one occasion firing 3500 rounds in five hours. Lee tanks pushed up from Dimapur finally broke the Japanese siege by employing bulldozers to make tracks for them. Kohima was relieved on 20 April 1944 and reinforced by the 2 British Infantry Division. The Japanese were thereafter pushed back by the 2 British Infantry Division and 7 Indian Infantry Division flown in from the Arakan. The siege and the battle left 2337 British and Indian soldiers dead.

The Japanese invasion of India had been halted at the tennis court adjoining the DC's Bungalow at Kohima. The tennis court is marked with concrete lines and preserved within the cemetery. Driving back the Japanese, the 2 British Infantry Division advanced along the Manipur Road while 7 Indian Infantry Division pursued them eastwards through Chakabama and beyond to the Chindwin. Earlier, while in Manipur, I had located the spot near my Brigade Headquarters at Senapati where tanks of 3rd Carabiniers of 2 British Infantry Division from Kohima and troops of 1/17 Dogras of 5 Indian Infantry Division from Imphal had linked up after the siege at Mile 109 (48 Km South of Kohima on the road to Imphal) on the morning of 22 June 1944. A formal link up took place at 2'o clock in the afternoon between the Commanders of 33 Corps and 2 British Division from Kohima and of 9 Indian Infantry Brigade from Imphal. Unfortunately, nothing marked the spot, however, a masonry plaque on the road outside Kohima indicated the commencement of the advance from that spot after the siege.

> British – Too many guns, tanks and troops. Japanese going, but back in six months.
> —Japanese writing on abandoned village wall near Kohima

Amidst its turbulent and violent past, three things stood out at

Chakabama – the profusion of rose bushes in bloom, incredibly colourful butterflies as big as one's open palm and, a result of someone's past effort, abundant pear trees with a surfeit of fruit in season. Our medical officer, having tested the water from the spring which was the source for the camp, declared it to be better than any branded bottled mineral water!

> Probably one of the greatest battles in history ... the British/Indian Thermopylae
> —Lord Louis Mountbatten, Supreme Allied Commander

# IF...

Rudyard Kipling, born in Bombay on 30 December 1865, returned to India as a 17-year-old fresh out of school in England and began working as a newspaper reporter in Lahore. Then as a sub-editor, he struggled to get out each day's edition of the *Civil and Military Gazette*. Writing fiction and poetry in his spare time, he would fill up the left-over space in the newspaper with his poems and stories, often under a pseudonym.

His plots dealt mainly with courage and sacrifice associated with life in the Army and the exotic colours, sounds, sights and mysteries of India which he assimilated effortlessly. He came to be the 'chief propagandist of empire', and his writings became the inspiration for many to serve in India. As a 'barrack room balladeer' the common British soldier saw him as articulating their concerns and held him in high esteem. This found expression in his stories in *Soldiers Three*. He was awarded the Nobel Prize for Literature in 1907, the first for English language and the youngest recipient till date. His prodigious output in verse covered a vast canvas, including his personal life.

*Mother of Cities to me,*
*For I was born in her gate,*
*Between the palms and the sea,*
*Where the world-end steamers wait.*
—Rudyard Kipling, *To the City of Bombay*

Kipling saw his only son grow up and display some qualities he admired, amongst others the handling of adversity with fortitude, and set great hopes by him. He wanted his son to follow in the footsteps of great men he had known. If his son could live by their values, if he could .... Penning his thoughts for his twelve-year-old took the shape of *If.* It became a classic and was translated into 27 languages. It was framed and affixed above the writing table in each cadet's room at the National Defence Academy, Kharakvasla, on its inception. The poem was also on the desk of Kaiser Wilhelm. Its most famous line '*If you can meet with triumph and disaster and treat those two imposters just the same*' appears on the wall of the tunnel between the dressing room and the entrance at Wimbledon Centre Court. It was voted Britain's most popular poem in a BBC poll.

When World War I broke out, Kipling arranged his son John's commission in the Irish Guards of the British Army, even though he was unfit due to poor eyesight. Tragically, John, for whom *If* was written, was killed in action at the Battle of Loos on the Western Front on 27 September 1915, aged just 17 years. *If* lives on.

*If you can keep your head when all about you*
*are losing theirs and blaming it on you;*
*If you can trust yourself when all men doubt you,*
*but make allowances for their doubting too;*
*If you can wait and not be tired of waiting,*
*or being lied about, don't deal in lies,*
*or being hated don't give way to hating,*
*and yet don't look too good, nor talk too wise;*
*If you can dream and not make dreams your master;*
*If you can think and not make thoughts your aim;*
*If you can meet with triumph and disaster*
*and treat those two imposters just the same;*
*If you can bear to hear the truth you have spoken*
*twisted by knaves to make a trap for fools,*
*or watch the things you gave your life to, broken,*
*and stoop and build 'em up with worn out tools;*
*If you can make one heap of all your winnings*
*and risk it on one turn of pitch and toss,*
*and lose and start again at your beginnings*

*and never breathe a word about your loss;*
*If you can force your heart and nerve and sinew*
*to serve your turn long after they are gone,*
*and so hold on when there is nothing in you*
*except the will, which says to them 'Hold On';*
*If you can talk with crowds and keep your virtue*
*or walk with kings nor lose the common touch;*
*If neither foes nor loving friends can hurt you;*
*If all men count with you, but none too much;*
*If you can fill the unforgiving minute*
*with sixty seconds' worth of distance run,*
*yours is the Earth and everything that's in it,*
*And – which is more – you'll be a man my son!*

After the War, as literary adviser to the Imperial War Graves Commission, it was his idea to engrave 'A Soldier Of The Great War – Known Unto God', on the graves of unidentified soldiers. Ironically, his son's body was never found, though seventy-five years later, an unidentified grave was attributed to him and marked as such. In lament for his son's death, and the terrible casualties for a cause projected by leaders now seen as futile, he wrote:

*If any question why we died,*
*Tell them, because our fathers lied.*

Kipling died on 18 January 1936 and then two days later, when King George V died, a newspaper wrote 'The King is gone, and has taken his trumpeter with him'.

# ARMIES OF THE PRINCES

On 23 September 1918, in a unique action, the mounted troops of Mysore and Hyderabad Lancers captured Mt Carmel, while the Jodhpur Lancers routed the Turk defenders and captured Haifa in Palestine as part of Allenby's offensive. There is no other recorded instance of mounted cavalry capturing a fortified town. On 26 October 1918, the Mysore Lancers and two squadrons of Jodhpur Lancers charged the enemy and helped capture Aleppo. The troops belonged to the Indian State Forces – the soldiers of the Princes of India. When New Delhi was laid out, on the roundabout on the erstwhile Roberts Road in front of the Commander-in-Chief's residence (today Teen Murti Bhavan), a memorial to the 15 Indian Imperial Service Cavalry Brigade was erected and unveiled in 1931. The *Teen Murtis,* or three statues, are lancers from the Hyderabad, Mysore and Jodhpur State Forces. The brigade had served on the Western Front and was part of the Battle of Cambrai in 1917. If the lancers of Jodhpur, Mysore and Hyderabad were famous as mounted troops, the foot soldiers of Patiala and Jaipur were renowned infantry just as the sappers of Faridkot and Malerkotla had an enviable reputation as combat engineers. The Jaipur Transport Corps was the only transport unit in the history of the Indian Army to win a battle honour when they were so honoured at Sheiba in Mesopotamia in World War I.

An army, a flag and a seal have been the indispensable symbols of sovereignty and statehood. Throughout recorded history, the Indian subcontinent has not been an exception. The most visible symbol, as also the most potent instrument of governance being the army, the hereditary Indian rulers lavished special care and attention to maintain and field their armies. The personal protection of the ruler was logically one of the prime functions of his army. Invariably, the elite of their troops were styled as 'Bodyguards', the most famous among them being the Swai Man Guards of Jaipur and the Jammu and Kashmir Bodyguards, besides the mounted troops of Holkar of Indore. Loyalty to the ruler was the *sine qua non* of these troops, reflected in the case of the Jodhpur Lancers in their nickname – *Jo Hukum* – whatever the order. Some families had served in the same units for four or five generations.

The formation of the (British) Indian Army may be dated to 1748 when Major Stringer Lawrence came out to India to be appointed the commander of all the East India Company's forces in India, or to 1768, when the first sepoy battalions were formed in Bombay. On the other hand, some erstwhile Indian princely units, which are perpetuated in the Indian Army today, lay claim to their origins in antiquity with an indeterminate date of raising. The Mewar Infantry, today 9 Grenadiers, was raised in 1303 and carries the honour of having fought at Haldighati on 18 June 1576. The 1000 camel mounted sowars who accompanied Rao Bikaji from Jodhpur in 1465 and enabled him to establish the independent kingdom of Bikaner are today the 13 Grenadiers. 15 Punjab, the erstwhile I Patiala Rajindra Infantry, was raised on Baisakhi Day, 13 April 1705, by Ala Singh, the founder of Patiala State. The Nabha Akal Infantry, today 14 Punjab, was raised in 1757. The Swai Man Guards of Jaipur were raised sometime in the mid-sixteenth century as the bodyguards of Raja Man Singh, Commander-in-Chief of Akbar's army. Two of the oldest artillery units surviving in the Indian Army and forming part of the 23 Field Regiment are the Bikaner Bijay Battery raised in 1650 and the Gwalior Horse Battery raised sometime in the mid-1700s.

Many of the state forces units were trained and officered by Europeans, especially the French, after the Napoleonic wars. Thus it was no surprise that at the Delhi Coronation Durbar in 1911 the words of command and designations of commanders in some of these units were in French.

Through the long process of consolidation of British rule in India, while some territories were directly taken over and administered by the

British, two-thirds of the Indian Empire was controlled and ruled by native Indian princes under the suzerainty of the British Crown through treaties and alliances. However, two prominent articles in all treaties were the ban on any diplomatic relations with outside powers and war amongst states. Complementing the British-Indian Army, the armies of the princes, or the Indian State Forces, were part of the total military capability of the Raj. Prior to 1857, some rulers had entered into agreements with the East India Company to maintain forces within or near their states for which the Company provided officers. These were designated as Subsidiary Forces and were swept away after 1857. Then there were the 'Contingent Forces' which were of the states itself with liability for imperial service. They were the precursors of the 'Imperial Service Troops'.

The Panjdeh Incident, when the Russians seized Panjdeh Oasis opposite Heart on 31 March 1885, brought the imperial powers of Britain and Russia to the brink of open hostilities. The perceived Russian threat through the North-West Frontier in the late 1880s prompted the Crown to utilise the manpower and material resources of the Indian states for military purposes. This resulted in the 'Imperial Service Scheme' being initiated in 1887. Thus the 'Imperial Service Troops', as distinct from the feudal forces of the states, came into being. These troops were trained and equipped to standards comparable to the Indian Army and had a similar liability towards active service under British control. Though initially infantry and cavalry units were so organised, by 1890, some states had converted the infantry to sappers. By World War I, twenty-nine states were part of the Imperial Service Troops Scheme, and the total strength of all ranks was 7673 Cavalry, 373 Artillery, 741 Sappers, 10,298 Infantry, 34 Signals, 637 Camel Corps and 2723 Transport Corps making a total of 22,479. The scheme underwent changes after the Great War, and by 1939, all state forces were designated as Indian State Forces and classified based on their organisation, training and equipment. By 1947, forty-four states maintained such forces with a total strength of about 75,000.

Though the states had no treaty obligation to serve outside India, Patiala had provided 1100 men for the 1879 Afghan War. The Imperial Service Troops first saw action in the Chitral Campaign of

1891-95 where Kashmir troops were employed, including in the famous defence of Chitral Fort in 1895. In the Frontier War of 1897 units from Gwalior, Jaipur, Jind, Kashmir, Malerkotla, Nabha, Sirmoor and Patiala took part. A detachment of the Kapurthala Infantry died fighting to the last man in the Kermana defile. Alwar, Bikaner, Jodhpur and Malerkotla sent detachments with the International Force to China during the Boxer Rebellion in 1901. The Bikaner Camel Corps went to Somaliland in 1902.

At the outbreak of war in 1914, the 22,479 Imperial Service Troops from 29 states fielded a total of fifteen cavalry regiments, thirteen infantry battalions, two mountain batteries, four companies of engineers, three camel corps and seven transport corps. 18,500 states' troops and 27,000 non-combatants in the labour corps served overseas during the war, besides providing troops for duty on the North-West Frontier. Hyderabad, Mysore, Patiala and Bikaner troops served in Egypt and Palestine. Jodhpur Lancers and Sappers from Tehri Garhwal along with transport units from Bharatpur, Gwalior, and Indore served on the Western Front. East Africa saw troops from Bharatpur, Faridkot, Gwalior, Jind, Kapurthala, Kashmir and Rampur, with the Faridkot Sappers particularly distinguishing themselves. 2754 State Forces troops were killed or wounded. These troops were frequently used to provide immediate reinforcements to similar Indian Army units suffering heavy casualties. State Forces won a total of 689 gallantry awards during the war. Men from the states were also recruited into the Indian Army.

Distinct from the armies of the states were contingents, like the Hyderabad Contingent, which drew officers from the regular Indian Army, and were linked to the states in as much as their maintenance was underwritten and paid for by the rulers out of revenues generated from specified territories like Berar from Hyderabad. The Hyderabad Contingent was formed in 1798. Two battalions of the Contingent were styled by the British resident as Russell's Brigade in 1812. The contingent was transferred to the East India Company in 1853. In 1903 the contingent was merged into the Indian Army; the cavalry regiments and the infantry battalions ultimately becoming the Deccan Horse and the Kumaon Regiment. Service in the Hyderabad Contingent was much sought after by British officers for the good pay and allowances. Any extravagance was justified by the nonchalant 'Nizzy will pay'. The Gwalior Contingent, though one of the elite forces and consisting of seven infantry regiments, two cavalry regiments and five artillery batteries, was consumed by the events of 1857.

The post World War 1 review and reforms in 1920 addressed the organisation, equipment and role of the state forces, and accordingly, they were classified into three categories under the 'Indian States Forces Scheme'. The first, categorised as Field Service Units, were organised, equipped and trained like the Indian Army and had similar unconditional liability for war. The second category consisted of such states which were provided arms and equipment by the Crown at cost price and could be called for active service. The third category consisted of militia type units. This system encompassed some 50,000 men, with forty-nine states within its ambit, ranging from divisional-sized forces from Kashmir, Gwalior and Hyderabad to states with one platoon.

When World War II came, the states' units served alongside the Indian Army in all theatres. Five battalions from Bahawalpur, Hyderabad, Jind, Mysore and Kapurthala were lost when the British garrison at Singapore surrendered in February 1942. The J&K artillery and Nabha infantry won laurels at Keran and in Italy. The Jaipur and Jodhpur Infantry distinguished themselves in the North African and Italian Campaign. At the end of the war, 98 state forces units had served outside their states.

The standing and military capability of a state was reflected in the gun salute entitlement of its ruler. The states were divided into three divisions. Rulers of 118 First Division States were entitled to gun salutes and were known as the 'Salute States'. Kashmir and Gwalior were entitled the highest 21 till 1917 when Hyderabad, Mysore and Baroda were also elevated from 19 to 21 for their war services. Others followed in odd-numbered descending order from 19 (Bhopal, Indore, Kalat, Kohlapur, Travancore and Udaipur) to 17 (Bikaner and Patiala) and so on till 9. The Second Division comprised 117 states and the remaining 330 were in the Third Division. The Chamber of Princes constituted on 08 February 1921 at the Diwan-e-Aam, Red Fort, Delhi through the efforts of Bikaner and Patiala were all 'Gun Salute' states.

The innate military ardour and warlike endeavours of the Kshatriya princes appealed to their senses no matter how circumscribed the opportunity due to the prevailing circumstances. The growing Indian aspirations to seek entry into the commissioned ranks of the army were attempted to be partially mollified by opening such avenues to young men from the Indian royalty. Accordingly, the Imperial Cadet College was created by Lord Curzon at Dehradun in 1901. A contingent of the Imperial Cadet Corps under the Honorary Commandant, Sir Partap Singh, was present at the Delhi Durbar of 1911. As the graduates were not intended to be appointed to regimental duties, but merely to fill staff appointments; it was short lived and was soon closed down. It was later reopened as the Prince of Wales Royal Indian Military College in 1922 and is today the Rashtriya Indian Military College. The campus is still referred to as *Rajwara Camp* by the locals. On the establishment of the Indian Military Academy at Dehradun in 1932, 40 cadets were selected of which 10 were from the state forces. Others followed. Gobinder Singh stood second in the order of merit among the 29 cadets of the first batch who passed out and later became the Commandant of the Indian Military Academy.

The Maharajas of Kashmir, Bikaner, Jodhpur, Jaipur and Patiala were honorary generals of the British-Indian Army, and at one time or the other, were members of the Imperial War Council. Other rulers carried lesser honorary ranks. Some like Sir Pratap Singh of Jodhpur and Ganga Singh of Bikaner led their troops during the Boxer Rebellion in China in 1901. Sir Pratap Singh again led his troops in France and Palestine in the First World War at the age of 70, and Ganga Singh served on the staff of the Commander-in-Chief in France and also led the Bikaner Camel Corps (*Ganga Risala*) against the Turks in defence of the Suez Canal in February 1915. Major Dalpat Singh, who had won a Military Cross in the Jordan Valley, was killed leading the charge at Haifa in 1918. 18 rulers had served in various theatres of the war. The Maharaja of Bundi won a Military Cross leading his troops in Burma in World War II. Major General Ganga Singh, the Maharaja of Bikaner, had been a member of the Imperial War Council in 1917. India was a separate signatory to the Treaty of Versailles in 1919 at the end of the Great War, and a founding member of the League of Nations. It was the only non-independent territory to have this status. As a signal honour, Ganga Singh was the sole Indian or 'non-white' representative at the signing of the treaty on 28 June 1919. William Orpen's iconic painting *The Signing of Peace* in the Imperial War Museum, London shows an imposing Ganga Singh in uniform with the traditional *safa*. He became Chancellor of the Chamber of Princes in 1921.

On 15 August 1947, 44 states maintained units under the Indian State Forces (ISF) scheme aggregating a total of 75,311 personnel. There were also a large number of non-ISF scheme units consisting of police and ceremonial guards. The inevitable post World War II reforms and reorganisation had yet to be implemented when Independence came along with the immediate military challenge in Jammu and Kashmir. The initial brunt was borne by the J&K State Forces. Brigadier Rajinder Singh, Chief of Staff J&K State Forces, was killed leading his troops near Uri and was awarded the country's first Maha Vir Chakra. Two companies of 6 J&K Infantry, under Lieutenant Colonel Sher Jung Thapa, held out under siege at Skardu for six months, enabling Leh to be reinforced and, ultimately, Ladakh to be saved. Among the first troops to be inducted from outside was 1 Patiala Rajindra Infantry. Guns of the Patiala Mountain Battery were airlifted to Srinagar on 30 October 1947 and came into action on the airfield to disperse the raiders. The main body of the battery under Major Kuldip Singh, MC, marched with the animals and reached in April 1948. 1 Patiala and the J&K Mountain Battery played a major role in forcing the Zojila and pushing on up to Kargil as part of 77 Parachute Brigade in 1948. When 1 Patiala Rajindra Infantry came out in December 1948 it had won no less than eight Mahavir Chakras and sixteen Vir Chakras. The Suket Infantry, similarly, had a distinguished record in the J&K Operations.

After Independence, the future of the State Forces along with the States themselves had to be addressed. Consequent to the merger of the Princely States into the Indian Union, the military forces of these states were taken over by the Government of India. The States were viewed as four groups. The first two groups comprised states like Rampur which were to be merged into their neighbouring province and those which were to be administered as provinces under Chief

Commissioners. Their forces were taken over by the Government of India and absorbed into the Indian Army or mustered out. The third group consisted of Hyderabad and Mysore. The fourth group was made up of those states which were formed into unions like the Patiala and East Punjab States Union – PEPSU – under a Raj Pramukh. Hyderabad, Mysore, Travancore and Cochin forces were placed under the control of the Indian Army on 01 April 1950. Forces of the union states were merged into the Indian Army on 01 April 1951. Bahawalpur State Forces were the only ones to go to Pakistan and were merged into the Baluch Regiment in 1956. While all Indian State Forces units were merged into existing Indian Army regiments and units, the Jammu and Kashmir Infantry was transferred en bloc in 1957 and retained as the Jammu and Kashmir Rifles. The merger signalled the end of the old order. Some old units were disbanded while the legitimate aspirations of others could not be accommodated; one such being the claim of the Jaipur Swai Man Guards to be embodied into the newly created Brigade of Guards which was constituted by picking up the four oldest battalions of the Indian Army. By the end of World War II and Independence, the regular Indian Cavalry regiments had been mechanised. The only surviving horse cavalry units were those of the State Forces. These were amalgamated and perpetuated into 61 Cavalry which survives as the only horsed cavalry regiment in service in the world. The regiment adopted the Mysore crest of the mythological double-headed bird, the Gandabherunda. Among the amalgamated constituents the Regiment has 39 battle honours.

The colours of 17 state forces units were laid to rest at the Chetwood Hall of the Indian Military Academy, Dehradun on 06 April 1956. The proud legacy of the state forces lives on today with the unit titles suffixed with the states name and the old state forces crest displayed within the units or affixed alongside the regimental crest on cards and letterheads. Needless to say these state forces units added to the rich heritage of the Indian Army.

## THE LEGACY

| | | |
|---|---|---|
| 1 Gwalior Lancers, Jaipur | | |
| 2 Gwalior Lancers, Jaipur | | |
| Kachhawa Horse | | |
| Jodhpur Lancers | | |
| Patiala Lancers | | |
| Dungar Lancers | | |
| Mangal Lancers | | |
| Mysore Lancers | | |
| Mewar Lancers | | |
| Saurashtra Horsed Cavalry | | 61 Cavalry |
| Gwalior Mountain Battery | 74 (Gwalior) Mountain Battery | |
| Patiala Mountain Battery | 75 (Patiala) Mountain Battery | |
| Jammu and Kashmir Mountain Battery | 76 (J&K) Mountain Battery | 23 Mountain Regiment |
| Bikaner Bijay Mountain Battery | 83 (Bikaner) Field Battery | |
| Gwalior Scindia Mountain Battery | 84 (Scindia) Field Battery | |
| Patiala Field Battery | 85 (Patiala) Field Battery | 41 Field Regiment |
| J&K Bodyguard Cavalry | 60 Heavy Regiment | |
| Bahawalpur Mountain Battery | 14 Field Regiment Pak Army | |
| 1 Faridkot Field Company | 368 Field Company (Faridkot) | 51 Engineer Regiment |
| 2 Faridkot Field Company | 94 Field Company (Faridkot) | 59 Engineer Regiment |
| Tehri Garhwal Field Company | 84 Field Company (Tehri Garhwal) | 54 Engineer Regiment |
| Mandi Field Company | 95 Field Company (Mandi) | 54 Engineer Regiment |
| Sirmoor Field Company | 100 Field Company (Sirmoor) | 51 Engineer Regiment |
| Malerkotla Field Company | 369 Field Company (Malerkotla) | 58 Engineer Regiment |
| Sirmoor Brass Band | Bengal Engineer Group Centre Band | |

(All the above sapper units are part of the Bengal Sappers)

| | | |
|---|---|---|
| Jind Infantry | 13 Punjab (Jind) | |
| Nabha Akal Infantry | 14 Punjab (Nabha Akal) | |
| 1 Patiala Rajindra Infantry | 15 Punjab (Patiala) | |
| 2 Patiala Rajindra Infantry | 16 Punjab (Patiala) | |
| 1 Mysore Infantry | 8 Madras (Mysore) | |
| 1 Travancore Infantry | 9 Madras (Travancore) | |
| 2 Travancore Infantry | 16 Madras (Travancore) | |
| 1 Cochin Infantry | 17 Madras (Cochin) | |
| Kutch State Forces | 7 Grenadiers | 9 Mechanised Infantry |
| Baria, Idar, Lunawada and Rajpipla State Forces | 8 Grenadiers | |
| Mewar Infantry, Alwar Jey Paltan, Bharatpur Infantry and Kota Umed Infantry | 9 Grenadiers (Mewar) | |
| Bikaner Ganga Risala and Jaisalmer Camel Corps | 13 Grenadiers (Ganga Jaisalmer) | |
| Kolhapur Infantry | 19 Maratha LI (Kolhapur) | |
| Baroda Lancers, 1 Baroda Infantry and 2 Baroda Inf | 20 Maratha LI (Baroda) | 10 Mechanised Infantry |
| 2 Hyderabad Infantry | 22 Maratha LI (Hyderabad) | |
| Jaipur Sawai Man Guards | 17 Rajputana Rifles (Sawai Man) | |
| Bhavnagar Lancers, Bhavnagar Infantry, Dharangadra Infantry, Nawanagar Infantry and Porbandar Infantry | 18 Rajputana Rifles (Saurashtra) | 11 Mechanised Infantry |
| Bikaner Sadul Infantry | 19 Rajput (Bikaner) and 5 Field Regiment | |
| Jodhpur Sardar Infantry | 20 Rajput (Jodhpur) | |
| Chamba, Mandi, Sirmoor and Suket Infantry | 16 Dogra | |
| 4 Gwalior Infantry | 14 Kumaon (Gwalior) | 5 Mechanized Infantry |
| 1 Indore Infantry | 15 Kumaon (Indore) | |
| 1,2,3,4,7 and 9 Jammu and Kashmir Infantry | 1,2,3,4,7 and 9 Jammu and Kashmir Rifles | |
| 1 Tripura Manikya Rifles | 6 Assam | |
| Kapurthala Military Band | Regiment of Artillery Military Band | |
| 1,2,3 and 4 Bahawalpur Infantry | 8,9,20 and 21 Baluch, Pak Army | |
| Gwalior Pony Company | 10 Animal Transport Company, ASC | |

# THE MEN WHO SAVED LADAKH

> The land is so barren and the passes so high that only the best of friends or fiercest enemies would want to visit us.
>
> —A Ladakhi saying

Ladakh, the crown on India's map, was the transit route of trading caravans to and from Central Asia, with Leh as the communications and barter hub. The three valleys formed by the Indus, Zanskar and Shyok rivers provided the natural routes amidst mountains towering up to 18,000 feet. Branching off from the Silk Route, caravans from Chinese Turkistan crossed over the Karakoram Pass moving along the Shyok River and onto Leh and thence along the Indus to Skardu and Gilgit east of Leh. On another branch southwards from this route was Kargil and across the Zojila lay Srinagar. Leh was connected to Manali over the Rohtang Pass on the south-east. The high-altitude cold desert averages 11,000 feet along the Indus which runs through Ladakh from east to west.

Following the First Anglo-Sikh War 1845-46 and the signing of the Treaty of Amritsar on 16 March 1846, Jammu and Kashmir, including Ladakh and Baltistan, was acquired by Maharaja Gulab Singh. British strategic interest in Baltistan, bordering Afghanistan and Russia, ensured constant interference in this region and culminated in the entire region of Nagar, Hunza, Gilgit and Skardu being leased by the Maharaja to the British in 1935 for 60 years. With the impending lapse of British paramountcy on 15 August 1947, the region was to technically and legally revert to Jammu and Kashmir State on that date. It was handed over by the British Political Agent to the Governor of Gilgit appointed by the Maharaja of Jammu and Kashmir on 30 June 1947. In a grave error of judgement, the British officers, including the commander of the Gilgit Scouts, were retained by the Maharaja. A coup was staged by these officers on 31 October 1947 and the Governor imprisoned. Major Brown hoisted the Pakistani flag on 03 November 1947 and handed over the administration to Pakistan. By December 1947, the small garrison at Skardu was besieged and in concert with the tribal invasion of other parts of the state, Pakistan aided tribals had advanced up the Shyok and Indus valleys, the objective being Leh and ultimately the entire Ladakh. The Skardu garrison under Lieutenant Colonel Sher Jang Thapa of the State Forces held out for six months which proved crucial in delaying the enemy advance towards Leh.

Leh at that time was garrisoned by a platoon of 33 men of the State Forces. With no other means available to reinforce the garrison, Major Prithi Chand and Captain Khusal Chand with 14 men of 2 Dogra and two platoons of the State Forces set out from Srinagar on foot on 16 February 1948, across the Zojila. They were accompanied by the British trained Sonam Norbu, the first engineer from Ladakh. He carried Rs 13,000 for constructing an airstrip at Leh. The party reached Leh on 08 March 1948. The Zojila had been crossed on foot during the winters perhaps for the first time. The alternate route for reinforcements was from Manali over the Rohtang Pass which was too long and only negotiable on foot. It too was impassable in winters.

Major Prithi Chand commenced raising 7 J&K Militia amongst whom was a young man named Chewang Rinchen – later Colonel Chewang Rinchen, Maha Vir Chakra and Bar, Sena Medal.

Construction of the airstrip between the Indus river bed and the town began on 12 March 1948 and a 2300-yard long makeshift airstrip was ready by 06 April 1948. It was an outstanding achievement by any standard. Norbu had spent Rs 10,891. On 06 April 1948, he sent the following signal to Brigadier Harbaksh Singh, Commander, 163 Infantry Brigade, in Kashmir:

> 2300 yards runway serviceable (.) remainder 500 yards needs enormous cutting and filling which will be done if found necessary on landing (.) small igloo hut can be constructed with balance

> amount out of thirteen thousand sanctioned for landing ground(.) send planes immediately (.) weather most favourable early morning and noon (.)

As no instructions were received for constructing the igloo, he deposited the remaining amount of Rs 2109 in the treasury.

By 22 May 1948, Zojila, Kargil, Khaltsi and Tharu, along the Indus on the outskirts of Leh, had been captured by the raiders. The land route from Srinagar was no longer available. The enemy was at the gates of Leh. With no other means of reinforcements, it could only be saved by an air link.

In the pleasant surroundings of cherry trees at Baramulla, Major General Thimayya invited Air Commodore Mehar Singh, commanding the Air Force in J&K, in the third week of May to a strawberry cream party – a weakness of Mehar Singh. While Thimayya urged Mehar Singh to help relieve Leh, Mehar Singh explained that the Dakota aircraft were not designed to operate at such altitudes. They were not pressurized, had no oxygen for the crew, and limited power to fly over the 18,000 foot high mountains. The weather en route was unknown and unpredictable. The Air Force then had only one squadron of Dakota transport aircraft and was very heavily committed in ongoing operations in Kashmir and Poonch. Thimayya then offered to go along with the first aircraft and share the risks with the Air Force. Mehar Singh not only relented but also decided to pilot the first aircraft to Leh. It was a mutual agreement between the two with no clearance from higher headquarters.

The airstrip at Leh was at an altitude of approximately 11,000 feet. No one had landed piston engine transport aircraft at such altitudes at that time. The airfield was aligned in a bowl with only one direction for approach and landing. The hills on the other side precluded any scope for 'going around' in case the approach was not right – in short, it had to be right the first time. With no pressurisation, no oxygen equipment, no maps, no navigation aids, and no prior familiarisation with the landing strip, Mehar Singh took off in a Dakota on 24 May 1948 with Flight Lieutenant SD Singh as co-pilot and with General Thimayya on board. Thimayya also took along a 24 year old war artist – Sarabjit Singh – who recorded much of the J&K operations on film and canvas. Flying above 18,000 feet and after negotiating the Zojila, Namikla and Fotula they landed at Leh. Aviation history had been created.

The weather did not permit flying for the next six days. An attempt on 31 May was frustrated by bad weather. Then on 01 June, Air Commodore Mehar Singh led a flight of six Dakotas with a company of 2/4 Gurkha Rifles along with essential supplies and ammunition. After dropping the stores near the airfield Air Commodore Mehar Singh landed the first aircraft. The others followed. Leh had been reinforced. Immediately on landing, the company of Gurkhas pushed westwards to hold the raiders. The local population had not seen a motor vehicle, leave alone an aircraft, and hurriedly brought fodder for the 'flying horses'! A tenuous air bridge in the prevailing monsoon conditions was thereafter established.

As Zojila, Dras and Kargil were in enemy hands, the only land route available was from Manali over the Rohtang Pass, a distance of over 475 km. A company of 2/8 Gurkha Rifles under Major Hari Chand was moved from Ferozepur to Manali on 28 May 1948. The company consisting of 151 men and carrying 600 rifles with 60,000 rounds of ammunition and supplies set out on foot with all available porters and ponies. After traversing the over 17,000-foot high Baralachala, Lachulung and Tanglang passes, the column reached Leh on 05 July 1948.

Another company of 2/8 Gurkha Rifles under the commanding officer, Lieutenant Colonel HS Parab, was moved from Ferozepur to Srinagar on 17 August. The Commanding Officer and the company were airlifted to Leh on 23 August. The remainder of the battalion moved on foot across the Rohtang pass reaching Leh on 18 September. Before being airlifted to Leh, Colonel Parab had been appointed the Military Governor of Ladakh by a charter signed by Bakshi Gulam Mohammad. His orders from General Thimayya were 'You will defend Leh at all costs'. On arrival, he assumed command of all troops in Ladakh and set about pushing the raiders back.

Further reinforcements and supplies were air-landed thereafter and also carried across Rohtang on foot. Leh was saved, and the enemy pushed back. Zojila was captured on 01 November 1948 and Kargil on 23 November 1948. Colonel Parab's troops advancing from Leh linked up with those advancing from Kargil on 24 November 1948. Further advance westward along the Indus was stalled by the winters setting in. The cease-fire followed on 01 January 1949.

These intrepid men had saved Ladakh.

Sonam Norbu joined the J&K Public Works Department, and later, as a Chief Engineer with the Border Roads Organisation, he was instrumental in the construction of the Srinagar-Leh road. Air Commodore Mehar Singh was awarded the Maha Vir Chakra for his role in the J&K Operations. He resigned from the Air Force in August 1948 and was killed in an air crash on 11 March 1952. General Thimayya went on to become the Chief of the Army Staff. Lieutenant Colonel Sher Jang Thapa was awarded the Maha Vir Chakra for the defence of Skardu. Major Hari Chand and Captain Khusal Chand were awarded the Maha Vir Chakra for their gallant actions in keeping the raiders at bay till Leh was finally relieved and secured. Chewang Rinchen was also awarded the Maha Vir Chakra. He led his troops in the capture of Turtuk in 1971 and was awarded a Bar to the Maha Vir Chakra. The other soldiers faded away.

In a small plot on the outskirts of Leh is an enclosed compound with dozen-odd graves, with passers-by barely noticing it. There lie some of those who were killed during the operations. Unsung, they too had helped save Ladakh.

# MOUNTAIN GUNNERS

> Whatever their rivalries, no cavalry or infantry officer would dispute the supreme excellence of the Mountain Batteries: the Indian Army was very proud of them.
> —Charles Chenevix Trench, *The Indian Army and the Kings Enemies 1900 - 1947*

Mountain Gunners and Mountain Artillery became extinct in 1985 when the last Mountain Regiment of the Indian Army was redesignated as a Field Regiment and equipped with field guns. It was curtains for nearly a century-and-a-half of a very exceptional and a unique breed of soldiers and animals.

The genesis of mountain artillery lay in Napoleon's famous victories at Austerlitz (1805), Jena-Auerstedat (1806), Friedland (1807) and Lutzen (1813) where his ability to quickly concentrate at the opponent's point of weakness and hard fighting carried the day. Gustavas Adolphus of Sweden (1594-1632) and Frederick the Great of Prussia (1712-1786) – 'Father of Mobile Artillery' – had first introduced horse artillery. Refining this concept, Napoleon introduced light horse-drawn artillery capable of galloping into action at the pace of the cavalry and bearing firepower at the point of decision where the slow, heavy and ponderous artillery of the day was unable to do so. He organised the *Grande Batterie* of up to a hundred centrally controlled guns employed en masse at close range at the critical point. The British quickly adapted and raised the first of the Royal Horse Artillery in 1793, which logically evolved into portable animal-pack artillery in mountainous terrains. A mule-pack mountain artillery was raised for employment in the Pyrenees by Wellington in the Peninsular Campaign 1813-14 against Napoleon. As the British in India advanced westwards and came up to the North-West Frontier and Afghanistan, mule-pack mountain artillery was introduced into the Indian Army – the first being the Hazara Mountain Train, raised locally in 1840, and later disbanded in 1843.

In 1851, the Hazara Mountain Train was again formed officially with six 3-pounder guns, forty-four mules and two elephants. Post 1857, all 'native' artillery was disbanded except for six batteries of the old East India Company – two from the Bombay Presidency and four of the Punjab Irregular Frontier Force (PIFFERS). As the Frontier commitment grew, by 1876, all were converted to mountain batteries and formed part of every Frontier operation including the famous march from Kabul to Kandahar. Of these originals, three survive in the Indian Artillery today, and 5 (Bombay) Mountain Battery raised on 28 September 1827 remains the oldest and the senior-most unit of the Indian Artillery. 28 September is, therefore, commemorated each year as 'Gunners Day'. The original six, along with the two that were raised later, remained on the Frontier till the end of the century. Technically, the mountain batteries formed part of the Royal Artillery establishment till they were merged into the Indian Artillery on 01 August 1939. Additionally, there were also the Indian State Forces batteries of J&K, Gwalior, Bikaner and Patiala.

By 1939, the original six had evolved into 5 (Bombay) Mountain Battery, 6 (Jacob's) Mountain Battery [raised in 1843], and four PIFFER batteries – 2 (Derajat) Mountain Battery (FF) [raised in 1849 from the remnants of the Khalsa Army's horse artillery], 1 Royal (Kohat) Mountain Battery (FF) [raised in 1851, again from the soldiers of the disbanded Sikh Army], 4 (Hazara) Mountain Battery (FF) [raised in 1851] and 3 (Peshawar) Mountain Battery (FF) [raised in 1853]. Bombay, Derajat and Hazara Batteries remain in the Indian Army today, while the other three went to Pakistan in 1947.

The artillery of the British-Indian Army between 1858 and 1935, when the Indian Artillery was reconstituted, consisted only of the Indian Mountain Artillery. At the outbreak of World War I, Indian Artillery was made up of twelve mountain batteries. The history of Indian Artillery in World War I is the history of Indian Mountain

Artillery. Between the 1880s and 1960s, the mountain guns in service evolved in design from the '2.5-Inch Rifled Muzzle Loading' (1879-1916) to a '10-Pounder' (1901-18) followed by a '2.75-Inch Breech Loading Gun' (1914-19) and finally a '3.7-Inch Howitzer' (1915-1960s). Besides, the regular high-explosive shells, these fired shrapnel, either over open sights or laid indirectly, or case-shot in dire, close range emergency. They could also fire the 'star' shell for illumination at night. The 3.7-Inch Howitzer was the longest serving gun, and some were even employed in 1971 and a few years later along the Line of Control in J&K. It first saw action in East Africa on 11 April 1918. Sturdy, reliable, consistent and accurate, it was an ideal mule-pack artillery gun. It became synonymous with mountain artillery. All mountain guns were designed with the gun barrel in two parts to form a load viable for a large and sturdy mountain artillery mule to carry in rough terrain. On coming into action, the two portions of the gun barrel were joined by a threaded 'junction nut' and hence the mountain gun was known as the 'Screw Gun'. Kipling popularised them with his poem *Screw Guns*:

*Smokin' my pipe on the mountings, sniffin' the mornin' cool,*
*I walks in my old brown gaiters along o' my old brown mule,*
*With seventy gunners be'ind me, an' never a beggar forgets*
*It's only the pick of the Army that handles the dear little pets —*
*'Tss! 'Tss! .....*

*They sends us along where the roads are, but mostly we goes where they ain't.*
*We'd climb up the side of a sign-board an' trust to the stick o' the paint .....*

*If a man doesn't work, why, we drills 'im an' teaches 'im 'ow to behave.*
*If a beggar can't march, why, we kills 'im an' rattles 'im into 'is grave*
*You've got to stand up to our business an' spring without snatchin' or fuss.*
*D'you say that you sweat with the field-guns?*
*By God, you must lather with us — 'Tss! 'Tss! ....*

*The eagles is screamin' around us, the river's a-moanin' below,*
*We're clear o' the pine an' the oak-scrub, we're out on the rocks an' the snow,*
*An' the wind is as thin as a whip-lash what carries away to the plains*
*The rattle an' stamp o' the lead-mules -- the jinglety-jink o' the chains — 'Tss! 'Tss! ....*

*There's a wheel on the Horns o' the Mornin', an' a wheel on the edge o' the Pit,*
*An' a drop into nothin' beneath you as straight as a beggar can spit:*
*With the sweat runnin' out o' your shirt-sleeves, an' the sun off the snow in your face,*
*An' 'arf o' the men on the drag-ropes to hold the old gun in 'er place — 'Tss! 'Tss!*

CJ Payne – 'Snaffles' – sketched the opening verse by observing the 3 (Peshawar) Mountain Battery (FF) live at Landi Kotal in 1928. The sketch converted the poem into a visual delight. Prints and paintings of the sketch are to be found in most Gunner messes and establishments.

Since 1862, the Mountain Batteries of the British-Indian Army were officered exclusively by officers seconded from the British Royal Artillery. They were the very best amongst them. Many were adventure seekers, eccentric and able men; often combining all three qualities. Such talented men competed to serve in an Indian Mountain Battery as it assured active service on the Frontier. Many stayed on. One served as Battery Commander for eighteen years. Another, having won the MC during the war, was released during the post-war downsizing. He enrolled as a gunner in a British Mountain Battery. He was again commissioned during the Second World War and won a DSO. The Mountain Batteries also held the added attraction of an independent command by a captain, later major, unlike the infantry or cavalry where companies and squadrons formed part of the regiment under a lieutenant colonel. The men were all Indian and the best available. They had to be strong, sturdy and well-built, with a minimum height of 5 feet 10 inches, to be capable of loading and unloading heavy gun parts on mules and handling the guns and ammunition over rough terrain. The small number of batteries in the only Indian artillery meant that there were always volunteers. Recruits of only the highest quality were accepted – they were 'big men with small guns'. The men, mountains and mules made an eclectic mix. Besides the Indian Mountain Batteries, the British Mountain Batteries in India had British officers and gunners and Indian muleteers.

Central to the Mountain Artillery was the mule – a hybrid offspring of a male donkey or ass (jack) and a female horse (mare) that had the endurance of a donkey and the strength of a horse. Patient, sure-footed, stoic and stubborn – 'stubborn as a mule' – it was less fussy about food and fodder than a horse but more particular about the water. As a veterinary officer put it:

> Horses are more particular about their food and less particular about their water than mules;
> Mules are less particular about their food and more particular about their water than horses;
> Hence if you have to water a mixed force of horses and mules, water your mules first.

The mule was also less prone to disease and had a longer lifespan. The Mountain Artillery Mule – Mule MA – was a specially bred big, broad animal capable of carrying a heavier load than the General Service Mule – Mule GS. The MA mule was an elite creature above 14 hands and 2 inches (as tall as an Army horse) and those designated as gun-mules were even bigger. The big, strong, trusty, tireless and faithful battery mule was the stuff of stories and folklore of the mountain artillery. It commanded much affection and respect. These mules came from North America, Argentina and China, but did not come cheap. An untrained mountain artillery mule could cost upwards of Rs 900 in 1939.

The number of mules in a battery varied with the number of guns and the ammunition to be carried. Later, the introduction of mechanical transport to carry part of the ammunition reduced their numbers. By the end of World War II, a 3.7-Inch Howitzer battery of four guns had 12 horses, 94 MA mules and 24 GS mules. The howitzer was broken up into eight mule-loads carried by the 'fighting mules' in the order of march as they were required to be assembled, these being Carriage, Wheels and Axle, Pivot, Cradle, Trail Legs, Shield and Slipper, Breech and Chase. The Breech being the heaviest at 247 lbs or 112 kg, the mule carrying this load had to be the biggest and strongest. The battery mules were the highest priority. At the end of the day's march, they had to be groomed, fed and watered before the mule drivers did anything for themselves. Then followed the care and maintenance of the guns and finally the men. Injury or sickness were serious matters. The regimental VO (Veterinary Officer) was next in importance to the CO (Commanding Officer). On the order 'Halt Action Front' or 'Rear Limber-up' they were trained to gallop to their gun-flag or gun and form a circle around it in the order of their unloading and assembling the gun or dismantling and loading it and held steady without demur till offloaded or loaded. Having off-loaded the gun and ammunition, at a given signal, they would follow the Battery Havildar Major to be led off to the 'Wagon Lines' – the administrative area set up away from the gun position. If under fire or when ordered, they would lie down on their sides. A mule slipping and falling down a deep *khud* would quickly scramble back to its original place in the line of march. An animal not up to the mark would be drilled, disciplined and relegated to carrying water or panniers with tools.

All mules were generally assigned a 'Hoof Number' and were known as such, however, some were given names like horses. A tailless mule was appropriately and affectionately named *Landi!* A 35-year-old veteran *Kandhar*, with six campaign medals to his credit, marched from Ambala to Delhi and back for the Delhi Durbar in 1911. And while a mule could kick, they rarely did. The popular soldier's axiom was to never go in front of an officer or behind a mule, but contrary to popular belief, mules were seldom ill-tempered or dangerous. Any tendency of being ill-tempered was controlled by the driver with training, patience and care, supplemented with handfuls of jaggery. Rarely, if ever, was a mule cast for being vicious. Visiting or inspecting officers were often invited to smack any mule on the rump to demonstrate their training and steadiness which was generally declined politely! In fact, the 'Ordnance Mule' could even be said to have a 'personality' and was 'dignified'! During the siege and battle of Kohima in April 1944, a Mountain Regiment had only one small tent. A visiting senior officer, on his asking who enjoyed this luxury, was told it was *Memsahib* – the regiment's favourite mule and which was being cared for in anticipation of winning in the horse-show after the war!

The bond between the gunners and the battery mules was akin to family ties. Mules MA were generally 'put down' by 15 years of age. *Granny*, a Mule MA which had always led the Hazara Battery into action, being the first mule with the gun parts, was officially declared by the VO as no longer required due to its age (but not ability) and classified to be 'cast and destroyed'. All personnel of the battery then decided to retain her and pooled in to pay for her upkeep. *Granny* continued to carry loads till the age of 28. When *Granny* finally died at 35, its hoofs were cast in silver and are retained as such to this day.

*The keen head and the long cocked ear and the nostril quivering wide,*
*The beamy back and quarters broad and these are all allied,*
*To a temper kind tho' oft maligned by some untutored fool,*
*The finest friend that God's designed the Mountain Battery mule.*
— From *The Gunner*, 1964

Availability of horses allowed the cavalry to indulge in polo. The mountain artillery devised 'Mule O', a six-a-side game played astride bareback mules with pick-handles and a football. There were other sports like mounted tug-of-war and bareback wrestling.

The mountain gunners' boast was that they could go anywhere where a man and a mule could put a foot and climb any slope a man could negotiate without pulling himself up by his hands.

*As me and my companions were scrambling up a hill,*
*The path was lost in rolling stones, but we went forward still;*
*For we can wriggle and climb, my lads, an turn up everywhere*
*And it's our delight on a mountain height, with a leg or two to spare!*

*Good luck to every sergeant, then, that lets us pick our road:*
*Bad luck to all the driver-men that cannot pack a load!*
*For we can wriggle and climb, my lads, and turn up everywhere,*
*And it's our delight on a mountain height, with a leg or two to spare!*
—Rudyard Kipling's *Screw-Gun Mules* from *Parade Song of the Camp Animals*

It was a remarkable sight to see a good Mountain Battery coming into 'crash' action. It was the finest example of 'regulated stampede', 'controlled chaos', 'time and motion' and 'synchronised teamwork' between man and mule. What would appear to the uninitiated eye to be a disorderly assembly of mules and soldiers would suddenly stream into position, there would be a brief pause with much exertion and heaving of lumps of metal, and in a minute or two, the animals would be led off at a run leaving six or four sturdy guns with their detachments kneeling smartly round them. All this while there was no shouting or any other noise other than the clang of metal being assembled. A shell would be on the target within three minutes of the commencement of coming into action. An old and distinguished mountain gunner recalls that as a Gun Position Officer of one of the original Mountain Batteries in 1951, he recorded a gun detachment bringing a gun into action and ready to fire in an incredible 44 seconds. As someone recorded — 'Only three things are worth seeing in India: the Taj Mahal, an Indian Cavalry Regiment charging and a Mountain Battery coming into action'.

On the line of march, Mountain Gunners always out-marched even the Light Infantry, keeping up a steady clip of up to four and a half mile per hour, mile after mile and day after day. The officers customarily never rode their horses and instead marched alongside except when required to move up and down the column. A Mountain Battery on the Frontier in 1878 covered 75 miles in 48 hours while another covered 47 miles in 24 hours in Burma in 1942. A former mountain gunner writing in *The Daily Telegraph* in 1957 recorded: "My Mountain Battery had been 60 years on the Frontier when I joined in 1924. We were the supreme footsloggers and climbers. A traditional march was from 'Pindi to Quetta, 600 miles; another Quetta to Ambala, 700. We trained as we marched, resting only on Sundays. The officers' horses had the best of it, they were never mounted on the line of march....". Relief of Mountain Batteries deployed on the Frontier from Quetta up to Chitral was carried out by a battery marching from, say, Dehradun or Ambala. It would cover about twenty miles in darkness or the early part of the day and set up camp. A hockey match with the neighbouring village team in the afternoon was followed by a gathering with old soldiers over dinner and the march resumed early next morning. Any suitable youth brought along by the veterans was 'enrolled' and marched with the battery the next day. Camping grounds earmarked along the main routes are seen today as open patches surrounded by the urban sprawl.

Up to World War I, the Mountain Artillery batteries had depots at Quetta, Abbottabad and Dehradun. At the outbreak of the war, they were amalgamated at Dehradun in 1915 as the Mountain Artillery Training Centre. It moved to Lucknow in 1921, and then to Ambala in 1928, where it stayed till 1948 when it moved to Deolali and finally to nearby Nasik.

On 15 August 1947, 22 Mountain Regiment consisted of 4 (Hazara) (FF), 5 (Bombay) and 7 (Bengal) Mountain Batteries. 2 (Derajat) Mountain Battery (FF) was transferred to 22 Mountain Regiment from 24 Mountain Regiment in 1949, when the latter was converted to a medium regiment. In 1951, an Army Order designated 22 Mountain Regiment as the *corps d'elite* of the Indian Artillery in recognition of the past services of its four batteries over the previous 124 years, symbolised by 34 'Battle Honours' held by these old units. A mounted ceremonial parade was held below Rajauri Fort in 1952 where a newly designed *corps d'elite* red and blue lanyard was presented to the Regiment by the General Officer Commanding of the Division. This was to be worn only by the *corps d'elite*. However, in due course, it was adopted by all Mountain Batteries and finally by the Regiment of Artillery. The Kohat Mountain Battery had been designated 'Royal' after the First World War and entitled to wear a white lanyard on the right shoulder. It went to Pakistan in 1947.

In the humiliating withdrawal from Tawang in 1962, a Mountain Battery was the only unit to march back to the plains along with their complete complement of men, guns, equipment, mules and weapons.

When the mule-based Mountain Artillery began converting to towed Field Artillery, the Drivers Mountain Artillery (DMA) were remustered as Drivers Mechanical Transport (DMT) and allotted to Field Artillery units. Considering their residual service and grounding with animals, training them new skills was seen as impractical, however, these stalwart men proved to be extremely useful in handling the heavy artillery ammunition.

Consequent to the resurrection of the Indian Artillery on 15 January 1935, the Mountain Artillery was merged into the Indian Artillery in 1939. The historical lineage and foundation of the Indian Artillery today is, in fact, that of the Mountain Artillery. Increasing road construction and extension into remote areas, lighter towed-guns, and finally, even helicopters for lifting the guns sounded the *Last Post* for the Mountain Artillery and Gunner. The Regimental War Memorial erected at the Nasik Centre unveiled on 19 May 1981 has a 3.7-Inch Howitzer and a Mountain Gunner on a raised pedestal. When the Indian Regiment of Artillery commemorated its Golden Jubilee of Raising in 1985, the Commemorative Postage Stamp released on the occasion also depicted a 3.7-Inch Howitzer and a Mountain Gunner.

# THE UNKNOWN SOLDIER

IN MEMORY OF
THOSE WHO SET OUT TO SERVE THE NATION'S CAUSE
AND
DID NOT RETURN
—Inscribed on the memorials at
Leh (Ladakh) and Bathinda (Punjab)

By 1914, conscription and industrial methods had produced mass armies of millions in Europe. The railways could speedily transport and reinforce them wherever required. Inevitably, when the fighting started, the casualties were on an equally massive scale. Newspapers carried page after page of black print listing the dead. By the end of the Great War, a sense of universal loss and grief prevailed. Of the dead, more than four million could never be found or identified. They became the 'Unknown Soldiers'.

David Railton, an Army Chaplain on the Western Front, was deeply moved by seeing a grave in 1916 marked with a makeshift cross with a pencil written 'An Unknown British Soldier'. By 1918, the sheer numbers of such graves had overwhelmed him. In 1920, he suggested that an unidentified soldier from the battlefield of France be buried in Westminster Abbey 'amongst the Kings' to honour all the unknown dead of the war. Prime Minister David Lloyd George supported the idea strongly. King George V too felt that the unknown soldiers must be honoured as they had died 'For King and Country'.

Meanwhile, for the Victory Parade on the second anniversary of the signing of the Armistice, a plaster and wood Cenotaph designed by

Edwin Lutyens was erected in front of Whitehall, London, to commemorate the war dead. It was intended to be a temporary structure to be dismantled after the parade. However, strong public sentiment demanded that it be made permanent. It was accordingly reconstructed exactly in stone. Similar cenotaphs were to come up later in commonwealth countries worldwide.

To select the 'Unknown Soldier' four bodies from unmarked graves from the battlefields of Aisne, Somme, Arras and Ypres were exhumed and placed in identical coffins and covered with the Union Jack in a makeshift chapel near Arras on 09 November 1920. The same night the local military commander went into the chapel and placed his hand on one of them. This was sealed with iron bands and the other three re-buried. The coffin was carried with due ceremony aboard the Cruiser *HMS Verdun* and brought to England. On 11 November the coffin, placed on a gun carriage and escorted by Field Marshals, Admirals and Marshal of the Air Force, was brought to the Cenotaph. Silent crowds lined the streets, and a Field Marshal's 19-gun salute was fired. The King unveiled the Cenotaph at 11 am on 11 November 1920 and placed a wreath on the coffin which was then accompanied by him to Westminster Abbey. Outside the Abbey, a Guard of Honour composed of 100 gallantry awards recipients, including 74 VCs, saluted the coffin. The body was lowered into the Abbey floor and covered with earth brought from the battlefields of France. It soon caught the public imagination, and more than 1.25 million people filed past in the next one week. Since 1923, Royal Brides married at the Abbey have their bouquets laid on the tomb the day after the wedding.

In France, the idea of honouring an unknown soldier had been mooted in 1916. It was formally accepted and announced on 12 November 1919. Eight unknown bodies were exhumed from French cemeteries of the Western Front and placed in identical caskets on 10 November 1920. The caskets were repositioned a number of times en route to Verdun to ensure anonymity and avoid identification of the place from where the bodies were exhumed. At Verdun, a young French soldier was asked to select a casket which was then taken and placed in the chapel on the first floor of the Arc de Triomphe at the western end of the Champs-Élysées in Paris on 11 November 1920. It remained there till 28 January 1921 when it was buried. The plan originally had been to bury the Unknown Soldier in the Pantheon; however, a strong public opinion demanded that he be buried beneath the Arc de Triomphe.

On 04 March 1921, the United States Congress resolved to have an unknown American soldier of World War I buried at the Arlington National Cemetery outside Washington DC. Accordingly, the Unknown Soldier was brought back from France and buried in the Memorial Amphitheatre. Situated on a prominent hillock, the site overlooks Washington DC. Though not designated as such, it is known as the Tomb of the Unknown Soldier. The body had been randomly selected on 24 October 1921 from amongst four exhumed from American cemeteries in France. In 1930, a sculpted marble block was placed over the grave. Unknown soldiers were subsequently brought and buried alongside from battlefields of World War II, Korea and Vietnam.

The President of the United States of America awarded the Medal of Honour to the British Unknown on 17 October 1921 which was personally presented by General of the Army Pershing. Britain awarded the Victoria Cross to the American Unknown conferred by Admiral of the Fleet Beatty on 11 November 1921.

Soviet Russia commemorated the twenty-fifth anniversary of the Battle of Moscow in World War II in December 1966 by bringing the body of an unknown soldier from a mass grave 40 km from Moscow, the closest the Germans had reached, and burying him at the Kremlin Wall in the Alexander Garden in Moscow. Earth from the battlefields of Leningrad, Kiev, Stalingrad, Minsk and Smolensk, amongst others, was brought and placed in the grave.

The British and French memorials to the Unknown Soldier aroused similar sentiments and desire in Australia in the 1920s. It was opposed by the Imperial War Graves Commission (IWGC) which had been set up in December 1917 for war graves and memorials to soldiers killed in the Great War. The IWGC placed a blanket ban on removing any body from the battlefields. The strong sense of being a British Dominion, and the Unknown Soldier in Westminster Abbey being representative of all Empire and Dominion soldiers, also tempered the demand. It finally found expression in 1993 on the 75th

Anniversary of the end of the Great War. An Australian soldier's remains were exhumed from France and interned in the Hall of Memory of the Australian War Memorial in Canberra on 11 November 1993. Canada and New Zealand followed in 2000 and 2004.

Indian casualties from the Western Front were evacuated to Southampton and brought to Brighton where military hospitals for the Indian Army were set up. Those dying at Brighton of wounds were cremated nearby in Patcham. At the site of cremation, The Chattri Memorial was erected, a first of its kind dedicated to the members of the Indian Army who fought in World War 1. It was dedicated on 21 February 1921. The local newspaper recorded: 'For East came to West in a strange romantic way when, on these Sussex Downs, the ashes were burned of Hindu warriors born in remote villages in faraway Hindustan, for whom the wildest imagination could never have suggested at their birth that their funeral fires would be fanned by the winds that swept these Sussex hills'.

Another memorial to the 4742 Indian soldiers who fell during World War 1 on the Western Front and have no known grave was unveiled on 07 October 1927 at Neuve Chapelle, France, it being the site of the first major action fought by the Indian Corps as a single unit and achieving a breakthrough in the German line. Addressing the Indian Army contingent present on the occasion, Marshal Ferdinand Foch said, 'Return to your homes in the distant, sun-bathed East and proclaim how your countrymen drenched with their blood the cold northern land of France and Flanders ... tell all India that we shall watch over their graves with the devotion due to all our dead. We shall cherish above all the memory of their example'.

Perhaps the maximum casualties suffered by the British and Commonwealth troops on the Western Front were in the Ypres Salient and the fighting nearby. Thousands and thousands had marched out to the front over the moat and rampart and the eastern gate of the old fortifications of the Belgian town of Menin. Amongst the nearly 2,00,000 dead in the five offensives in and around the Salient, the remains of nearly 90,000 were never found, declared 'Missing Believed Killed'. This included Indian troops. In 1927, the old Eastern Gate, much damaged by shelling, was replaced by a single span memorial hall 36.5 meters long and 20 meters wide with archways at both ends 9 meters wide and 14.5 meters high. The inside walls have panels inscribed with the names of 54,389 officers and men whose remains were never found. The memorial was dedicated on 24 July 1927, and except for the duration of the Second World War, all traffic through it is closed at 2000 hrs when a bugler sounds the last post. Indian troops landed in France in September and October 1914 and were rushed to Ypres Salient to hold the German advance. Amongst the 1,30,000 Indian troops, 9000 died. The Western end of the gate has panels dedicated to the Indian troops. In March 2011, a memorial to the Indian dead in the shape of a pedestal with the Sarnath Lions was erected adjacent to the North Wall of the gate. Menin gate is amongst the most visited war memorials in the world.

*This man in his own country prayed we know not to what Powers.*
*We pray Them to reward him for his bravery in ours.*
—Rudyard Kipling, *Hindu Sepoy In France*

The Somme battlefield claimed 4,20,000 British casualties. The first day of the offensive on 01 July 1916 saw the maximum killed in a single day in British military history. In memory of the 72,246 who died here and have no known grave, a memorial was unveiled on 01 August 1932. It commemorates the dead of the Somme battlefields of July 1915 to March 1918. The 140-foot high structure is the largest Commonwealth memorial to the unknown in the world. A commemorative ceremony is held here on 01 July every year.

The plan for the new capital of Delhi envisaged some form of a commemorative arch at the end of the West-East ceremonial boulevard (King's Way now Rajpath) starting from the Viceroy's House (Rashtrapati Bhavan). Prompted by Indian nationalists, the IWGC gave it a concrete shape by proposing an All India War Memorial.

*Lo! I have flung to the East and the West*
*Priceless treasures torn from my breast,*
*And yielded the sons of my stricken womb*
*To the drum-beats of the duty, the sabres of doom.*
*Gathered like pearls in their alien graves*
*Silent they sleep by the Persian waves,*

*Scattered like shells on Egyptian sands,*
*They lie with pale brows and brave, broken hands,*
*They are strewn like blossoms mown down by chance*
*On the blood-brown meadows of Flanders and France.*
—Sarojini Naidu, *The Gift of India, 1915*

Edwin Lutyens, the main architect of New Delhi and a member of the IWGC, designed the memorial based on the Arc de Triomphe of Paris. The symmetry is derived from a square divided into three horizontal and vertical sections. The central section of the nine squares encloses a circle the upper half of which is the arch of the structure. Unlike the Arc de Triomphe and other similar monuments, it does not have any figural decorations. Two huge sandstone urns with stone pine cones growing out of them signify heroic death and rebirth though these are Roman concepts and alien to any Indian symbolism. The 42 meters high and 9.1 meters wide red sandstone structure has a shallow bowl on top intended to be filled with oil and lit on special occasions to signify holy smoke, but has rarely been used as such. Names of 13,516 war dead, representative of all the war dead, and who have no known grave are inscribed on the memorial.

The foundation stone of the memorial was laid on 10 February 1921 by the Duke of Connaught. On this occasion the Deccan Horse (9 Deccan Horse), 21 (Kohat) Mountain Battery (FF) (1 Medium Regiment (SP) Pakistan Army), 3rd Sappers and Miners (Bombay Sappers), 6th Jat Light Infantry (1 Jat Light Infantry – 2 Mechanised Infantry), 34th Sikh Pioneers (Sikh Light Infantry), 39th Garhwal Rifles (1 Garhwal Rifles – 6 Mechanised Infantry), 59th Scinde Rifles (FF) (1 Frontier Force, Pakistan Army), 117th Marathas (5 Maratha Light Infantry), and 5th Gurkha Rifles (FF) were honoured with the title of 'Royal' in recognition of their distinguished war time services.

The All India War Memorial, now popularly called India Gate, was inaugurated by the Viceroy, Lord Irwin on the late afternoon of 12 February 1931. The ceremonial fire and smoke were generated as a lone bugler sounded the last post and a guard of honour drawn up of veterans of the Great War from the Indian Army and the State Forces reversed arms. The Central India Horse horsemen with red and white pennons on their lances lined the King's Way.

Following the 1971 War, a black marble plinth with a reversed rifle and helmet, and with four urns at the corners with a permanent flame was erected below the India Gate Arch. It was unveiled by Prime Minister Indira Gandhi on 26 January 1972. *Amar Jawan* inscribed on the plinth signifies the Immortal Soldier. It has come to be identified as India's Tomb of the Unknown Soldier.

All Tombs of the Unknown have a solemn ceremonial guard round the clock all days of the year. Visiting heads of state usually lay wreaths.

A nation reveals itself not only by the men it produces but also the men it honours, the men it remembers.

*Soldier, rest! Thy warfare o'er,*
*Dream of fighting fields no more:*
*Sleep the sleep that knows not breaking,*
*Morn of toil, nor night of waking.*
—Sir Walter Scott, *Lady of the Lake*

# REVEILLE AND RETREAT

On a cold, foggy January night in 1961, my father and I boarded a train from the Old Delhi Railway Station bound for Dehradun. It had a steam locomotive, and we settled into an old-world wood-panelled coupe. The morning saw us being woken by the cries of hawkers selling tea in earthen *kullas* at Haridwar. The train chugged along through thick forests of *sal,* while we dressed and were soon at Dehradun. Taking a station-wagon taxi, we arrived at the Rashtriya Indian Military College – the RIMC – with the snow-covered hills of Mussoorie in the background.

I was one of the fourteen 'new cadets' joining that term. We were ushered into the Headmaster's office where I was 'handed over', and my father departed. Soon enough I was handed out the olive green uniform – starched cotton in those days – which, except for the three years of khaki at the National Defence Academy, I was to don for the next five decades. My fellow cadets were to be my comrades-in-arms and lifelong friends. Some were to make the ultimate sacrifice in the line of duty. I had been initiated into the brotherhood of arms.

> A mysterious fraternity born out of smoke and danger of death.
> —Stephen Crane, *The Red Badge Of Courage*

The customary farewells and courtesy calls were all done. My personal baggage had already been dispatched home, the official bungalow in Lutyen's Delhi handed over and the time to 'hang my uniform' had come. The last farewell tea had been hosted in the morning. In the afternoon, I walked down the steps of South Block on to the road leading to Rashtrapati Bhavan. It was a pleasant March day with a few scattered clouds in the surprisingly clear blue sky. I got into my waiting staff car and we drove off down the slope of Raisina Hill and to the Officers Mess in Delhi Cantt. On reaching my room, I looked into the full-length mirror and said to myself: 'Well, it has been a long and interesting journey. I have worn my uniform with honour and pride. My father would have been proud of me too'. Then I took off my uniform and hung it for the last time. It was 'farewell to the trumpets' and 'following the drum'. Early next morning I drove off to my hometown. I was now an 'Old Soldier'.

*Try as he will, no man breaks wholly loose*
*From his first love, no matter who she be,*
*Oh, was there ever a sailor free to choose*
*That didn't settle somewhere near the sea?*
—Rudyard Kipling, *The Virginity*